LIBRARY OF NEW TESTAMENT STUDIES

658

Formerly the Journal for the Study of the New Testament Supplement series

Editor
Chris Keith

Editorial Board
Dale C. Allison, Lynn H. Cohick, R. Alan Culpepper,
Craig A. Evans, Jennifer Eyl, Robert Fowler, Simon J. Gathercole,
Juan Hernández Jr., John S. Kloppenborg, Michael Labahn,
Matthew V. Novenson, Love L. Sechrest, Robert Wall,
Catrin H. Williams, and Brittany E. Wilson

The Concept of Canon in the Reception of the Epistle to the Hebrews

David Young

t&tclark
LONDON · NEW YORK · OXFORD · NEW DELHI · SYDNEY

T&T CLARK
Bloomsbury Publishing Plc
50 Bedford Square, London, WC1B 3DP, UK
1385 Broadway, New York, NY 10018, USA
29 Earlsfort Terrace, Dublin 2, Ireland

BLOOMSBURY, T&T CLARK and the T&T Clark logo are trademarks of
Bloomsbury Publishing Plc

First published in Great Britain 2022
This paperback edition published in 2023

Copyright © David Young, 2022

David Young has asserted his right under the Copyright, Designs and Patents Act,
1988, to be identified as Author of this work.

For legal purposes the Acknowledgments on pp. xi–xii constitute an
extension of this copyright page.

All rights reserved. No part of this publication may be reproduced or transmitted
in any form or by any means, electronic or mechanical, including photocopying,
recording, or any information storage or retrieval system, without prior permission
in writing from the publishers.

Bloomsbury Publishing Plc does not have any control over, or responsibility for, any
third-party websites referred to or in this book. All internet addresses given in this book were
correct at the time of going to press. The author and publisher regret any inconvenience caused if
addresses have changed or sites have ceased to exist, but
can accept no responsibility for any such changes.

A catalogue record for this book is available from the British Library.

Library of Congress Cataloging-in-Publication Data
Names: Young, David, 1951– author.
Title: The Concept of canon in the reception of the Epistle to the Hebrews / David Young.
Description: London ; New York : T&T Clark, 2021. |
Series: The library of New Testament studies, 2513-8790 ; 658 |
Includes bibliographical references and index. |
Summary: "This volume highlights the complex development of the Pauline
corpus and the larger Christian canon, by exploring the reception of the Epistle
to the Hebrews in early Christianity"– Provided by publisher.
Identifiers: LCCN 2021016667 (print) | LCCN 2021016668 (ebook) |
ISBN 9780567701343 (hb) | ISBN 9780567701350 (epdf) | ISBN 9780567701374 (epub)
Subjects: LCSH: Bible. Hebrews–Canon.
Classification: LCC BS2775.55 .Y68 2021 (print) | LCC BS2775.55 (ebook) |
DDC 227/.8706–dc23
LC record available at https://lccn.loc.gov/2021016667
LC ebook record available at https://lccn.loc.gov/2021016668

ISBN: HB: 978-0-5677-0134-3
PB: 978-0-5677-0138-1
ePDF: 978-0-5677-0135-0
ePUB: 978-0-5677-0137-4

Series: Library of New Testament Studies, volume 658
ISSN 2513–8790

Typeset by Newgen KnowledgeWorks Pvt. Ltd., Chennai, India

To find out more about our authors and books visit www.bloomsbury.com
and sign up for our newsletters.

I dedicate this work in memory of my father, Harold E. Young, whose passing coincided with the beginning of my doctoral studies. I am grateful for his example of doing small things with great love.

Contents

List of Figures	ix
List of Tables	x
Acknowledgments	xi
List of Abbreviations	xiii

1 The History of Hebrews' Reception History: Methodological
   Considerations and a Review of the Scholarly Literature
   on Hebrews' Reception 1
      Introduction 1
      Tracing the Reception of Hebrews 3
      Previous Scholarship Concerning the Reception History of Hebrews ... 6
      Conclusions 13

2 Translating Authorship into Authority: The Reception of Hebrews in
   Fourth-Century Discourses on Christian Scriptures 15
      Introduction 15
      Arguments over Authenticity 15
      Christian Discourses about Authoritative Scriptures in the Fourth Century ... 19
         Eusebius of Caesarea 19
         Athanasius of Alexandria 29
         Rufinus of Aquileia 33
         The Muratorian Fragment 40
         Jerome and Augustine 44
      Conclusions 47

3 Quoting Hebrews: Patristic Citations of Hebrews in the Second and
   Third Centuries 49
      Introduction 49
      Expressions of Utility in Ancient Compositional Practice ... 50
      The Diverse Utilization of Hebrews among Patristic Writers ... 55
         Justin Martyr 55
         Tertullian of Carthage 59

		Clement of Alexandria	63
		Origen of Alexandria	66
	Conclusions		72
4	Editing Paul: Hebrews among Editions of the Pauline Corpus		75
	Introduction		75
	Creating an Edition in Antiquity		77
	The Reception of Hebrews in Greek Editions of Paul's Letters		82
		P^{46}: An Early Edition of Paul's Letters	82
		P^{13}: An Amateur Edition of Paul's Letters?	84
		Evidence for Editions of Paul within Larger Collections	85
		Coislinianus: A Witness to the Euthalian Edition of Paul's Letters	95
	The Reception of Hebrews in the Earliest Latin Editions of Paul's Letters		99
		The Distinctive Treatment of Hebrews in Codex Claromontanus	99
		The Competing Traditions Regarding Hebrews in Codex Fuldensis	103
	Conclusions		105
5	Translating Paul: The Role of Latinity in the Reception of Hebrews		107
	Introduction		107
	The Omission of Hebrews from the Initial Translation of the *Corpus Paulinum*		108
	The Rise of Latinity		114
	The Impact of Latinity on the Reproduction of Christian Scriptures		118
		The Latin Revisions of Jerome and Rufinus	120
		Greek-Latin Bilinguals	123
	Conclusions		128
6	Concluding Reflections		129

Appendix	133
Bibliography	139
Ancient Sources Index	153
Biblical Passages Index	155
Modern Authors Index	159

Figures

1	Subscription for Revelation in Codex Alexandrinus	87
2	Tailpiece for Acts in Codex Alexandrinus	90
3	Tailpiece for Catholic Epistles in Codex Alexandrinus	91
4	Tailpiece for Pauline Epistles in Codex Alexandrinus	92
5	Subscription for Philemon in Codex Sinaiticus	93
6	Divine Testimonies in Codex Coislinianus	97
7	Subscription to Hebrews in Codex Coislinianus	98
8	Subscription to Colossians, Superscription to Philippians in Codex Claromontanus	100
9	Catalogue of Scriptures in Codex Claromontanus	101
10	Subscription to Philemon in Codex Claromontanus	102
11	Bilingual Editions of Paul	109
12	Prologue and Beginning of Hebrews in Codex Augiensis	111

Tables

1 Eusebius' Catalogue of Scriptures   22
2 Latin Translations of Hebrews   112

Acknowledgments

One of the most valuable lessons I have learned over the course of this project has more to do with the process of its production than its content: scholarly work, like so many other important endeavors in life, requires a community. The scholar's community is often not immediately visible as it is frequently composed of persons separated from the researcher by time or distance who are made accessible only by the artifacts they have created. Among the truly great treasures included in the privilege of research, however, are the communities that are immediately present, the people who offer support and share their wisdom along the way. Three communities have been essential means of grace and support to me in seeing this project through to its completion.

I owe a tremendous debt of gratitude to the community of scholars who have mentored, supported, and encouraged me throughout this project. Among the many to whom I owe thanks, my advisor, Jennifer Knust, deserves special recognition. She has enriched this project immeasurably through countless conversations and revisions, numerous insights from her own research, and a keen ability to refine an argument. In addition to her contributions to my research, I am perhaps even more appreciative of the many intangible ways she has taught me what it means to be a scholar, both by her own example and her constant challenge and encouragement to improve my own work. Many books could not contain the appropriate expressions of gratitude for her mentorship.

Other members of the scholarly community to whom I am grateful include David Frankfurter, who offered feedback on early drafts and has been a source of wisdom and insight throughout my program. The other members of my committee, Alejandro Botta, Shively Smith, Tommy Wasserman, and Zsuzsanna Varhelyi, also deserve thanks for the time, energy, and insight they have offered as part of my committee as well as the other numerous ways they have provided assistance and guidance. Bryan Stone has also offered meaningful support on a number of occasions throughout my program. I am thankful for Eldon Epp whose class on New Testament manuscripts and textual criticism was pivotal in setting me on the path that led to this dissertation and who has continued to offer support in related endeavors ever since. I am also grateful to my colleagues Alexis Felder Boyer, Chang Seon An, Andrew Henry, Scott Possiel, Jordan Conley, and David Malamud for their friendship, encouragement, and intellectual partnership as well as the truly unique conversations we have shared together. My gratitude also extends to my undergraduate and seminary professors who first set me on the path toward biblical scholarship and continue to serve as mentors, particularly Andy Johnson and Bill Malas.

I am also exceedingly grateful for my church community, Lowell First Church of the Nazarene. I owe special appreciation to Rev. John Megyesi and those who have faithfully participated in my Sunday School class. In a world where there seems to be an ever-growing chasm between the academy and the church, I am truly appreciative of a pastor and a community who have provided space, resources, and opportunity to wrestle with some of the more difficult questions posed by biblical scholarship. I am thankful for a class and a congregation who have been willing to do the hard work of dialogue around challenging issues. I must also express thanks to the people of Clinton First Church of the Nazarene whom I served as pastor prior to beginning this program. They gave me the opportunity to learn what it means to be a pastor and offered me nothing but blessing when I decided to pursue further studies. My work as a scholar will always be influenced by our time together.

My family is the final community to which I owe a debt of thanks. Jessica Young, your wit and charm are a delight. I am blessed beyond measure to share life with you, to pursue our passions together, and to enjoy some sparkling conversation along the way. Hannah, Malachi, and Esther, you are my greatest joy and pride. There is no greater privilege I could ever enjoy than being your father. I am grateful to be part of a family that promised each other that this degree would not come at the cost of our relationship with one another and to have come to this point believing that promise has been fulfilled. I am thankful for my mom, Lana Young, who has provided care and faithful support throughout my life as well as her continued prayers throughout this program. I am also grateful to count Mark and Joy Metcalfe among my family. They have offered continuous support in a variety of forms, the absence of which would have made the completion of this degree much more difficult, if not impossible.

Abbreviations

Abbreviations follow the list of abbreviations in *The SBL Handbook of Style: For Ancient Near Eastern, Biblical, and Early Christian Studies* (2nd ed., ed. Billie Jean Collins et al. [Peabody, MA: Hendrickson, 2014]).

Some common abbreviations include the following:

BCE	**Before the Common Era**
CCSL	Corpus Christianorum Series Latina
CE	Common Era
f.	folio
Grec.	Greek, denoting a Greek manuscript
LCL	Loeb Classical Library
LXX	Septuagint
MS(S)	manuscript(s)
NT	New Testament
OT	Old Testament
PQ	*Primum quaeritur*
TC	Testimonia Collection
Vg	Vulgate
VL	Vetus Latina, Old Latin

1

The History of Hebrews' Reception History: Methodological Considerations and a Review of the Scholarly Literature on Hebrews' Reception

Introduction

Scholarship concerning the reception of New Testament texts has often operated in a manner akin to the old trick for finding one's way through a maze: start at the end, working your way back to the start, and the one path that leads to the desired destination is easily found, avoiding the many dead ends along the way. That is to say that reception histories of New Testament books have frequently begun with an anachronistic presupposition: each distinct book will inevitably be placed alongside the others and recognized as "canonical," and the scholarly task is therefore to enumerate the process that led to this presupposed canonization.[1] The "end of the maze" in this case is usually the twenty-seven books of Athanasius' list, and the goal is to identify the key turns in the path that eventually led to the collection known as the New Testament. This line of inquiry is pursued for any given writing in the New Testament by utilizing the historical evidence relevant to that writing to reconstruct its path toward canonicity. As a result, a variety of evidence ranging from lists of authoritative writings to patristic citations to New Testament manuscripts are marshaled to serve the single purpose of reconstructing the path of a given writing toward a canonicity that must necessarily be achieved. Recently, however, a number of scholars have challenged the homogeneous treatment of these various kinds of evidence, arguing instead that each citation, canon list, and manuscript must be placed in its own distinct social context if the various means for interacting with sacred writings in early Christianity are to be more clearly understood.[2] When this careful attention to social context is applied to the use and

---

[1] Hans von Campenhausen, *The Formation of the Christian Bible*, trans. J. A. Baker (Philadelphia: Fortress Press, 1972); Harry Y. Gamble, *The New Testament Canon: Its Making and Meaning* (Philadelphia: Fortress Press, 1985); Bruce M. Metzger, *The Canon of the New Testament: Its Origin, Development, and Significance* (New York: Oxford University Press, 1987); David Trobisch, *The First Edition of the New Testament* (Oxford: Oxford University Press, 2000).

[2] David Brakke, "Scriptural Practices in Early Christianity: Towards a New History of the New Testament Canon," in *Invention, Rewriting, Usurpation: Discursive Fights over Religious Traditions*

reproduction of the work known as the Epistle to the Hebrews, a complex story of the epistle's reception emerges, which complicates a simple dichotomy of acceptance or rejection. The Epistle to the Hebrews was written about, quoted, and reproduced to a variety of ends in ancient Christianity, and its reception was influenced by a wide array of factors including its utility in theological arguments, its relationship to the Pauline corpus, its omission from that corpus when it was first translated into Latin, and, to a lesser extent, the lists of sacred scriptures produced by fourth- and fifth-century theologians.

The reception history of Hebrews serves to problematize the notion that such diverse kinds of evidence may be subsumed under a single project of determining when a writing became "canonical." While patristic citations of Hebrews indicate that the work could be cited in support of a writer's theological argument at a very early stage, this fact alone does not establish the work's place among a broadly accepted list of authoritative "sacred scriptures" as determined at a later stage of history. Likewise, though lists of "approved" scriptures began to be enumerated in the fourth century, the manuscripts that include Hebrews share neither the order of writings nor the concerns represented by these lists. On the contrary, these manuscripts can be interpreted as embodiments of distinctive hermeneutic, technological, and linguistic frameworks; each manuscript witness indicates some editorial effort to determine which writings should be included within its own folia, either by the editors of an exemplar or those who produced the manuscript in question, but no single manuscript resolves the location of Hebrews within a preordained collection. No one manuscript, no specific editor, and no single patristic writer settled the question of how Hebrews fits within a larger gathering of apostolic writings, at least not in a definitive manner. Furthermore, the treatment of Hebrews in these manuscripts appears to have been influenced not by an attempt to establish a settled canon but by the book's availability in the language in which a given manuscript was reproduced; accidents of history linked to geography, language, and local book culture were as significant in determining this work's inclusion into collections of scriptures as theological judgments regarding its value.[3]

in *Antiquity*, ed. Jörg Ulrich, Anders-Christian Jacobsen, and David Brakke (Frankfurt am Main: Peter Lang, Internationaler Verlag der Wissenschaften, 2011), 263–80. See also John Guillory, *Cultural Capital: The Problem of Literary Canon Formation* (Chicago: University of Chicago Press, 1993); Jennifer Knust, "Miscellany Manuscripts and the Christian Canonical Imaginary," in *Ritual Matters: Material Remains and Ancient Religion*, ed. Jennifer Knust and Claudia Moser (Ann Arbor: University of Michigan Press, 2017), 99–118; D. F. McKenzie, *Bibliography and the Sociology of Texts* (New York: Cambridge University Press, 1999); Eva Mroczek, *The Literary Imagination in Jewish Antiquity* (New York: Oxford University Press, 2016); and Hindy Najman, "The Vitality of Scripture Within and Beyond the 'Canon,'" *Journal for the Study of Judaism* 43, nos. 4–5 (2012): 497–518.

[3] The liturgical reading of Christian writings was likely an important factor in a work's reception as well. Tertullian's description of churches that were recipients of apostolic letters as "the very thrones of the apostles" witnesses to the importance of local traditions with regard to a writing's reception. The Muratorian Fragment separates works to be read in church from those that should not be read publicly. Augustine's criteria "to prefer those accepted by all the catholic churches" may be in part a reference to the writings the churches have chosen to read in worship. Unfortunately, explicit references to the liturgical reading of Hebrews are rare. Tertullian's statement that Hebrews is "better received by the churches" than the Shepherd may be a reference to liturgical reading. Likewise, Jerome's comment that Hebrews is "received not only by the churches of the East but also by all Church writers of the Greek language" and "is celebrated in the daily readings of the Churches"

Tracing the Reception of Hebrews

David Brakke has called for scholars of ancient Christianity to resist a long-standing trend in the study of early Christian writings: the tendency to search for clues capable of documenting the purportedly inevitable establishment of a fixed New Testament canon. As he states,

> And so it is simply anachronistic to ask writers of the second century which books were in their canon and which not—for the notion of a closed canon was simply not there. We must not continue to place Christian authors on a trajectory that leads inevitably to Athanasius's supposedly definitive list of 367.[4]

As Brakke's observation highlights, the search for a "canon" among writers who cannot and did not share the concept obscures the specific contexts and priorities that informed decisions about which texts would be authorized and why, while also flattening diverse evidence into a single interpretive framework. Dimitri Krytatas makes a similar point in an analysis of references to Christian scriptures in martyrological literature. "A distinction between documents considered sacred and documents that were held to be heretical or profane was taken for granted," he observes, but sacred documents were rarely, if ever, described as "bound all together." Thus, early-fourth-century accounts about the impact of "the Great Persecution" also suggest that Christian groups held neither consistent ideas about which texts were sacred nor a consistent set of practices binding particular sets of books together.[5] Even in the fourth century, after the notion of canon emerged as a topic for open discussion, neither the concept of canonicity nor the particular lists of church leaders determined for all Christians everywhere what would be read from that moment forward. On the contrary, such lists appear to be the concern of a very specific group of Christians who were in fact unable to reproduce their decisions in any meaningful way. "Canon" as a concept is anachronistic prior to the fourth century and remains a misleading guide to later Christian scriptures as well.[6] The case of Hebrews offers one striking illustration of this broader problem.

---

provides evidence that some churches were regularly reading Hebrews as a part of their worship. The limited availability of early evidence regarding the liturgical reading of Hebrews (such evidence is characteristically sixth-century or later) places a close study of such reading beyond the scope of the current project. Nevertheless, reading practices undoubtedly impacted perceptions of the work's authority, as Tertullian's comments indicate.

[4] Brakke, "Scriptural Practices in Early Christianity," 266.

[5] He continues, "*I take this observation to be a further indication that the canon was originally mainly a theoretical notion of interest to church leaders and theologians*" (Dimitris J. Kyrtatas, "Historical Aspects of the Formation of the New Testament Canon" in *Canon and Canonicity: The Formation and Use of Scripture*, ed. Einar Thomassen [Copenhagen: Museum Tusculanum Press, 2009], 34. Italics mine).

[6] Marcion's collection of Paul's letters (*Apostolikon*) and his edition of the Gospel of Luke (*Euangelion*) as well as Irenaeus' defense of the fourfold gospel collection have been cited frequently as second-century precursors to the later concept of canon. The available evidence, however, does not suggest that either of these authors intended these collections to function as "canon" in the later sense of the term. It remains unclear whether Marcion's utilization of the Gospel of Luke and Paul's epistles was an intentional choice or merely a matter of what was available to him. Ulrich Schmid, "Marcion and the Textual History of Romans: Editorial Activity and Early Editions of the New Testament," *Studia*

The present work builds on the observations of Brakke, Krytatas, and others to reopen the question of the reception of Hebrews.[7] Like previous scholars, I also review the citations of Hebrews by early Christian writers, consider the explicit judgments of theologians and ecclesiastical councils, and survey extant manuscripts of this document.[8] Unlike these scholars, however, I seek to understand the historical contexts and settings that enabled particular judgments about texts to be made.[9] As Brakke has emphasized, reflections on the authority of a given text are dependent upon the social contexts in which scholars did their work, the aims such reflections were designed to serve, and the practical circumstances in which such judgments could be realized.[10] Even the famous list of books in Athanasius' thirty-ninth *Festal Letter* should not be seen as an attempt to impose a canon where one did not previously exist but to offer an alternative to the less fixed academic canon, the boundaries of which could shift since its authority did not reside in the canon itself but in the teacher who utilized it.[11] As a result, the more illuminating question for understanding the reception and

---

Patristica 54 (2013): 105–8. Marcion's attempt to limit which writings were considered beneficial for Christians is clearer in his exclusion of the Jewish scriptures, an exclusion that had far more to do with eliminating what Marcion saw as a corrupting Jewish influence than establishing a set of canonical scriptures. Lee Martin McDonald, *The Formation of the Biblical Canon: 2 Volumes* (New York: T&T Clark, 2017), 148. Furthermore, the response of other Christian writers

> was to reject Marcion not by imitating but by contradicting him, and insisting that far more books had authority in the church than he was prepared to allow. In principle, what Christian writers of the second century defend is the variety and profusion of Christian texts, just as they also defend the continued acceptance and use of the Old Testament. (John Barton, "Marcion Revisited," in *The Canon Debate*, ed. Lee Martin McDonald and James A. Sanders [Peabody, MA: Hendrickson, 2002], 343)

"Irenaeus neither articulates nor assumes a 'Christian canon' in the later sense of that phrase. Instead, buttressing the church on all sides against the threat of heresy, he weaves a sophisticated argument about how multiple authoritative Christian documents (i.e. 'gospels') can paradoxically bear witness to an essentially singular Truth" (Annette Yoshiko Reed, "ΕΥΑΓΓΕΛΙΟΝ: Orality, Textuality, and the Christian Truth in Irenaeus' 'Adversus Haereses,'" *Vigiliae Christianae* 56, no. 1 [2002]: 15).

[7] Eva Mroczek's work on the Psalms is helpful in illustrating this same point. She argues that the "book of Psalms" was not merely an uncompleted work in the Second Temple Period but that it did not exist as a category:

> But to say that no sense of a "book of Psalms" as a coherent and bounded work emerges is not only to make the chronological argument that the Psalter was still fluid, not fixed or closed, in the Second Temple period. This observation is crucial to reconstructing the history of the book of Psalms, and to placing its precursors onto a timeline of how the Bible came to be. But to describe the evidence on its own terms—to imagine how the landscape might have looked to a person in the first century, who did not have access to such a timeline—we must make a stronger claim: the "book of Psalms" did not exist as a conceptual category in the Second Temple period. This was not the way that psalms traditions were imaginatively construed. (Mroczek, *Literary Imagination in Jewish Antiquity*, 33)

[8] Harry Gamble considers the importance of these different types of evidence in *Making and Meaning*, 23.

[9] Cf. Guillory, *Cultural Capital*, 28, as cited in Brakke, "Scriptural Practices in Early Christianity," 268: "An individual's judgment that a work is great does nothing in itself to preserve that work, unless that judgment is made in a certain institutional context, a setting in which it is possible to insure the reproduction of the work, its continual reintroduction to generations of readers."

[10] Brakke, "Scriptural Practices in Early Christianity," 269.

[11] David Brakke, "Canon Formation and Social Conflict in Fourth-Century Egypt: Athanasius of Alexandria's Thirty-Ninth '*Festal Letter*,'" *Harvard Theological Review* 87, no. 4 (October 1994): 398.

utilization of a given scripture is not "How did we get Athanasius' canon?" but "What are the various ways early Christians were interacting with and reproducing their scriptures?"

The question of Hebrews' canonicity was not the only, or even a primary, factor in the question of its reception. Early Christians were interacting with Hebrews in a variety of ways beyond merely asking whether or not it was canonical. Christian writers alluded to Hebrews' distinctive theology when developing their own perspectives; they also adapted Hebrews' list of biblical proofs regarding the status of Jesus. But a concept of "canon" was not a factor in these uses. Instead, as Margaret Mitchell has helpfully demonstrated, patristic citations of Paul's letters existed within an agonistic framework that these writers imitated from their classical counterparts. "The whole point, indeed the 'end' of interpretation ... is the interpretation that is useful or beneficial. Paul and his ancient interpreters had in common strategic variability according to a recognized set of commonplaces for where meaning is to be found—in the letter or in the spirit."[12] If the question of canonicity or authority is set aside, then another important concept in the interaction of early Christians with their scriptures emerges—usefulness. These quotations and allusions demonstrate that the document was available and useful to that author's argument. Of course, this availability and usefulness implies a certain kind of limited authority, namely, that the document carries enough weight that the writer found its arguments persuasive, or if well known or directly cited, that the author assumes the audience would find a quotation from the document persuasive. The categories of usefulness and authority and later determinations of "canonicity" are therefore not mutually exclusive.

The manuscripts that include Hebrews among their contents provide another window into the interactions of early Christians with this document. A proper contextualization of the evidence also highlights just how indeterminate issues of canon and authority were in the production of these manuscripts. This is true in the simplest sense that the many manuscripts that contain various New Testament books do not reflect the canon lists of the fourth century. In addition to the fact that entire New Testaments are relatively rare in the manuscript tradition, the collections that do exist often include writings not found in Athanasius' list. In the case of Hebrews in particular, the epistle continues to be treated distinctively among Paul's letters, particularly in Latin-dominant contexts. Of course, the production of a manuscript entails some of the same choices about what writings to include and the order in which to include them. However, the available evidence suggests that the decisions of church leaders were not neatly reproduced in the actual material representations of the church's scriptures.

What does seem to be determinative for the production of these manuscripts are the same kinds of questions that were important for the production of an edition of any author's works in the ancient world—questions of authentic authorship and the place of a given work within an edition of the author's corpus of works. This can be seen in

---

[12] Margaret Mary Mitchell, *Paul, the Corinthians, and the Birth of Christian Hermeneutics* (New York: Cambridge University Press, 2012), 107–8.

the case of Hebrews quite clearly in the Latin manuscript tradition where questions about its Pauline authorship lead to its distinctive treatment among Paul's letters. As Eric Sherbenske has shown, various editions of the *corpus Paulinum* were both shaped by interpretative tradition and vehicles of interpretation themselves. That is, the arrangement of Pauline letter collections and the accompanying paratextual features provided an interpretive framework through which the Pauline letters themselves were to be understood. He explains,

> In the transmission and alteration of the text, the selection and arrangement of the content, and deployment of paratexts (such as prologues, bioi, hypotheses, kephalaia), editors tacitly (and sometimes explicitly) presented the reader with an interpretation of the accompanying edition. An edition was thus the product of interpretation and, in turn, sought to shape subsequent interpretation.[13]

While the manuscript tradition and pronouncements of church leaders surely must have exerted some minimal degree of mutual influence on one another, their concerns were by no means identical. Manuscripts are materializations of interpretations that in turn impact later interpretations, but not necessarily in direct ways.

Tracing the diverse array of placements, languages, and material representations of Hebrews alongside patristic citations and other references enables a better understanding of the mechanisms that led to its diverse reception. Placing patristic citation habits within a context of ancient editorial practice provides a means for identifying the scholarly procedures that informed writers in general. A detailed analysis of the treatment of Hebrews in the Latin manuscript tradition also highlights another category of evidence: the significance of bilingualism and the rise of Latinity for the reception history of this specific book. The availability of Hebrews in Latin played a substantial role in determining its reception and association with the *corpus Paulinum*. As this analysis shows, Hebrews provides a particularly striking example of the shifting category of "sacred scripture."

Previous Scholarship Concerning the Reception History of Hebrews

The declarations of fourth- and fifth-century theologians concerning the authority of Christian scriptures have played a prominent role in scholarly reconstructions of Hebrews' reception history just as they have in the reception histories of many other New Testament writings. In the case of Hebrews, however, the majority of scholarship has not considered the fourth century to be merely a moment of recognition for the place of authority that Hebrews already held but a critically

---

[13] Eric W. Scherbenske, *Canonizing Paul: Ancient Editorial Practice and the Corpus Paulinum* (New York: Oxford University Press, 2013), 16.

important *turning point* in the history of Hebrews' reception. This is because much of the previous scholarship on Hebrews has regarded the book as broadly accepted in the East from a very early stage but neglected, or even rejected, in the West *until the fourth century* when the opinions of Jerome and Augustine produced a decisive shift in the book's Western reception. As a result, the fourth century is also often regarded as a natural point of conclusion in the study of Hebrews' reception since this century is positioned as the juncture at which Hebrews ascended to canonical status in both East and West. Although earlier scholarship has contributed valuable insight into Hebrews' reception history by highlighting the uneven nature of that reception, Clare K. Rothschild has complicated this scholarly portrait of a dichotomous East/West divide in Hebrews' reception, which is only unified in the fourth century by drawing attention to the many pieces of evidence that fail to fit neatly into this narrative.

William Hatch's 1936 essay "The Position of Hebrews in the New Testament Canon" offers a representative example of the earlier approach.[14] Hatch maintains the framework of Hebrews' early acceptance in the East with its initial rejection in the West throughout his work. He claims this as the reason for Hebrews' position after Philemon: when it was finally recognized as scripture in the West it was simply appended to the end of the Pauline corpus. In support of this claim, he cites the absence of Hebrews from the Muratorian Fragment and the Marcionite prologues as well as the peculiar language of the Council of Carthage, which cites thirteen unnamed letters of Paul only to add "*eiusdem ad Hebraeos una*."[15] Hatch also views the fourth century as the decisive turning point for Hebrews' reception, stating, "Thus Hebrews occupied this position in the Latin-speaking churches of the West as early as the end of the fourth century, and it always retained this place in the Western Church."[16] Hatch concludes his essay with a portrayal of the Church as "a universal or Catholic fellowship" that was initially characterized by diversity but moved toward an inevitable unity in which "local usage should give way to more or less uniform standards of belief and practice."[17]

Bruce Metzger similarly characterizes Hebrews' reception in terms of early acceptance in the East and initial rejection in the West until its acceptance in the fourth century. Metzger's presentation of Hebrews' reception in the East is largely dependent on the opinions passed down through the scholars at Alexandria as

---

[14] William H. P. Hatch, "The Position of Hebrews in the Canon of the New Testament," *Harvard Theological Review* 29, no. 2 (1936): 133–51.
[15] "And also one to the Hebrews" (ibid., 144).
[16] Ibid., 145.
[17] Ibid., 151:

> Diversity was everywhere the rule in the early period, whereas uniformity was the note of a later age. The Church was a universal or Catholic fellowship. Local Christian communities, wherever they might be, were not isolated units. They were rather integral parts of a living organism, members of the body of Christ. Hence it was inevitable that in the course of time local usage should give way to more or less uniform standards of belief and practice.

reported by Eusebius. Pantaenus,[18] Clement,[19] and Origen[20] each defend the Pauline authorship of Hebrews to varying degrees according to Eusebius even while they recognize that there are obstacles to making such a claim, chief among them the absence of Paul's name on the document. Metzger portrays Hebrews' reception in the West, on the other hand, as a writing that was occasionally quoted by Western authors but not fully accepted as authoritative until the fourth century. He notes that Hippolytus, Tertullian, Hilary, and Lucifer all quote Hebrews though this does not mean that the opinion of these authors is uniform with reference to Hebrews. Although Hippolytus

---

[18] Eusebius, *Hist. eccl.* 6.14.4, trans. J. E. L Oulton, LCL 265 (Cambridge, MA: Harvard University Press, 1932), 46–7; Metzger, *Canon of the New Testament*, 130:

> ἐπεὶ ὁ κύριος, ἀπόστολος ὢν τοῦ παντοκράτορος, ἀπεστάλη πρὸς Ἑβραίους, διὰ μετριότητα ὁ Παῦλος, ὡς ἂν εἰς τὰ ἔθνη ἀπεσταλμένος, οὐκ ἐγγράφει ἑαυτὸν Ἑβραίων ἀπόστολον διά τε τὴν πρὸς τὸν κύριον τιμὴν διά τε τὸ ἐκ περιουσίας καὶ τοῖς Ἑβραίοις ἐπιστέλλειν, ἐθνῶν κήρυκα ὄντα καὶ ἀπόστολον [since the Lord, being the apostle of the Almighty, was sent to the Hebrews, Paul, through modesty, since he had been sent to the Gentiles, does not inscribe himself as an apostle of the Hebrews, both to give due deference to the Lord and because he wrote to the Hebrews also out of his abundance, being a preacher and apostle of the Gentiles.]

[19] *Hist. eccl.* 6.14.2 (Oulton: LCL 265:46–7); Metzger, *Canon of the New Testament*, 134:

> καὶ τὴν πρὸς Ἑβραίους δὲ ἐπιστολὴν Παύλου μὲν εἶναί φησιν, γεγράφθαι δὲ Ἑβραίοις Ἑβραϊκῇ φωνῇ, Λουκᾶν δὲ φιλοτίμως αὐτὴν μεθερμηνεύσαντα ἐκδοῦναι τοῖς Ἕλλησιν, ὅθεν τὸν αὐτὸν χρῶτα εὑρίσκεσθαι κατὰ τὴν ἑρμηνείαν ταύτης τε τῆς ἐπιστολῆς καὶ τῶν Πράξεων· ῥμὴ προγεγράφθαι δὲ τὸ "Παῦλος ἀπόστολος" εἰκότως· ἱκἙβραίοις γάρ," φησίν, "ἐπιστέλλων πρόληψιν εἰληφόσιν κατ᾽ αὐτοῦ καὶ ὑποπτεύουσιν αὐτόν, συνετῶς πάνυ οὐκ ἐν ἀρχῇ ἀπέτρεψεν αὐτούς, τὸ ὄνομα θείς. [And as for the Epistle to the Hebrews, he says indeed that it is Paul's, but that it was written for Hebrews in the Hebrew tongue, and that Luke, having carefully translated it, published it for the Greeks; hence, as a result of this translation, the same complexion of style is found in this Epistle and in the Acts: but that the [words] "Paul an apostle" were naturally not prefixed. For, says he, "in writing to Hebrews who had conceived a prejudice against him and were suspicious of him, he very wisely did not repel them at the beginning by putting his name."]

[20] *Hist. eccl,* 6.25.11-14 (Oulton: LCL 265:76–9); Metzger, *Canon of the New Testament*, 138:

> Ἔτι πρὸς τούτοις περὶ τῆς Πρὸς Ἑβραίους ἐπιστολῆς ἐν ταῖς εἰς αὐτὴν Ὁμιλίαις ταῦτα διαλαμβάνει· "ὅτι ὁ χαρακτὴρ τῆς λέξεως τῆς Πρὸς Ἑβραίους ἐπιγεγραμμένης ἐπιστολῆς οὐκ ἔχει τὸ ἐν λόγῳ ἰδιωτικὸν τοῦ ἀποστόλου, ὁμολογήσαντος ἑαυτὸν ἰδιώτην εἶναι τῷ λόγῳ, τοῦτ᾽ ἐστὶν τῇ φράσει, ἀλλ᾽ ἐστὶν ἡ ἐπιστολὴ συνθέσει τῆς λέξεως Ἑλληνικωτέρα, πᾶς ὁ ἐπιστάμενος κρίνειν φράσεων διαφορὰς ὁμολογήσαι ἄν. πάλιν τε αὖ ὅτι τὰ νοήματα τῆς ἐπιστολῆς θαυμάσιά ἐστιν καὶ οὐ δεύτερα τῶν ἀποστολικῶν ὁμολογουμένων γραμμάτων, καὶ τοῦτο ἂν συμφήσαι εἶναι ἀληθὲς πᾶς ὁ προσέχων τῇ ἀναγνώσει τῇ ἀποστολικῇ. Τούτοις μεθ᾽ ἕτερα ἐπιθέρει λέγων·ἐγὼ δὲ ἀποφαινόμενος εἴποιμ᾽ ἂν ὅτι τὰ μὲν νοήματα τοῦ ἀποστόλου ἐστίν, ἡ δὲ φράσις καὶ ἡ σύνθεσις ἀπομνημονεύσαντός τινος τὰ ἀποστολικὰ καὶ ὥσπερ σχολιογραφήσαντός τινος τὰ εἰρημένα ὑπὸ τοῦ διδασκάλου. εἴ τις οὖν ἐκκλησία ἔχει ταύτην τὴν ἐπιστολὴν ὡς Παύλου, αὕτη εὐδοκιμείτω καὶ ἐπὶ τούτῳ· οὐ γὰρ εἰκῆ οἱ ἀρχαῖοι ἄνδρες ὡς Παύλου αὐτὴν παραδεδώκασιν. τίς δὲ ὁ γράψας τὴν ἐπιστολήν, τὸ μὲν ἀληθὲς θεὸς οἶδεν, ἡ δὲ εἰς ἡμᾶς φθάσασα ἱστορία ὑπὸ τινῶν μὲν λεγόντων ὅτι Κλήμης, ὁ γενόμενος ἐπίσκοπος Ῥωμαίων, ἔγραψεν τὴν ἐπιστολήν, ὑπὸ τινῶν δὲ ὅτι Λουκᾶς, ὁ γράψας τὸ εὐαγγέλιον καὶ τὰς Πράξεις." [Furthermore, he thus discusses the Epistle to the Hebrews, in his *Homilies* upon it: "That the character of the diction of the epistle entitled To the Hebrews has not the apostle's rudeness in speech, who confessed himself rude in speech, that is, in style, but that the epistle is better Greek in the framing of its diction, will be admitted by everyone who is able to discern differences of style. But again, on the other hand, that the thoughts of the epistle are admirable, and not inferior to the acknowledged writings of the apostle, to this also everyone will consent as true who has given attention to

quotes it, Metzger claims he did not rank it as scripture.[21] Tertullian attributes the epistle to Barnabas while Hilary stands out among Western writers by attributing Hebrews to Paul.[22] Cyprian, on the other hand, fails to cite Hebrews at all.[23]

Metzger notes that Hebrews is also omitted from two Latin lists of books, the Cheltenham canon (James and Jude also omitted) and the Muratorian Fragment (James also omitted).[24] Metzger's interpretation of the Muratorian Fragment is particularly indicative of how deeply he regards the divide between East and West in terms of Hebrews' reception. The provenance of the Fragment has been debated among scholars, a point that could be considered to complicate the East/West divide in Hebrews' reception. Metzger, however, regards Hebrews' lack of authority in the West prior to the fourth century as so certain that it can be used as evidence for the Fragment's Western provenance. Despite Metzger's confidence about the poor reception of Hebrews in the West prior to the fourth century, he regards Hebrews' acceptance into canonical status as all but complete by the time of Jerome[25] and Augustine.[26]

reading the apostle." Further on, he adds the following remarks: "But as for myself, if I were to state my own opinion, I should say that the thoughts are the apostle's, but that the style and composition belong to one who called to mind the apostle's teachings and, as it were, made short notes of what his master said. If any church, therefore, holds this epistle as Paul's, let it be commended for this also. For not without reason have the men of old time handed it down as Paul's. But who wrote the epistle, in truth God knows. Yet the account which has reached us [is twofold], some saying that Clement, who was bishop of the Romans, wrote the epistle, others, that it was Luke, he who wrote the Gospel and the Acts."]

[21] "Although he did not rank the Epistle to the Hebrews as Scripture, he makes frequent quotations from it, particularly in his *Commentary on Daniel*" (Metzger, *Canon of the New Testament*, 150).

[22] Tertullian will be discussed at length in the chapter on patristic citations. His attribution of the epistle to Barnabas is limited to a single occurrence with specific rhetorical aims though he quotes the epistle frequently without specifically referencing it as his source. Metzger and Gamble disagree about Hilary's attribution of Pauline authorship. See footnote 28 for more details. Ibid., 159, 232.

[23] Metzger argues that the absence of Hebrews in Cyprian's writing is unlikely to have been the result of a lack of awareness of Hebrews on Cyprian's part since he studied the works of Tertullian who discusses it. Thus, Metzger concludes that Cyprian "obviously did not regard it as canonical" (ibid., 162).

[24] The Muratorian Fragment is discussed at length in the next chapter. I have not given as much attention to the so-called Cheltenham canon for several reasons:

1. Hebrews' omission from this list has not been a major point of scholarly discussion in reconstructions of Hebrews' reception as its omission from the Muratorian Fragment has.
2. The list is not really a "canon" but a stichometric list that enumerates the lines in each work for the purposes of book production.
3. Hebrews' omission from the list is assumed and not stated directly since the letters of Paul are counted as thirteen rather than fourteen.
4. This notation of thirteen Pauline letters rather than fourteen could easily be the result of scribal error since the difference between the two numbers in Latin is a single "I."

Despite these factors, the absence of Hebrews from a Latin list intended for book production could possibly serve as further evidence that Hebrews was omitted from the earliest Latin editions of the *corpus Paulinum*, as I argue in the final chapter. Edmon Gallagher and John Meade, *The Biblical Canon Lists From Early Christianity: Texts and Analysis* (New York: Oxford University Press, 2017), 188–93.

[25] Metzger portrays Jerome's acceptance of Hebrews as an acknowledgment of an emerging consensus, stating that "contrary to his quarrelsome and sometimes irascible temperament, when it comes to the books of the New Testament, he is content to acquiesce to the list of those that were then in general use" (Metzger, *Canon of the New Testament*, 236).

[26] The settled nature of the canon is more or less complete in Metzger's opinion upon reaching the time of Augustine, which he regards as "a natural terminus in our survey of debate concerning the closing of the New Testament canon." With regard to Hebrews, Metzger remarks that Augustine includes

Harry Gamble reproduces and even intensifies the bifurcation between Hebrews' reception in East and West found in Hatch and Metzger. Gamble states explicitly, "Hebrews, as noted earlier, was early associated with the Pauline Epistles in the East, but its fate in the West was very different. There it was almost wholly neglected until the fourth century."[27] Gamble cites much of the same evidence as Hatch and Metzger in his interpretation. Still, he also notes that Clement of Rome appears to have utilized the letter at a very early stage, "but during the second century it commanded almost no interest in the western church."[28] He adds that although Tertullian knew Hebrews, he made very little use of it. Furthermore, Gamble argues, what use Tertullian did make of Hebrews was likely problematic because he appealed to its teaching against a second repentance, a position that stood in opposition to the developing penitential theology of the Western church as a whole.[29]

Gamble's reconstruction of Hebrews' reception also places great emphasis on the role of church leaders in the process of Hebrews' eventual acceptance.[30] While Gamble notes that many forces played a role in deciding which writings were ultimately included in the New Testament—"political rivalries, cultural differences, and theological orientations"[31] are a few that he mentions—he highlights "the opinions of respected theologians" as being "widely influential."[32] This is especially true, he claims, in the case of writings like Hebrews and Revelation that faced a more difficult path to acceptance. Even so, he points out, ecclesiastical decisions could often do little more than "confirm standing practice."[33] Additionally, Gamble notes that "the history of the canon cannot be completely separated

---

Hebrews as one of the fourteen epistles of Paul but in his later works "he assiduously avoids calling it by the Apostle's name." Nevertheless, Metzger concludes, "he had no scruples as to its canonicity" (ibid., 236–7).

[27] Harry Gamble, "The New Testament Canon: Recent Research and the Status Quaestionis," in *The Canon Debate*, ed. Lee Martin McDonald and James A. Sanders (Peabody, MA: Hendrickson, 2002), 284–5:

> The relation of Hebrews to Paul and his letters is an old chestnut. Clement of Rome apparently knew and used Hebrews, but it subsequently commanded little interest or comment in the western church. Tertullian knew it and attributed it to Barnabas, but it was otherwise neglected until the fourth-century. In the East, however, it was well known: Clement of Alexandria fully acknowledged it as a letter of Paul, and Origen, though famously uncertain about its authorship, clearly regarded it as an authoritative document. Its inclusion in P46 shows its close eastern association with Paul.

[28] Gamble, *Making and Meaning*, 47.
[29] Ibid., 47, 52.
[30] Gamble references the inclusion of Hebrews among the twenty-seven books of the New Testament at the councils of Hippo and Carthage even while they express hesitancy over the Pauline authorship of Hebrews. He claims that the path for this acceptance was made by Hilary of Poitiers, Ambrose of Milan, and Rufinus of Aquileia, "all of whom used it as canonical while nevertheless regarding it as anonymous" (ibid., 56). One may note here the contradictory representations of Hilary by Metzger, who says Hilary stands out among Western authors by attributing Hebrews to Paul, and Gamble, who says Hilary regarded Hebrews as anonymous. The confusion likely arises from *De. Trin.* 4.11 where Hilary is arguing against the claim that Jesus is created. Hilary portrays his opponents as citing "what Paul writes to the Hebrews" in Hebrews 1:4 in their favor. It is unclear whether the attribution of Pauline authorship to Hebrews is a part of Hilary's portrayal of his opponents or representative of his own opinion about Hebrews' authorship.
[31] Ibid., 66.
[32] Ibid., 65.
[33] Ibid., 66.

even from so ordinary a matter as *the history of book manufacture* in the ancient world."[34] Specifically, he correlates the "relatively fixed content" of the New Testament in the fourth century with the emergence of technology capable of producing codices that were large enough to contain all twenty-seven books. In Gamble's later work, *Books and Readers in the Early Church*, he argues that an early Pauline letter collection was likely the impetus for the disproportionally high usage of the codex as opposed to the book roll among early Christians, thereby drawing another line of correlation between the process of book production and the reception history of New Testament documents.[35] Therefore, even as Gamble maintains the importance of fourth-century church leaders in Hebrews' acceptance in the West, he also invites further consideration of the impact of late ancient book cultures on the transmission of Hebrews.

The scholarly model of Hebrews' early acceptance in the East and initial rejection in the West can also be seen across a broad array of scholarship beyond Hatch, Metzger, and Gamble.[36] Many of the critical commentaries on Hebrews echo the opinion that Hebrews was accepted early in the East while suffering neglect in the West until the fourth century.[37] The same idea can be found among discussions about receptions of Paul,[38] the criteria of canonicity,[39] and the literary history of the New Testament.[40] The idea that Hebrews was met with early acceptance in the East and initial neglect in the West has been a persistent model for scholarly reconstructions of the reception of the Epistle to the Hebrews.

Clare K. Rothschild, however, has problematized this East/West dichotomy.[41] The evidence regarding Hebrews' reception does not divide neatly into a dichotomy of East

---

[34] Ibid., 67. Italics his.
[35] Harry Y. Gamble, *Books and Readers in the Early Church: A History of Early Christian Texts* (New Haven, CT: Yale University Press, 1995), 58–63.
[36] Hans von Campenhausen can also be included in this trajectory of scholarship. I have chosen not to write about his work at length because he gives very little attention to Hebrews specifically. Nevertheless, where he does write about Hebrews, he offers the same points that have been outlined above. He takes for granted Hebrews' rejection in the West and asserts that the idea that this rejection "is linked with anti-Montanism seems certain." He summarizes, "Only in the fourth century was Hebrews recognized in the West as Pauline, after it had long been canonized in the East, first under the influence of Origen and finally as a result of the conflict with Arianism" (*Formation of the Christian Bible*, 232–3).
[37] Harold W. Attridge, *Hebrews: A Commentary on the Epistle to the Hebrews* (Philadelphia: Fortress Press, 1989), 3; Paul Ellingworth, *Hebrews* (Grand Rapids, MI: Eerdmans, 2015), 34–6; Luke Timothy Johnson, *Hebrews: A Commentary* (Louisville: Westminster John Knox Press, 2006), 3–4; Craig R. Koester, *Hebrews* (New Haven, CT: Yale University Press, 2001), 19–24. Koester recites much of the same evidence in the framework of East and West but stops short of claiming Hebrews' rejection in the West.
[38] Richard I. Pervo, *The Making of Paul: Constructions of the Apostle in Early Christianity* (Minneapolis, MN: Fortress Press, 2010), 27, 29, 120.
[39] Einar Thomassen, ed., *Canon and Canonicity: The Formation and Use of Scripture* (Copenhagen: Museum Tusculanum Press, 2009), 22.
[40] Gerd Theissen, *The New Testament: A Literary History* (Minneapolis, MN: Fortress Press, 2011), 209–10.
[41] Her concluding reflection on the matter is particularly insightful:

> References "East and West" are less useful categories today than in the past. Increasing sophistication of scientific research dedicated to understanding the earliest phase of development of the Christian church renders such general designations unnecessarily vague … Too often similarities between groups are emphasized over distinctions between

and West, she shows, nor does it suggest that Jerome and Augustine represented a radical break from the traditions that preceded them.[42] She notes that among modern scholars, the thesis that Hebrews was rejected in the West is most commonly founded on two pieces of evidence: the absence of the treatise from the Muratorian Fragment and Eusebius' report about Gaius, the Presbyter of Rome who opposed Hebrews. Neither the Fragment nor Eusebius' report, however, offer strong support for Hebrews' rejection in the West. Rothschild regards Hebrews' omission from the Fragment as a poor foundation on which to build an argument for Hebrews' rejection given the uncertainty over the Fragment's provenance. Furthermore, Rothschild argues, even if the Western provenance and the early date of the Fragment were certain, Hebrews' omission as evidence of its rejection is in fact an argument from silence. That is, nowhere in the document is Hebrews' explicitly rejected, though the Epistle to the Laodiceans and the Epistle to the Alexandrians are.[43]

Rothschild gives more detailed attention to the second piece of evidence often cited in arguments for Hebrews' rejection in the West: Eusebius' comment that Hebrews is disputed by some at Rome.[44] Eusebius reports that some have rejected Hebrews even as he categorizes it among Paul's fourteen "well known and undisputed" epistles. He also says that he will say more later concerning what others "who lived before our time" have said about the epistle. As Rothschild points out, however, this later comment by Eusebius must be related to a report about Gaius in Book Six (6.20.3) since he does not bring the topic up anywhere else.[45] There Eusebius offers only Gaius in support of his claim that "some in Rome" reject the Epistle. Whereas Eusebius' comments in 3.3 might leave the impression that a large contingent of the Roman church rejected Hebrews, his clarification in 6.20 suggests that this rejection was the act of a single presbyter in response to very specific concerns about "Montanism."[46] Furthermore, Rothschild argues, the very fact that Gaius felt compelled to undercut Hebrews' authority by rejecting its Pauline authorship may suggest just how widely it was being

---

individuals. In this way stereotypes are propagated which, on account of their simplicity and convenience, instantly convert to axioms in the field. Such tenets, however, lack the flexibility to accurately reflect our sources. (Clare K. Rothschild, *Hebrews as Pseudepigraphon: The History and Significance of the Pauline Attribution of Hebrews* [Tubingen: Mohr Siebeck, 2012], 43)

[42] "the 'accepted versus rejected' approach to Hebrews' early reception history lacks sufficient nuance to represent the primary sources accurately" (ibid., 43).

[43] Ibid., 21–4.

[44] "τοῦ δὲ Παύλου πρόδηλοι καὶ σαφεῖς αἱ δεκατέσσαρες· ὅτι γε μὴν τινες ἠθετήκασι τὴν πρὸς Ἑβραίους, πρὸς τῆς Ῥωμαίων ἐκκλησίας ὡς μὴ Παύλου οὖσαν αὐτὴν ἀντιλέγεσθαι φήσαντες, οὐ δίκαιον ἀγνοεῖν· καὶ τὰ περὶ ταύτης δὲ τοῖς πρὸ ἡμῶν εἰρημένα κατὰ καιρὸν παραθήσομαι" ["And the fourteen letters of Paul are obvious and plain, yet it is not right to ignore that some dispute the Epistle to the Hebrews, saying that it was rejected by the church of Rome as not being by Paul, and I will expound at the proper time what was said about it by our predecessors"] (*Hist. eccl.* 3.3.3 [Oulton, LCL 153:192–3]).

[45] Rothschild, *Hebrews as Pseudepigraphon*, 24–5.

[46] *Hist. Eccl.* 6.20 (Oulton, LCL 265:64–7):
Ἦλθεν δὲ εἰς ἡμᾶς καὶ Γαΐου, λογιωτάτου ἀνδρός, διάλογος, ἐπὶ Ῥώμης κατὰ Ζεφυρῖνον πρὸς Πρόκλον τῆς κατὰ Φρύγας αἱρέσεως ὑπερμαχοῦντα κεκινημένος· ἐν ᾧ τῶν δι' ἐναντίας τὴν περὶ τὸ συντάττειν καινὰς γραφὰς προπέτειάν τε καὶ τόλμαν ἐπιστομίζων, τῶν τοῦ ἱεροῦ ἀποστόλου δεκατριῶν μόνων ἐπιστολῶν μνημονεύει, τὴν πρὸς Ἑβραίους μὴ συναριθμήσας ταῖς λοιπαῖς, ἐπεὶ καὶ εἰς δεῦρο παρὰ Ῥωμαίων τισὶν οὐ νομίζεται τοῦ ἀποστόλου τυγχάνειν. [And there has reached

read at the time. Gaius would not have considered it a genuine threat if it were not already a widely read and highly venerated document.[47] As Rothchild's analysis shows, the two primary pieces of evidence usually submitted in defense of Hebrews' supposed rejection in the West, namely the Muratorian Fragment and Eusebius' comments about the Roman church, have failed to prove the matter as conclusively as has often been thought.

Additionally, Rothschild draws attention to a number of other Western authors who witness to Hebrews' value in the West. The earliest of these is Clement of Rome who quotes Heb 1:3–4.[48] Tertullian also states that Hebrews is more widely used than the Shepherd of Hermas. Furthermore, the Shepherd itself appears to be offering a response to Heb 6:4–6 in that it "refutes belief in a single repentance, the only prior example of which is Hebrews."[49] Although this is a refutation of Hebrews' theology, it may serve to demonstrate just how well known Hebrews was at the time. In addition to these works, Rothschild also notes allusions to Hebrews among the works of Polycarp, Justin Martyr, Hippolytus, and Irenaeus.[50] In light of this evidence, Rothschild concludes that Jerome and Augustine do not represent a major turning point in Hebrews' reception. On the contrary, even as these two writers approve of Hebrews' inclusion among lists of authoritative works, they both continue to express doubts about its authorship. Rothschild notes that their opinions largely reflect the tradition leading up to them, an acceptance of Hebrews mixed with questions about its authorship.[51]

Conclusions

Rothschild's careful analysis of the literary sources has demonstrated that the reconstruction of Hebrews' reception as one of early acceptance in the East and

---

us also a Dialogue of Gaius, a very learned person (which was set a-going at Rome in the time of Zephyrinus), with Proclus the champion of the heresy of the Phrygians. In which, when curbing the recklessness and audacity of his opponents in composing new Scriptures, he mentions only thirteen epistles of the holy Apostle, not numbering the Epistle to the Hebrews with the rest; seeing that even to this day among the Romans there are some who do not consider it to be the Apostle's.]

[47] Rothschild, *Hebrews as Pseudepigraphon*, 25.
[48] Attridge, *Hebrews*, 6; Rothschild, *Hebrews as Pseudepigraphon*, 29:

"*Who, being the brightness of his majesty, is by so much greater than angels as he has inherited a more excellent name.*" For it is written thus, "*Who makes his angels spirits, and his ministers a flame of fire.*" But of his Son the Master said thus, "*You are my son; Today have I begotten thee. Ask of me and I will give you the heathen for your inheritance, and the ends of the earth for your possession.*" And again he says to him, "*Sit at my right hand until I make your enemies a footstool for thy feet.*" Who then are the enemies? Those who are wicked and oppose his will.

[49] Rothschild, *Hebrews as Pseudepigraphon*, 30.
[50] Many of these allusions are so weak, however, that it is not entirely clear that they are references to Hebrews rather references to the LXX texts that Hebrews quotes. Rothschild notes disagreement about Irenaeus' knowledge of Hebrews. Eusebius reports (*Hist. eccl.* 5.26.3) that Irenaeus knew Hebrews while Robert Grant argues from Irenaeus' extant writings that he knew nearly the entire New Testament except Hebrews. Rothschild, *Hebrews as Pseudepigraphon*, 30–1; Robert Grant, *Irenaeus of Lyons* (New York: Routledge, 1996), 1.
[51] Rothschild, *Hebrews as Pseudepigraphon*, 34–5.

initial rejection in the West inadequately captures the varied and nuanced manner in which Hebrews was received among early Christians. The present work builds on this insight through a detailed scrutiny of the various social contexts in which Hebrews was utilized and reproduced. The lists of Christian scriptures produced in the fourth and fifth centuries were the product of elite Christian intellectuals demonstrating their mastery of Greek *paideia*, particularly the methods of Greek bibliography, and were not representative of the reception of Christian scriptures prior to them or determinative for the reproduction of Christian scriptures after them. Patristic citations of Hebrews prior to the fourth century followed the compositional and citational practices common in antiquity; these writers cited the text of Hebrews as "inartificial proofs" in their arguments about the proper interpretation of Christian scriptures. The material reproductions of Hebrews that survive suggest the influence of ancient editorial practice on the creation of manuscripts that include Hebrews, as many of these manuscripts, particularly those written in Greek, indicate a close relationship between Hebrews and editions of the Pauline corpus. Latin manuscripts of Hebrews, on the other hand, reveal some hesitation regarding the inclusion of Hebrews among Paul's letters, a hesitation, I argue, that is the result of an initial omission of Hebrews from translations of the *corpus Paulinum* into Latin. The absence of Hebrews from Latin editions of Paul's letters and its inclusion after 2 Thessalonians in Greek editions posed a question to editors who consulted both as they sought to produce new Latin editions: should Hebrews be included among editions of the *corpus Paulinum*? The result, I argue, was a compromise consistent with the principles of ancient editorial practice as works of questionable authenticity were often placed at the end of an authorial edition. Therefore, Hebrews' position after Philemon in the majority of later manuscripts and modern printed Bibles represents uncertainty about its relationship to the Pauline corpus as a result of its divergent treatment in early Greek and Latin editions of Paul's letters.

2

Translating Authorship into Authority: The Reception of Hebrews in Fourth-Century Discourses on Christian Scriptures

Introduction

Highly educated Christian theologians in the fourth and fifth centuries frequently employed their elite training to create lists of Christian writings that delineated those that were acceptable and authoritative from those that were not. Although these lists have often been treated as if they were widely determinative for the use and reproduction of Christian scriptures, they were more likely the prerogative of a limited number of well-educated individuals since their creation required skills similar to those used by ancient bibliographers to determine a writing's authorship. Christian theologians who had been trained in these bibliographic skills as a part of their education utilized them to subtly new ends in their attempt to establish definitive lists of acceptable Christian writings. Since this bibliographic methodology included reporting the opinions of previous scholars, fourth-century theologians presented the thoughts of earlier Christian writers in support of their lists of acceptable scriptures. This resulted in lists that had the appearance of being rooted in long-standing tradition even though earlier Christian writers created no such lists of scriptures themselves. By doing so, fourth-century theologians retrojected their own growing desire for a clear delineation of Christian scripture upon the works of earlier writers for whom such a concern would have been largely alien. The bibliographic method that began as an endeavor entirely concerned with authorship was slowly transformed into a similar yet distinct means for establishing the authority of Christian writings through a combination of authorship, orthodoxy, and acceptance among the churches—a transformation that is especially apparent in the reception of the Epistle to the Hebrews and debates about its authorship.

Arguments over Authenticity

When fourth-century theologians began to make arguments about which writings should be counted among acceptable Christian scriptures, they did so in a way that bore remarkable resemblance to the bibliographic methods of the Greek and Roman authors before them. In the context of Greek scholarship, the custom of listing books by genre and author was initiated by Callimachus of Cyrene, the third-century BCE librarian of the great Alexandrian collection, who sought to organize the library's holdings. His *Pinakes*, or index, was a detailed catalogue of every scroll in his library that sorted the library's contents by both genre and author. The reconstruction of Callimachus' method from the relevant sources suggests that he sought to classify authors according to the kind of writings they composed. He then arranged the authors in each class alphabetically and included any biographical information about the author he could find. The author's works were listed under his or her name with the opening words of the work cited as well. (In some cases, the opening words of a work served as the title while in others they served to distinguish it from another work of the same title.) Finally, the number of lines in the work were included, presumably as a further guarantor of authenticity.[1]

The organization of the library by author required that Callimachus separate the works he regarded as an author's authentic writings from those regarded as spurious.[2] In order to accomplish this task, Callimachus employed the resources available to him in the Alexandrian library, including the biographical information about each author that Callimachus himself had assembled.[3] Most frequently, however, Callimachus repeatedly returned to two criteria: the opinion of previous writers on a work's authorship (even noting when the opinions of previous authors differed) and his own judgments of a work's style.[4] In instances where the reports of previous opinions were limited or entirely unavailable, Callimachus appears to have had no qualms about

---

[1] Rudolf Pfeiffer, *History of Classical Scholarship from the Beginnings to the End of the Hellenistic Age.* (Oxford: Clarendon Press, 1968), 130; Rudolf Blum, *Kallimachos: The Alexandrian Library and the Origins of Bibliography* (Madison: University of Wisconsin Press, 1991), 153:

> The layout of the papyrus-rolls in the Alexandrian library seems to have resembled that of the clay tablets in the oriental libraries in one or perhaps two significant points. The title of a work was regularly placed at the end of the roll and of the tablet (in contrast for instance to the practice in the Egyptian papyri), and in "catalogues" not only this title, but also the "incipit" was cited. On tablets and rolls the number of lines was occasionally counted, and these "stichometrical" figures were put at the end and sometimes as running figures in the margins; they appear again in the library-catalogues.

[2] Blum, *Kallimachos*, 236:

> Even though only a few remarks of a critical nature by Kallimachos have come down to us, it is nevertheless clear from the character of his cataloging that he sought above all to find out who had been the real authors of many works whose attribution was disputed or questionable, and at least to distinguish the genuine works of an author from the spurious ones. For example, if the copies of the same work bore the name of three different authors, he could not list it under each name; this would have been inventorying not cataloging. It is therefore unlikely that he made notes of literary criticism only occasionally and as an afterthought after having finished his catalog, as some researchers have thought. Rather, literary criticism constituted an integral part of the cataloging process that he performed.

[3] Ibid., 233. For other reference works created by Callimachus, see Francis J. Witty, "The Other Pinakes and Reference Works of Callimachus," *The Library Quarterly* 43, no. 3 (1973): 237–44. For the place of the Alexandrian library among the other great libraries of history, see Ian Willison, "On the History of the Archival Library and Scholarship in the West since the Alexandrian Library: An Overview," *Alexandria* 25, no. 3 (2014): 87–110.

[4] Blum, *Kallimachos*, 149, 158–9, 246.

making his own declarations about the work's authenticity based on his judgments of its style as compared to the other works attributed to the same author.[5] Once all of these factors were taken into consideration, Callimachus could label a work as authentic, spurious, or, in some cases, simply note that is was disputed without making a final judgment.

The influence of Callimachus' bibliographic method extended well beyond his own lifetime as the *Pinakes* continued to be expanded by his successors even after his death.[6] Later Alexandrian philologists also compiled editions of classic poetry and included biographies of the authors. These biographies often included a list of the author's works, distinguishing between those regarded as authentic and those regarded as spurious.[7] Although adopting Callimachus' critical method, later bibliographers naturally disagreed with some of his conclusions. Dionysios of Halicarnassus, for example, writing in the first century BCE cited instances where he believed Callimachus to be incorrect and even called into question Callimachus' ability to make such judgments at all.[8] The important point for the current study, however, is that even if later bibliographers judged Callimachus inept at carrying out his own methodology, they continued to employ that methodology themselves.

This practice continued into the Roman era as well. During the imperial period, excerpts of bibliographic works were compiled into handbooks focused on a single genre or class of authors. One of the most well-known creators of such compilations was Diogenes Laertius.[9] In his works describing the lives of important philosophers, Diogenes carefully catalogues the authentic works of the philosophers he discusses. In doing so, he often reports the opinions of previous bibliographers regarding the authenticity of a given work, labeling them either authentic, spurious, or disputed, much as Callimachus had done. One such example occurs in Diogenes' discussion of Phaedo:

> Of the dialogues which bear his name the Zopyrus and Simon are genuine; the Nicias is doubtful; the Medius is said by some to be the work of Aeschines, while others ascribe it to Polyaenus; the Antimachus or The Elders is also doubted; the Cobblers' Tales are also by some attributed to Aeschines.[10]

---

[5] Ibid., 232.
[6] Ibid., 182:
> We may be sure that the successors of Kallimachos followed his example, i.e. they endeavored to identify the works contained in newly acquired scrolls, to distinguish between authors with identical names, to indicate also others by relevant data about their persons, to separate authentic works from spurious ones, etc. If and when they were successful, they recorded the authors and their works in the appropriate classes, just as Kallimachos had done. Thus, the Alexandrian Pinakes contained also biographical data on authors who lived after Kallimachos.

[7] Ibid., 183.
[8] Ibid., 159. For a concise list of later literary references to Callimachus, see Francis J. Witty, "The Pínakes of Callimachus," *The Library Quarterly: Information, Community, Policy* 28, no. 2 (1958): 132–6.
[9] Blum, *Kallimachos*, 183.
[10] "διαλόγους δὲ συνέγραψε γνησίους μὲν Ζώπυρον, Σίμωνα, καὶ διστανζόμενον Νικίαν, Μήδιον, ὅν φασί τινες Αἰσχίνου, οἱ δὲ Πολυαίνου· Ἀντίμαχον ἢ Πρεσβύτας. καὶ οὗτος διστάζεται· σκυτικοὺς

Dungan notes that an important aspect of Diogenes' catalogue is that he seeks to record the state of the current discussion rather than to end it. He does offer a definitive opinion where the authenticity of a work seems to be in little, if any, doubt. Where there are disputes, however, he allows those disputes to stand rather than seeking to settle them.[11]

The tradition of arguing over the authentic authorship of important literary works was well established among Greek and Roman writers by the time Christian theologians began to debate the authority of Christian scriptures. Although the work of bibliographers revolved primarily around authorship, their work was also about much more than merely assigning a name to a given text. Authorship was itself inherently a means of authorizing the legitimacy of a written work by attaching it to the authority of a respected author.[12] Such judgments were often made based on the reports of previous bibliographers, one's own judgments about a work's style, and any biographical data that could be assembled about the author. Therefore, when educated Christian intellectuals of the fourth century utilized their training in bibliographic methodology to produce arguments about the authority of various Christian writings, they stood in a long tradition of translating authorship into authority. They also subtly transformed this method, however, in a manner that reflected their own concerns for a clearer delineation of Christian writings and thereby Christian identity as well.[13] Whereas their bibliographic predecessors sought to determine a work's authorship by virtue of its coherence to an author's other known works and the expressed opinions of previous scholars, educated Christian intellectuals judged a work by these ideas as well as the writing's coherence to an emerging concept of orthodoxy and its acceptance among Christian churches and writers.[14] Fourth-century theologians thus utilized

---

λόγους· καὶ τούτους τινὲς Αἰσχίνου φασί" (*De vit phil.* 2.64 [Hicks, LCL 184:233]). See also 3.57-62 for an example of a more extensive evaluation, in this case, of works attributed to Plato.

[11] David L. Dungan, *Constantine's Bible: Politics and the Making of the New Testament* (Minneapolis, MN: Fortress Press, 2007), 39.

[12] "In this sense, the function of an author is to characterize the existence, circulation, and operation of certain discourses within a society" (Michel Foucault, *Language, Counter-Memory, Practice: Selected Essays and Interviews* [Ithaca, NY: Cornell University Press, 1977], 124). "Works receive attribution only when it is useful to perform certain kinds of discursive work with regard to some present social enterprise" (Karen King, "What Is an Author?: Ancient Author-Function in the Apocryphon of John and the Apocalypse of John," in *Scribal Practices and Social Structures among Jesus Adherents: Essays in Honour of John S. Kloppenborg*, ed. William E. Arnal et al. [Leuven: Peeters, 2016], 41).

[13] "As a means of conceptualizing late ancient religious difference, grammatical techniques also allowed for the articulation of a temporal break that could then be construed as a break between preexistent religious entities, whose derived subjects necessarily occupied different cultural, religious, and physical spaces" (Catherine M. Chin, *Grammar and Christianity in the Late Roman World* [Philadelphia: University of Pennsylvania Press, 2007], 170).

[14] Use of the term "orthodoxy" here is not meant to suggest a well-established, homogeneous Christianity from which "heresies" knowingly departed. Recent scholarship has highlighted the extent to which later concepts of orthodoxy, much like later concepts of canon, have often been assumed in discussions of an early period in which no clear orthodoxy had emerged among the varieties of early Christianities. Furthermore, early Christian writings that do discuss orthodoxy and heresy often employ such rhetoric as a means of self-differentiation with the depiction of the heretical other serving to define the boundaries of what a given author seeks to delineate as orthodox. Eusebius exhibits these same characteristics in his use of the term "orthodoxy" with regard to the content of Christian writings. I have employed the term in an attempt to reflect Eusebius' perspective with regard to these writings without judgment regarding how accurately his rhetoric represents the diversity of early Christianity. David Brakke, *The Gnostics Myth, Ritual, and Diversity in Early*

their bibliographic training in a manner that was remarkably consistent with this educational tradition even while subtly transforming the parameters of that method in a manner that allowed them to address the needs of an emerging Christian identity.

Christian Discourses about Authoritative Scriptures in the Fourth Century

Eusebius of Caesarea

In the opening lines of his *Ecclesiastical History*, Eusebius states that his primary aims are to provide a record of succession from the apostles of Jesus to his own time, to list the church's leaders and their works, to number "those who in each generation were the ambassadors of the word of God either by speech or pen," and to outline the various heresies that have arisen along the way.[15] Therefore, from the very beginning, Eusebius characterizes his work as a kind of catalogue in which one of the matters he intends to catalogue is the written works of those who were "ambassadors of the word of God."[16] Eusebius' catalogue of Christian scriptures may best be understood in light of established bibliographic methods for determining authorship. Like his bibliographic predecessors, Eusebius was also concerned with establishing the authorship of the Christian writings he discussed and he attempted to do so by reporting the opinions of previous church leaders about these writings. However, Eusebius subtly shifted the parameters of these established bibliographic methods so as to address his own concerns in such a way that a writing's status came to encompass much more than just authorship; a work was established as recognized by a mixture of authorship, acceptance, and orthodoxy, not always in equal parts or an established order. In his

---

Christianity (Cambridge, MA: Harvard University Press, 2010); Karen L. King, "Factions, Variety, Diversity, Multiplicity: Representing Early Christian Differences for the 21st Century," *Method & Theory in the Study of Religion* 23, no. 3 (2011): 216–37.

[15] *Hist. eccl.* 1.1.1 (Oulton, LCL 153:7):

> Τὰς τῶν ἱερῶν ἀποστόλων διαδοχὰς σὺν καὶ τοῖς ἀπὸ τοῦ σωτῆρος ἡμῶν καὶ εἰς ἡμᾶς διηνυσμένοις χρόνοις, ὅσα τε καὶ πηλίκα πραγματευθῆναι κατὰ τὴν ἐκκλησιαστικὴν ἱστορίαν λέγεται, καὶ ὅσοι ταύτης διαπρεπῶς ἐν ταῖς μάλιστα ἐπισημοτάταις παροικίαις ἡγήσαντό τε καὶ προέστησαν, ὅσοι τε κατὰ γενεὰν ἑκάστην ἀγράφως ἢ καὶ διὰ συγγραμμάτων τὸν θεῖον ἐπρέσβευσαν λόγον, τίνες τε καὶ ὅσοι καὶ ὁπηνίκα νεωτεροποιίας ἱμέρῳ πλάνης εἰς ἔσχατον ἐλάσαντες, ψευδωνύμου γνώσεως εἰσηγητὰς ἑαυτοὺς ἀνακεκηρύχασιν, ἀφειδῶς οἷα λύκοι βαρεῖς τὴν Χριστοῦ ποίμνην ἐπεντρίβοντες.

[16] Indeed, one might argue that the *Ecclesiastical History* is a compilation of many kinds of catalogues.

> Eusebius' preferred word for a list of sacred writings, or any list, for that matter, as we have noted again and again in the translations throughout this chapter is catalogue. He uses "catalogue" to describe Melito's list of Jewish scriptures in 4.26.12. The group of Paul's letters in 3.25.2 is a "catalogue." The entire list of Christian writings categorized in 3.25 is referred to as a "catalogue." In 1.12.1, Eusebius catalogues apostles; in 3.4.4, Paul's fellow workers; in 3.38.1, the writings of Ignatius; in 5.17.2 Christian prophets; In 6.32.3, Origen's corpus. And, of course, Christian martyrs are catalogued as well (5.21.5). (Gregory Allen Robbins, "'Peri Ton Endiathekon Graphon': Eusebius and the Formation of the Christian Bible" [PhD diss., Duke University, 1986], 155)

assessment of Hebrews among other Christian writings, Eusebius continued to use the categories familiar to previous bibliographers, but he infused new layers of meaning into those categories in order to address the pressing questions of the fourth century about separating those scriptures that were authoritative from those that were not.

Eusebius introduces his most complete catalogue of Christian scriptures in 3.25.1-7, utilizing the familiar categories of bibliographic method—accepted, disputed, and spurious—but he does so to new ends.[17] Authorship is an important concern of Eusebius' catalogue, and he seeks to establish the authorship of these Christian writings in a manner that is similar to the methods of Callimachus or Diogenes; he presents the opinions of his predecessors and makes judgments about the coherence of a work's content with its presumed authorship, both methods which would have been familiar to previous bibliographers. However, Eusebius has also subtly shifted the manner in which these methods for establishing authorship worked. This shift can be seen most clearly in the criteria Eusebius uses to distinguish the "disputed" works from those he judges as heretical: ecclesiastical writers never referred to the latter; these differed from the apostolic writings in style and phraseology, and they were not orthodox in their content. The second of these criteria—the reference to the style of these works—is entirely consistent with the kind of judgment one might find among Eusebius' bibliographic predecessors.[18] The shape of the other two criteria, however, has been subtly expanded to fit the unique needs of Eusebius' own circumstance. In

---

[17] *Hist. eccl.* 3.25.1-7 (Oulton: LCL 153:257-9):
At this point it seems reasonable to summarize the writings of the New Testament which have been quoted. In the first place should be put the holy tetrad of the Gospels. To them follows the writing of the Acts of the Apostles. After this should be reckoned the Epistles of Paul. Following them the Epistle of John called the first, and in the same way should be recognized the Epistle of Peter. In addition to these should be put, if it seem desirable, the Revelation of John, the arguments concerning which we will expound at the proper time. These belong to the Recognized Books [ὁμολογουμένοις]. Of the Disputed Books [ἀντιλεγομένων] which are nevertheless known to most are the Epistle called of James, that of Jude, the second Epistle of Peter, and the so-called second and third Epistles of John which may be the work of the evangelist or of some other with the same name. Among the books which are not genuine [νόθοις] must be reckoned the Acts of Paul, the work entitled the Shepherd, the Apocalypse of Peter, and in addition to them the letter called of Barnabas and the so-called Teachings of the Apostles. And in addition, as I said, the Revelation of John, if this view prevail. For, as I said, some reject it, but others count it among the Recognized Books. Some have also counted the Gospel according to the Hebrews in which those of the Hebrews who have accepted Christ take a special pleasure. These would all belong to the disputed books, but we have nevertheless been obliged to make a list of them, distinguishing between those writings which, according to the tradition of the Church, are true, genuine, and recognized, and those which differ from them in that they are not canonical [ἐνδιαθήκους] but disputed, yet nevertheless are known to most of the writers of the Church, in order that we might know them and the writings which are put forward by heretics under the name of the apostles containing gospels such as those of Peter, and Thomas, and Matthias, and some others besides, or Acts such as those of Andrew and John and the other apostles. To none of these has any who belonged to the succession of the orthodox ever thought it right to refer in his writings. Moreover, the type of phraseology differs from apostolic style, and the opinion and tendency of their contents is widely dissonant from true orthodoxy and clearly shows that they are the forgeries of heretics. They ought, therefore, to be reckoned not even among spurious [νόθοις] books but shunned as altogether wicked [ἄτοπα]and impious [δυσσεβῆ].

[18] See his report of Origen's opinion about Hebrews at 6.25.11-14 for another example, discussed below.

the same way that earlier bibliographers reported the opinion of previous writers regarding a work's authorship, Eusebius refers to the work of earlier ecclesiastical writers to distinguish the disputed works from the heretical. Eusebius differs from his bibliographic predecessors, however, in that he does not say that these ecclesiastical writers made specific comments against the authorship of the works deemed heretical; it is enough that they failed to refer to them at all. Eusebius similarly expands the third criterion as well. It was not unusual for bibliographers to make judgments about authorship based on the coherence of a work's content with one's established authorial image; a work could be deemed spurious if the work's content was simply too disparate from an author's known works. Eusebius expands this notion when he claims that heretical works are not only dissonant with regard to the thoughts of Peter or Paul or any other apostolic writer but also dissonant from "true orthodoxy," a concept that, in his writings, encompasses a perceived agreement between all of these writers.

The adaptation and expansion of these criteria show that Eusebius is concerned not only with authorship but also with categories that go beyond it and derive their shape from a complex web of authorship, orthodoxy, and broad acceptance among the churches. It is important for Eusebius to establish some works based on authorship—specifically, their connection to an apostle—in the model of established bibliographic methods. On the other hand, he maintains some space for works that might be ruled out by these methods purely on the grounds of authorship but which are widely known across the church and are considered orthodox in content.[19] As a result, typical bibliographic terms like "disputed" and "spurious" take on a double meaning for Eusebius: a work can be disputed with regard to authorship as was the case in traditional bibliographic method, but it can also be disputed with regard to recognized status.[20]

Eusebius counts the four Gospels, the fourteen letters of Paul (including Hebrews), Acts, 1 John, and 1 Peter among the recognized works because they are orthodox, widely accepted, and their authorship by an apostle or an associate of an apostle is not in question.[21] He says that the status of James, Jude, 2 Peter, 2–3 John, the *Acts of*

---

[19] As Ehrman points out, these categories reinforced one another. A work was more likely to be judged as authentic with regard to authorship if its content was regarded as orthodox and it was widely accepted.

> Eusebius too was interested in knowing the actual authors of the early Christian writings. As one of his leading criteria he, the inveterate historian, looked to see how widely a book was used and attested by earlier authors. Writings that appear to have been unknown in earlier times were suspect, not just with respect to their canonicity but more specifically with respect to their authorship, two issues that were closely tied together (but by no means synonymous) in Eusebius' mind. Usage, though, was as important as content. (Bart D. Ehrman, *Forgery and Counterforgery: The Use of Literary Deceit in Early Christian Polemics* [New York: Oxford University Press, 2013], 89)

[20] In addition to using "spurious" as a term with regard to authorship, Eusebius can also use it to refer to heretical works as he does in 3.31.6, labeling them παντελῶς νόθων καὶ τῆς ἀποστολικῆς ὀρθοδοξίας ἀλλοτρίων. Edmon Gallagher and John Meade, *The Biblical Canon Lists from Early Christianity: Texts and Analysis* (New York: Oxford University Press, 2017), 106.

[21] Eusebius refers to these works as recognized or accepted here and later refers to them as ἐνδιάθηκον, a word some scholars have translated as "canonical," presumably because of an assumed similarity in function to this category in later Christian writings. Eusebius does use the word "canon" elsewhere but in a manner consistent with the uses of the word that preceded him, namely, as a rule or standard

Table 1 Eusebius' Catalogue of Scriptures

Recognized (ὁμολογουμένοις)	Four Gospels, Epistles of Paul, Acts of the Apostles, 1 John, 1 Peter	Possibly Apocalypse of John
Disputed (ἀντιλεγομένων): possibly apostolic, orthodox, and widely known, possibly recognized	James, Jude, 2 Peter, 2–3 John	
Spurious/ Disputed (νόθοις): definitively not apostolic but orthodox and somewhat widely known, less likely to be regarded as recognized	*Acts of Paul*, Shepherd, *Apocalypse of Peter*, *Barnabas*, *Didache*, and *Gospel according to the Hebrews*	Possibly Apocalypse of John
Heretical, Wicked, and Impious	Gospels of Peter, Thomas, and Matthias, Acts of Thomas, John, and others	

Paul, the *Shepherd*, the *Apocalypse of Peter*, the *Epistle of Barnabas*, the *Didache*, and the *Gospel according to the Hebrews* is disputed. However, within this larger disputed category he also describes the *Acts of Paul*, the *Shepherd*, the *Apocalypse of Peter*, *Barnabas*, the *Didache*, and the *Gospel according to the Hebrews* as spurious meaning that they are definitively not authored by an apostle or an associate of an apostle.[22] They are, nevertheless, "disputed" insofar as they are still widely read and accepted by many churches despite their definitively spurious status.[23] James, Jude, 2 Peter, and 2–3 John, on the other hand, are disputed both with regard to authorship and their recognized status. Indeed, these works are so widely read and orthodox in their content that the disputed status of their authorship is likely the only factor that keeps them out

---

rather than a list of writings. The only possible exception is in 6.25.3 where Eusebius says of Origen, "ἐν δὲ τῷ πρώτῳ τῶν εἰς τὸ κατὰ Ματθαῖον, τὸν ἐκκλησιαστικὸν φυλάττων κανόνα, μόνα τέσσαρα εἰδέναι εὐαγγέλια μαρτύρεται." One might read this as attesting to a canon of four Gospels but, as Robbins states,

> Given the way Eusebius uses κανόν elsewhere and the fact that, in 6.25.1 immediately preceding this passage, he refers to Origen's list of Old Testament scriptures as καταλόγου it seems reasonable to conclude that "the canon of the Church" here means the Church's tradition of accepting only four Gospels. This "ecclesiastical canon" is hardly a complete, closed list of scriptures, including Gospels, letters and other writings, "to which nothing could be added, nothing taken away. ("'Peri Ton Endiathekon Graphon," 153)

[22] Eric Junod, "D'Eusèbe de Césarée à Athanase d'Alexandrie en passant par Cyrille de Jérusalem: de la construction savante du Nouveau Testament à la clôture ecclésiastique du canon," in *Le canon du Nouveau Testament: regards nouveaux sur l'histoire de sa formation*, ed. Gabriella Aragione, Eric Junod, and Enrico Norelli (Genève: Labor et Fides, 2005), 178.

[23] Baum asserts that the difference between the two categories is Eusebius' own opinion regarding the authorship of the works. A. D. Baum, "Der Neutestamentliche Kanon Bei Eusebius (Historia Ecclesiastica 3.25.1–7) Im Kontext Seiner Literaturgeschichtlichen Arbeit," *ETL* 73 (1997): 307–48.

of the recognized category, a status to which they would presumably ascend if their authorship could be more firmly established (Table 1).[24]

Eusebius places the book of Revelation in two categories—both recognized and spurious—and fails to resolve the matter decisively. Such a lack of resolution is not outside the norms of bibliographic method, but Eusebius' treatment of Revelation does require extra attention since he already has a category available to him by which to note such ambiguity, the disputed works; yet he does not list the Apocalypse of John alongside James, Jude, 2 Peter, and 2 and 3 John.[25] Eusebius was persuaded by the argument of Dionysius of Alexandria that the Apocalypse was *not* written by the apostle John, son of Zebedee, but by another John who received a vision from the Lord and, furthermore, that it was only of value if it was read allegorically.[26] As a result, the Apocalypse could either be included in the "recognized" category on its merits as an orthodox vision from Jesus that was accepted by many if read properly or it could be demoted to the "spurious" subsection of the larger "disputed" category if others found it orthodox but not quite widely accepted enough to belong in the "recognized"

---

[24] For the view that "disputed" and "spurious" are virtually synonymous for Eusebius, see Everett R. Kalin, "The New Testament Canon of Eusebius," in *The Canon Debate*, ed. Lee Martin McDonald and James A. Sanders (Peabody, MA: Hendrickson, 2002), 393; Robbins, "'Peri Ton Endiathekon Graphon,'" 137–41.

[25] Dungan suggests that the difference between these categories is that the first (only disputed, not spurious) are "nevertheless known to most" while those considered not genuine Eusebius wishes to portray as less widely known: "On the other hand, this second group of 'disputed' writings, which Eusebius calls 'spurious,' were scarcely known or used by any of them [the bishops], as we can see from Eusebius' scanty or non-existent references elsewhere in his *History* to the *Epistle of Barnabas* or the *Institutions of the Apostles*" (*Constantine's Bible*, 74). Kalin provides a helpful catalogue of the various positions held by scholars regarding the number and shape of categories in Eusebius' catalogue ("New Testament Canon of Eusebius," 393–4).

[26] *Hist. eccl.* 7.24–25 (Oulton: LCL 265:198–9); Dungan, *Constantine's Bible*, 75; Ehrman, *Forgery and Counterforgery*, 48:

> Ἐπὶ τούτοις τὴν ὅλην τῆς Ἀποκαλύψεως βασανίσας γραφὴν ἀδύνατόν τε αὐτὴν κατὰ τὴν πρόχειρον ἀποδείξας νοεῖσθαι διάνοιαν, ἐπιφέρει λέγων· "συντελέσας δὴ πᾶσαν ὡς εἰπεῖν τὴν προφητείαν, μακαρίζει ὁ προφήτης τούς τε. 8φυλάσσοντας αὐτὴν καὶ δὴ καὶ ἑαυτόν. 'μακάριος' γάρ φησιν 'ὁ τηρῶν τοὺς λόγους τῆς προφητείας τοῦ βιβλίου τούτου κἀγὼ Ἰωάννης ὁ βλέπων καὶ ἀκούων ταῦτα.' καλεῖσθαι μὲν οὖν αὐτὸν Ἰωάννην καὶ εἶναι τὴν γραφὴν Ἰωάννου ταύτην οὐκ ἀντερῶ, ἁγίου μὲν γὰρ εἶναί τινος καὶ θεοπνεύστου συναινῶ· οὐ μὴν ῥᾳδίως ἂν συνθείμην τοῦτον εἶναι τὸν ἀπόστολον, τὸν υἱὸν Ζεβεδαίου, τὸν ἀδελφὸν Ἰακώβου, οὗ τὸ εὐαγγέλιον τὸ κατὰ Ἰωάννην ἐπιγεγραμμένον καὶ ἡ ἐπιστολὴ ἡ καθολική. τεκμαίρομαι γὰρ ἔκ τε τοῦ ἤθους ἑκατέρων καὶ τοῦ τῶν λόγων εἴδους καὶ τῆς τοῦ βιβλίου διεξαγωγῆς λεγομένης, μὴ τὸν αὐτὸν εἶναι. ὁ μὲν γὰρ εὐαγγελιστὴς οὐδαμοῦ τὸ ὄνομα αὐτοῦ παρεγγράφει οὐδὲ κηρύσσει ἑαυτὸν οὔτε διὰ τοῦ εὐαγγελίου οὔτε διὰ τῆς ἐπιστολῆς."
> [Moreover, after closely examining the whole book of the Apocalypse and demonstrating that it cannot be understood in the literal sense, he adds as follows: "After completing the whole, one might say, of his prophecy, the prophet calls those blessed who observe it, and indeed himself also; for he says: 'Blessed is he that keepeth the words of the prophecy of this book, and I John, he that saw and heard these things.' That, then, he was certainly named John and that this book is by one John, I will not gainsay; for I fully allow that it is the work of some holy and inspired person. But I should not readily agree that he was the apostle, the son of Zebedee, the brother of James, whose are the Gospel entitled According to John and the Catholic Epistle. For I form my judgement from the character of each and from the nature of the language and from what is known as the general construction of the book, that [the John therein mentioned] is not the same. For the evangelist nowhere adds his name, nor yet proclaims himself, throughout either the Gospel or the Epistle."]

category.²⁷ Eusebius' treatment of Revelation demonstrates that apostolic authorship is not a *necessary* criterion for recognized status; what is necessary is that a work does not misrepresent its authorship. Eusebius may recognize Revelation as having authentic authorship so long as it is understood that its author does not portray himself as John the apostle of Jesus. Furthermore, it is not primarily the authorship of Revelation but how widely known and used it is, a subject Eusebius leaves unsettled, which will ultimately decide whether it is recognized or not. In either case, however, Revelation does not belong in the disputed but not spurious category because its authorship is a settled matter in the mind of Eusebius; it was *not* written by an apostle or an associate of an apostle. Eusebius' treatment of Revelation, as well as the other works he discusses in his catalogue of scriptures at 3.25.1-7, illustrates the extent to which he has followed typical bibliographic methodology while also translating that method in a way that allows him to accommodate multiple criteria for evaluating the relative value of certain Christian writings where there had previously been only a concern for establishing authentic authorship.²⁸ Eusebius translated a methodology for discerning authentic authorship into a means of establishing a set of broadly accepted sacred writings.

This same utilization and adaptation of his bibliographic training is also on display in Eusebius' treatment of Hebrews and its relationship to the Pauline corpus:²⁹

---

²⁷ Although Eusebius says in 3.24.17-18 that there are opinions on both sides with regard to Revelation, he cites only the opinion in favor of it. Gallagher and Meade, *Biblical Canon Lists*, 105.

Τῶν δὲ Ἰωάννου γραμμάτων πρὸς τῷ εὐαγγελίῳ καὶ ἡ προτέρα τῶν ἐπιστολῶν παρά τε τοῖς νῦν καὶ τοῖς ἔτ᾽ ἀρχαίοις ἀναμφίλεκτος ὡμολόγηται, ἀντιλέγονται δὲ αἱ λοιπαὶ δύο, τῆς δ᾽ Ἀποκαλύψεως εἰς ἑκάτερον ἔτι νῦν παρὰ τοῖς πολλοῖς περιέλκεται ἡ δόξα· ὁμοίως γε μὴν ἐκ τῆς τῶν ἀρχαίων μαρτυρίας ἐν οἰκείῳ καιρῷ τὴν ἐπίκρισιν δέξεται καὶ αὐτή. [Of the writings of John in addition to the gospel the first of his epistles has been accepted without controversy by ancients and moderns alike but the other two are disputed, and as to the Revelation there have been many advocates of either opinion up to the present. This, too, shall be similarly illustrated by quotations from the ancients at the proper time.] (*Hist. eccl.* 3.24.17-18 [Oulton: LCL 153:254–7])

The orthodoxy of the Apocalypse is not in question here. Nor is it doubted that the writing has gained considerable currency among the churches. Some, however, consider it to be a forgery written in the name of the Apostle John, the son of Zebedee. If that is true, then it cannot be included among the "accepted" books. If, however, it can be proved that this book is genuine, that it was written by another John, in his own name, during the apostolic age, with no intention of deceiving the reader into believing that it was written by the Apostle John, then it would be appropriate to include it in this category. As we shall see, it is Eusebius' aim to establish that the Apocalypse is, in fact, genuine. (Robbins, "'Peri Ton Endiathekon Graphon,'" 117)

²⁸ This is succinctly apparent in Eusebius' summary of this section of his work. "We have now described the facts which have come to our knowledge concerning the Apostles and their times, the sacred writings which *they have left us*, those books which are disputed yet nevertheless are *used openly by many in most churches*, and those which are altogether fictitious and foreign to *our historic orthodoxy*. Let us now continue the narrative" (*Hist. eccl.* 3.31.6 [Oulton, LCL 153:273]). Italics mine.

²⁹ See also Eusebius' discussion of writings attributed to Peter at *Hist. eccl.* 3.3.3. Eusebius lists all the works he knows that are associated with Peter and proceeds to evaluate these works based on the opinions of those who have preceded him. The first epistle of Peter is accepted because "the ancient presbyters used it in their own writings" but the second epistle is not despite having "appeared useful to many." Likewise, the other works associated with Peter are rejected because "no ecclesiastical writer of ancient time or of our own has used their testimonies." Eusebius promises that he will follow this same procedure throughout his work, delineating which works are accepted

And the fourteen letters of Paul are obvious and plain, yet it is not right to ignore that some dispute the Epistle to the Hebrews, saying that it was rejected by the church of Rome as not being by Paul, and I will expound at the proper time what was said about it by our predecessors.[30]

In a manner consistent with bibliographic methodology, Eusebius states the generally accepted number of Paul's letters while also noting that some debate exists regarding the status of Hebrews. Eusebius keeps his promise to expound on what has been said about Hebrews by providing the opinions of no less than six of his predecessors. One of these is a direct clarification of his statement concerning Hebrews' status at Rome. In 6.20 Eusebius clarifies that this is a reference to the Dialogue of Gaius who did not count Hebrews among the Pauline Epistles, and, as a result, Eusebius reports there are some in Rome even into his own day who did not accept Hebrews as Pauline. However, Eusebius also draws attention to Clement of Rome, whose letter he cites as evidence of Hebrews' antiquity because of the parallels between the two writings. This is also the first of several reports by Eusebius in the *Ecclesiastical History* that an earlier writer believed that Paul had written Hebrews in the Hebrew language but that it was translated by someone else, in this case Clement himself.[31] Eusebius credits a similar idea to Pantaenus, Clement, and Origen, in the case of the former two adding the idea

---

or rejected, and even those regarded as doubtful, based not on his own opinion but on the opinion of "ecclesiastical writers in each period."

[30] I have ended the quote here so as to focus on Hebrews, but Eusebius continues,

> Nor have I received his so-called Acts among undisputed books. But since the same Apostle in the salutations at the end of Romans has mentioned among others Hermas, whose, they say, is the Book of the Shepherd, it should be known that this also is rejected by some, and for their sake should not be placed among accepted books, but by others it has been judged most valuable, especially to those who need elementary instruction. For this reason we know that it has been used in public in churches, and I have found it quoted by some of the most ancient writers. Let this suffice for the establishment of the divine writings which are undisputed, and of those which are not received by all. (*Hist. eccl.* 3.3.3 [Oulton, LCL 153:193])

[31] *Hist. eccl.* 3.38.1-3 (Oulton, LCL 153:289):

> ὥσπερ οὖν ἀμέλει τοῦ Ἰγνατίου ἐν αἷς κατελέξαμεν ἐπιστολαῖς, καὶ τοῦ Κλήμεντος ἐν τῇ ἀνωμολογημένῃ παρὰ πᾶσιν, ἣν ἐκ προσώπου τῆς Ῥωμαίων ἐκκλησίας τῇ Κορινθίων διετυπώσατο· ἐν ᾗ τῆς πρὸς Ἑβραίους πολλὰ νοήματα παραθείς, ἤδη δὲ καὶ αὐτολεξεὶ ῥητοῖς τισιν ἐξ αὐτῆς χρησάμενος, σαφέστατα παρίστησιν ὅτι μὴ νέον ὑπάρχει τὸ σύγγραμμα, ὅθεν δὴ καὶ εἰκότως ἔδοξεν αὐτὸ τοῖς λοιποῖς ἐγκαταλεχθῆναι γράμμασι τοῦ ἀποστόλου. Ἑβραίοις γὰρ διὰ τῆς πατρίου γλώττης ἐγγράφως ὡμιληκότος τοῦ Παύλου, οἱ μὲν τὸν εὐαγγελιστὴν Λουκᾶν, οἱ δὲ τὸν Κλήμεντα τοῦτον αὐτὸν ἑρμηνεῦσαι λέγουσι τὴν γραφήν· ὃ καὶ μᾶλλον ἂν εἴη ἀληθὲς τῷ τὸν ὅμοιον τῆς φράσεως χαρακτῆρα τήν τε τοῦ Κλήμεντος ἐπιστολὴν καὶ τὴν πρὸς Ἑβραίους ἀποσῴζειν καὶ τῷ μὴ πόρρω τὰ ἐν ἑκατέροις τοῖς συγγράμμασι νοήματα καθεστάναι. [Such writings, of course, were the letters of Ignatius of which we gave the list, and the Epistle of Clement which is recognized by all, which he wrote in the name of the church of the Romans to that of the Corinthians. In this he has many thoughts parallel to the Epistle to the Hebrews, and actually makes some verbal quotations from it showing clearly that it was not a recent production, and for this reason, too, it has seemed natural to include it among the other writings of the Apostle. For Paul had spoken in writing to the Hebrews in their native language, and some say that the evangelist Luke, others that this same Clement translated the writing. And the truth of this would be supported by the similarity of style preserved by the Epistle of Clement and that to the Hebrews, and by the little difference between the thoughts in both writings.]

that the reason Paul did not affix his name to it was out of modesty and so that he would not give offense to the Jewish audience he was addressing.[32]

Eusebius' presentation of Origen suggests the latter's own bibliographic training as Origen distinguishes Hebrews from the rest of Paul's writings on the basis of style. Origen states his own opinion on the matter (that the thoughts are those of the apostle even if the language is not), reports the opinions of his predecessors (that it was written by Clement of Rome or Luke), and finally leaves the debate open for discussion ("But who wrote the epistle, in truth God knows.").[33] However, Eusebius' ability to reshape bibliographic materials toward his own ends is visible in his treatment of Origen just as it was in Eusebius' own catalogue of scriptures. Eusebius' report of Origen's opinion concerning Hebrews occurs within a larger compilation and presentation of various quotations from Origen as though they were a single catalogue of scriptures.[34] Eusebius

---

[32] *Hist. eccl.* 6.14. (Oulton, LCL 265:47):

And as for the Epistle to the Hebrews, he says indeed that it is Paul's, but that it was written for Hebrews in the Hebrew tongue, and that Luke, having carefully translated it, published it for the Greeks; hence, as a result of this translation, the same complexion of style is found in this Epistle and in the Acts: but that the [words] "Paul an apostle" were naturally not prefixed. For, says he, "in writing to Hebrews who had conceived a prejudice against him and were suspicious of him, he very wisely did not repel them at the beginning by putting his name." Then lower down he adds: "But now, as the blessed elder used to say, since the Lord, being the apostle of the Almighty, was sent to the Hebrews, Paul, through modesty, since he had been sent to the Gentiles, does not inscribe himself as an apostle of the Hebrews, both to give due deference to the Lord and because he wrote to the Hebrews also out of his abundance, being a preacher and apostle of the Gentiles.

See footnotes 16 and 17 for Greek.

[33] *Hist. eccl.* 6.25.11-14 (Oulton, LCL 265:77):

Furthermore, he thus discusses the Epistle to the Hebrews, in his Homilies upon it: "That the character of the diction of the epistle entitled To the Hebrews has not the apostle's rudeness in speech, who confessed himself rude in speech, that is, in style, but that the epistle is better Greek in the framing of its diction, will be admitted by everyone who is able to discern differences of style. But again, on the other hand, that the thoughts of the epistle are admirable, and not inferior to the acknowledged writings of the apostle, to this also everyone will consent as true who has given attention to reading the apostle." Further on, he adds the following remarks: "But as for myself, if I were to state my own opinion, I should say that the thoughts are the apostle's, but that the style and composition belong to one who called to mind the apostle's teachings and, as it were, made short notes of what his master said. If any church, therefore, holds this epistle as Paul's, let it be commended for this also. For not without reason have the men of old time handed it down as Paul's. But who wrote the epistle, in truth God knows. Yet the account which has reached us [is twofold], some saying that Clement, who was bishop of the Romans, wrote the epistle, others, that it was Luke, he who wrote the Gospel and the Acts."

See footnote 18 for Greek. "This explanation captures perfectly the mild, judicious, learned, candid tone of a Greek philosopher discussing the authenticity of a writing that many experts consider sacred and believe to be genuine, but that others, impressed by the obviously non-Pauline style of the writing, refuse to admit is by the apostle – leaving the issue squarely on the fence" (Dungan, *Constantine's Bible*, 53).

[34] *Hist. eccl.* 6.25.1-10 (Oulton, LCL 265:75):

These things he inserts in the above-mentioned treatise. But in the first of his [Commentaries] on the Gospel according to Matthew, defending the canon of the Church, he gives his testimony that he knows only four Gospels, writing somewhat as follows: "… as having learnt by tradition concerning the four Gospels, which alone are unquestionable in the Church of God under heaven, that first was written that according to Matthew, who was

had to compile opinions from several of Origen's writings presumably because there was no one place in Origen's writings where he could have found such a list.³⁵ Even after compiling these quotations, the result is not a clean list of apostolic writings but a mere mentioning of New Testament authors. The content regarding Paul does not even mention how many letters Paul wrote or to whom he wrote aside from the lengthy discussion about Hebrews that Origen does not even regard as Pauline.³⁶ Finally, Eusebius presents this New Testament catalogue as though it were a complement to Origen's catalogue of Hebrew scriptures that precedes it. However, Origen is only recounting the catalogue of Jewish scriptures as he knew it and gives no indication that it is in any way binding for Christians or that it presupposes a corresponding New Testament. On the contrary, if Origen's use of various writings is any indication, he did not regard this catalogue as restrictive for his own work.³⁷ Therefore, Eusebius' treatment of Origen, especially Origen's opinion regarding Hebrews and its relationship to Paul's writings, provides a particularly illuminating example of Eusebius' willingness to present the work of earlier writers within a framework that serves his own agenda.

Eusebius' presentation of Irenaeus' opinion concerning Hebrews raises the question as to just how far Eusebius may have gone to adapt his reports about others to fit his own narrative. Eusebius claims that Irenaeus wrote "a little book of various discourses in which he mentions the Epistle to the Hebrews."³⁸ Irenaeus' own writings, on the

> once a tax-collector but afterwards an apostle of Jesus Christ, who published it for those who from Judaism came to believe, composed as it was in the Hebrew language. Secondly, that according to Mark, who wrote it in accordance with Peter's instructions, whom also Peter acknowledged as his son in the catholic epistle, speaking in these terms: 'She that is in Babylon, elect together with you, saluteth you; and so doth Mark my son.' And thirdly, that according to Luke, who wrote, for those who from the Gentiles [came to believe], the Gospel that was praised by Paul. After them all, that according to John. And in the fifth of his Expositions on the Gospel according to John the same person says this with reference to the epistles of the apostles: 'But he who was made sufficient to become a minister of the new covenant, not of the letter but of the spirit, even Paul, who fully preached the Gospel from Jerusalem and round about even unto Illyricum, did not so much as write to all the churches that he taught; and even to those to which he wrote he sent but a few lines. And Peter, on whom the Church of Christ is built, against which the gates of Hades shall not prevail, has left one acknowledged epistle, and, it may be, a second also; for it is doubted. Why need I speak of him who leaned back on Jesus' breast, John, who has left behind one Gospel, confessing that he could write so many that even the world itself could not contain them; and he wrote also the Apocalypse, being ordered to keep silence and not to write the voices of seven thunders? He has left also an epistle of a very few lines, and, it may be, a second and a third; for not all say that these are genuine. Only, the two of them together are not a hundred lines long.'"

This is followed by the discussion of Hebrews cited above.
³⁵ Robbins, "'Peri Ton Endiathekon Graphon,'" 88.
³⁶ Albert C. Sundberg, "Canon Muratori: A Fourth-Century List," *Harvard Theological Review* 66 (1973): 36–7.
³⁷ Kalin, "New Testament Canon of Eusebius," 389.
³⁸ *Hist. eccl.* 5.26.3 (Oulton: LCL 153:512–15):

> Ἀλλὰ γὰρ πρὸς τοῖς ἀποδοθεῖσιν Εἰρηναίου συγγράμμασιν καὶ ταῖς ἐπιστολαῖς φέρεταί τις αὐτοῦ πρὸς Ἕλληνας λόγος συντομώτατος καὶ τὰ μάλιστα ἀναγκαιότατος, Περὶ ἐπιστήμης ἐπιγεγραμμένος, καὶ ἄλλος, ὃν ἀνατέθεικεν ἀδελφῷ Μαρκιανῷ τοὔνομα εἰς ἐπίδειξιν τοῦ ἀποστολικοῦ κηρύγματος, καὶ βιβλίον τι διαλέξεων διαφόρων, ἐν ᾧ τῆς πρὸς Ἑβραίους ἐπιστολῆς καὶ τῆς λεγομένης Σολομῶνος Σοφίας μνημονεύει, ῥητά τινα ἐξ αὐτῶν παραθέμενος. καὶ τὰ μὲν εἰς ἡμετέραν ἐλθόντα γνῶσιν τῶν Εἰρηναίου τοσαῦτα. [In

other hand, suggest that he did not know the Epistle to the Hebrews.[39] Irenaeus never cites Hebrews, even in his extensive treatment concerning the quotations of Ps 110:1 in the Gospels, Paul, and Acts. Of course, it is possible that Eusebius is citing a work of Irenaeus that is no longer extant, but one wonders why Irenaeus would not even mention Hebrews in a lengthy discussion of a verse so central to Hebrews' argument. The only part of Irenaeus' work resembling a reference to Hebrews is the phrase τῷ ῥήματι τῆς δυνάμεως αὐτοῦ, which occurs in Heb 1:3 and in Adv Haer 2:30, 9.[40] Hebrews 1:3-4 is, however, widely considered to be a hymn borrowed by the author of Hebrews.[41] Given that this is the only possible reference to Hebrews in the entirety of Irenaeus, it may be more likely to assume that Irenaeus knew independently of the hymn rather than assume that he knew Hebrews and never once mentioned it elsewhere in his writings. If Eusebius encountered a similar parallel between Hebrews and Irenaeus' writings, the presentation of such a parallel as an explicit reference by Irenaeus to Hebrews would not be inconsistent with the manner in which Eusebius presents the discussion of Hebrews by other writers. Eusebius demonstrates an ability to adapt his reports about the opinions of previous writers to fit his own catalogue of scriptures.

Eusebius utilized the established bibliographic methods in which he had been trained as an educated member of society. In his catalogue of Christian writings and his comments about the works attributed to various Christian authors, he reported the opinions of his predecessors and noted where ambiguity remained regarding a work's authorship. However, Eusebius also transformed his bibliographic reports so that they included more than merely discussions of authorship, weaving in concerns about a writing's orthodoxy and acceptance among the churches. A writing's content and its use by earlier Christian writers could be used to support a work's authorial claims, but in some cases a work's content and broad appeal bolstered a work's acceptance even if it was known that it was not authored by an apostle or one of their associates. By infusing the categories of orthodoxy and acceptance among churches and earlier Christian writers into his bibliographic method, Eusebius expanded this method in order to address the growing concern for a delineation of Christian scriptures in the fourth century. This practice is especially evident in his catalogue of opinions regarding Hebrews and its relationship to Paul's writings. Eusebius reported the opinions of six different writers regarding Hebrews, even noting those who registered doubts about its Pauline authorship, but he did so in a manner that allowed Hebrews to be counted among the fourteen epistles of Paul.

addition to the published treatises and to the letters of Irenaeus, there is extant a concise and extremely convincing treatise of his against the Greeks, entitled Concerning Knowledge, and another which he has dedicated to a Christian named Marcian on the Demonstration of the Apostolic Preaching, and a little book of various discourses in which he mentions the Epistle to the Hebrews and the so-called Wisdom of Solomon, quoting certain passages from them. Such is the extent of our knowledge of the works of Irenaeus.]

[39] Robert Grant, *Irenaeus of Lyons* (New York: Routledge, 1996), 1.
[40] Ibid., 1, 39.
[41] Harold W. Attridge, *Hebrews: A Commentary on the Epistle to the Hebrews* (Philadelphia: Fortress Press, 1989), 41.

Athanasius of Alexandria

Athanasius' thirty-ninth *Festal Letter* is well known as the earliest extant list of New Testament writings to contain precisely the same twenty-seven works found in modern editions of the New Testament. Such a designation, while not historically incorrect, may not be the most insightful way of thinking about this document insofar as it predisposes modern readers to see Athanasius' list as the inevitable culmination of the formation of the New Testament. On the contrary, an analysis of the context surrounding Athanasius' *Festal Letter* indicates just how open-ended the conversation about the church's scriptures continued to be. The debates among educated elites in academic circles of Christianity about which scriptures were acceptable continued to resemble the flexible and fluid categories employed by Eusebius; works could potentially move between categories if the proper argument could be produced, and very few works were excluded as entirely unacceptable. Athanasius' letter sought to combat these fluid categories of scripture and the academic Christianity it represented even while he utilized some of the very same methods familiar to the scholarly variety of Christianity that he sought to oppose. Athanasius' letter modified bibliographic practice toward his own ends, a more fixed and definitive canon that placed ecclesial authority ahead of academic discourse. Athanasius was surely limited in his ability to accomplish such a goal.[42] Nonetheless, several features of his letter suggest that Athanasius' purpose was to close matters that other writers preferred to leave open in an attempt to locate authority in the scriptures themselves even as he retained some of the cataloging procedures adopted by Eusebius and other Greek scholars.

Several features of Athanasius' letter bear resemblance to Eusebius' catalogue of Christian scriptures. Much like Eusebius and his bibliographic predecessors, Athanasius portrays himself as merely reporting the tradition that had been handed down to him. He compares himself to Luke the evangelist giving an orderly account of the books that "are canonized, transmitted, and believed to be divine."[43] Athanasius also

---

[42] Gallagher and Meade, *Biblical Canon Lists*, 30:

> This thirty-ninth *Festal Letter* of Athanasius has become famous in modern times because it contains the first listing of the twenty-seven-book New Testament that would become standard. It did not immediately have the effect of standardizing the New Testament, and in truth its influence in this regard is open to question: rather than signaling the end of a process of defining the New Testament canon, this letter seems to have merely marked a point along the way. ... The New Testament list of Athanasius represents a minor point – not a decisive event – in a long process, then, because his letter does not seem to have settled anything for the wider church.

Bart D. Ehrman, *Lost Christianities: The Battles for Scripture and the Faiths We Never Knew* (Oxford: Oxford University Press, 2005), 230:

> Numerous scholars have unreflectively claimed that this letter of Athanasius represents the "closing" of the canon, that from then on there were no disputes about which books to include. But there continued to be debates and differences of opinion, even in Athanasius's home church. For example, the famous teacher of the late-fourth-century Alexandria, Didymus the Blind, claimed that 2 Peter was a "forgery" that was not to be included in the canon.

[43] *Ep. fest.* 39.16; Gallagher and Meade, *Biblical Canon Lists*, 121–2:

> Μέλλων δὲ τούτων μνημονεύειν, χρήσομαι πρὸς σύστασιν τῆς ἐμαυτοῦ τόλμης τῷ τύπῳ τοῦ εὐαγγελιστοῦ Λουκᾶ, λέγων καὶ αὐτός· Ἐπειδή πέρ τινες ἐπεχείρησαν ἀνατάξασθαι ἑαυτοῖς

demonstrates a concern for authorship similar to Eusebius and ancient bibliographers. In his dismissal of apocryphal works, he claims that heretics write whatever they want in these works and then add the name of an ancient author to them so that they might deceive "simple folk."[44] Finally, Athanasius' list bears resemblance to Eusebius' in that he also creates three categories for the works he evaluates, much as Eusebius had designated works as either recognized/accepted, disputed, or heretical.

Athanasius' work also diverges significantly from Eusebius, however, in his use of these categories. What Eusebius had called recognized or accepted, Athanasius now labels canonical.[45] Among the works deemed canonical, he delineates the four Gospels

> τὰ λεγόμενα ἀπόκρυφα καὶ μῖξαι ταῦτα τῇ θεοπνεύστῳ γραφῇ, περὶ ἧς ἐπληροφορήθημεν, καθὼς παρέδοσαν τοῖς πατράσιν οἱ ἀπ' ἀρχῆς αὐτόπται καὶ ὑπηρέται γενομενοι τοῦ λόγου, ἔδοξε κἀμοί, προτραπέντι παρὰ γνησίων ἀδελφῶν καὶ μαθόντι ἄνωθεν ἑξῆς ἐκθέσθαι τὰ κανονιζόμενα καὶ παραδοθέντα, πιστευθεντα τε θεῖα εἶναι βιβλία, ἵνα ἕκαστος, εἰ μὲν ἠπατήθη, καταγνῷ τῶν πλανησάντων, ὁ δὲ καθαρὸς διαμείνας χαίρῃ πάλιν ὑπομιμνησκόμενος
>
> As I begin to mention these things, in order to commend my audacity, I will employ the example of Luke the evangelist and say myself: Inasmuch as certain people have attempted to set in order for themselves the so-called apocryphal books and to mix these with the divinely inspired Scripture, about which we are convinced it is just as those who were eyewitnesses from the beginning and assistants of the Word handed down to our ancestors, it seemed good to me, because I have been urged by genuine brothers and sisters and instructed from the beginning to set forth in order the books that are canonized, transmitted, and believed to be divine, so that those who have been deceived might condemn the persons who led them astray, and those who have remained pure might rejoice to be reminded (of these things). (David Brakke, "A New Fragment of Athanasius's Thirty-Ninth *Festal Letter*. Heresy, Apocrypha, and the Canon," *Harvard Theological Review* 103, no. 1 [2010]: 60)
>
> See also his receiving of the tradition concerning the number of works in the Old Testament correlating to the number of letters in the Hebrew alphabet in *Ep. fest.* 39.17.

[44] "ἀλλὰ αἱρετικῶν ἐστιν ἐπίνοια, γραφόντων μὲν ὅτε θέλουσιν αὐτά, χαριζομένων δὲ καὶ προστιθέντων αὐτοῖς χρόνους, ἵνα ὡς παλαιὰ προφέροντες, πρόφασιν ἔχωσιν ἀπατᾶν ἐκ τούτου τοὺς ἀκεραίους" (*Ep. fest.* 39.21; Gallagher and Meade, *Biblical Canon Lists*, 126). "Rather, (the category of apocrypha) is an invention of heretics, who write these books whenever they want and then generously add time to them, so that, by publishing them as if they were ancient, they might have a pretext for deceiving the simple folk" (Brakke, "A New Fragment," 61).

[45] Athanasius is the first author known to use the term "canon" in this manner. The meaning of the Greek word κανόν is typically traced back to the word κάννα, denoting marsh reeds that were useful because of their straight and firm stalks. The term also became associated with the similarly shaped carpenter's rule or straight rod. By metaphorical extension, then, it was eventually used to refer to any standard or measure by which other objects were compared or evaluated. This meaning was most commonly applied in the arts, sculpture in particular, in which an artist's work could become the standard of excellence by which other works were judged. E. Dean Kolbas, *Critical Theory and the Literary Canon* (Ann Arbor: University of Michigan Press, 2001), 12. However, the term was additionally utilized in philosophy, ethics, and rhetoric to indicate a practice to be imitated or general guidelines for thinking and conduct. Anders Klostergaard Petersen, "Constraining Semiotic Riverrun," in *The Discursive Fight Over Religious Texts in Antiquity*, ed. Anders-Christian Jacobsen (Aarhus, DK: Aarhus University Press, 2009), 36. Christian uses of the term "canon" prior to the fourth century include Gal 6:16 where Paul uses the term in the sense of a rule or standard of practice with regard to circumcision and in 2 Cor 10:13 where it denotes the proper boundaries of Paul's God-given field of ministry. Similarly, 1 Clement praises women who run their households under the "rule of submission" and urges his audience to leave behind frivolous talk in favor of the "venerable rule of our tradition." Irenaeus has frequently been cited as signaling a turn toward the idea of canon as the standardization of a specific set of scriptures since he frequently uses the term "canon" and vigorously defends the four Gospels that would eventually be regarded as canonical. However, Irenaeus never uses the term "canon" to refer to a set of writings. Instead, he speaks of the κανών τῆς

by name, the Acts of the Apostles, seven Catholic Epistles that he lists by author, and finally the fourteen letters of Paul designated by recipient. Hebrews is listed after the two letters to the Thessalonians as one of the fourteen letters of Paul. Athanasius describes these canonical works as "the springs of salvation so that someone who thirsts may be satisfied by the words they contain. In these books alone the teaching of piety is proclaimed. Let no one add to or subtract from them."[46] The latter part of this statement is likely invoking the words of Deut 4:2 (LXX): "You shall not add to the word that I command you, nor take from it, that you may keep the commandments of the LORD." These words were often viewed as an inscriptional curse and were frequently reiterated by subsequent Jewish and Christian writers in an attempt to prevent the emendation of their works, which was so common among any written works in antiquity.[47] Athanasius applies this curse to all of the books that he lists as canonical, thereby defining his canon as a closed list that is not to be altered, a substantial deviation from Eusebius' much more open-ended categories.

Athanasius also employs a middle category that appears roughly equivalent to Eusebius' category of disputed writings, but the differences here are telling as well. Rather than calling these works disputed, Athanasius is clear that these works "have not been canonized, but have been appointed by the ancestors to be read by those who newly join us and want to be instructed in the word of piety."[48] Athanasius does not exhibit Eusebius' same flexibility with the ambiguous status of certain writings; for him a work is either canonized or not. In fact, Athanasius suggests reluctance at having to include this category at all, noting that he only adds it out of "necessity" and "for the sake of greater accuracy."[49] Although Athanasius lists a number of works in this category (Wisdom of Solomon, Wisdom of Sirach, Esther, Judith, Tobit, the *Didache*, and the Shepherd), one may note that with regard to writings associated with the New Testament, Athanasius has nearly evacuated this category entirely. Relative to Eusebius' catalogue, Athanasius has promoted James, Jude, 2 Peter, and 2–3 John into the canon while presumably demoting the *Acts of Paul*, *Epistle of Barnabas*, *Apocalypse of Peter*, and the *Gospel according to the Hebrews* to apocryphal and heretical status since he does not mention them here. Only the *Didache* and the Shepherd remain from Eusebius' catalogue in this in-between status. Athanasius' categorization of these

---

ἀληθείας that Annette Yoshiko Reed characterizes "as an extra-textual criterion for distinguishing true doctrine from heretical speculations, authentic texts from spurious compositions, and proper Scriptural interpretation from 'evil exegesis'" ("ΕΥΑΓΓΕΛΙΟΝ: Orality, Textuality, and the Christian Truth in Irenaeus' 'Adversus Haereses,'" *Vigiliae Christianae* 56, no. 1 [2002]: 13).

[46] "Ταῦτα πηγαὶ τοῦ σωτηρίου, ὥστε τὸν διψῶντα ἐμφορεῖσθαι τῶν ἐν τούτοις λογίων· ἐν τούτοις μόνοις τὸ τῆς εὐσεβείας διδασκαλεῖον εὐαγγελίζεται· μηδεὶς τούτοις ἐπιβαλλέτω, μηδὲ τούτων ἀφαιρείσθω τι" (*Ep. fest.* 39.19; Gallagher and Meade, *Biblical Canon Lists*, 124; Brakke, "A New Fragment," 61).

[47] Jennifer Knust and Tommy Wasserman, *To Cast the First Stone: The Transmission of a Gospel Story* (Princeton, NJ: Princeton University Press, 2018), 101. Michael J. Kruger, *Canon Revisited: Establishing the Origins and Authority of the New Testament Books* (Wheaton, IL: Crossway, 2012), 165.

[48] Ἀλλ' ἕνεκά γε πλείονος ἀκριβείας προστίθημι καὶ τοῦτο γράφων ἀναγκαίως, ὡς ὅτι ἔστι καὶ ἕτερα βιβλία τούτων ἔξωθεν, οὐ κανονιζόμενα μέν, τετυπωμένα δὲ παρὰ τῶν πατέρων ἀναγινώσκεσθαι τοῖς ἄρτι προσερχομένοις καὶ βουλομένοις κατηχεῖσθαι τὸν τῆς εὐσεβείας λόγον· (*Ep. fest.* 39.20; Gallagher and Meade, *Biblical Canon Lists*, 123–4; Brakke, "A New Fragment," 61).

[49] *Ep. fest.* 39.20; Brakke, "A New Fragment," 61.

works represents a movement toward categories that are more fixed and closed than those present in Eusebius' catalogue.

The rest of Athanasius' letter suggests, however, that his move toward a more fixed canon was not an end in itself but, as Brakke argues, an attempt to undercut the authority of charismatic teachers.[50] Indeed, most of the existing fragment reads as polemic against the idea that there could be any teacher other than Christ (and by extension, the canonical scriptures). In one of the very first extant lines of the letter, Athanasius states, "For the teaching of piety does not come from human beings; rather, it is the Lord who reveals his Father to those whom he wills because it is he who knows him."[51] Later he reminds his audience of James's caution against many becoming teachers and Jesus' own admonition that no one be called "teacher" except Jesus himself.[52] He argues that even those who are teachers are disciples of the one true teacher first and that he has not written the things in this letter as though he were a teacher but "I thus informed you of everything that I heard from my father."[53]

Athanasius regards these teachers as potentially dangerous because they do not care about the church or the faith of others as much as their own notoriety. He describes them as "people who do not see what is beneficial for the church, but who desire to receive compliments from those whom they lead astray, so that, by publishing new discourses, they will be considered great people."[54] Therefore, Athanasius also sees them as producers of heresy who lead away "simple folk" who are apparently too simpleminded to see that they are being duped by these intellectuals. Athanasius refers to these vulnerable "simple folk" multiple times throughout the letter as justification for strict observance to his canon.[55] If only the faithful will limit themselves to Athanasius' list of canonical scriptures and adhere only to the teaching of those who do the same, they will not be led astray into heresy by those who reference a wide range of writings in their intellectual debates. Brakke summarizes Athanasius' goals succinctly when he states,

> Thus, Athanasius's promulgation of a closed canon was an attempt at social formation and control; it regulated divination and access to truth by restricting the books to be read (only these and no others), establishing an authoritative diviner

---

[50] Contrary to Brakke and Williams, Pedersen argues that it is not Athanasius' goal to undercut scholastic Christianity as a whole but only the specific Arian and Miletian teachers. Brakke concedes in his more recent work that he underestimated the degree to which Athanasius was refuting heresy in his work on the fragment in 1994. However, he maintains that Athanasius supported an episcopally centered brand of Christianity against a more scholastically oriented version. Given the repeated references to teachers generally, I find Brakke's argument persuasive. Nils Arne Pedersen, "The New Testament Canon and Athanasius of Alexandria's 39th *Festal Letter*," in *The Discursive Fight Over Religious Texts in Antiquity*, ed. Anders-Christian Jacobsen (Aarhus, DK: Aarhus University Press, 2009), 173; Brakke, "A New Fragment," 48.

[51] *Ep. fest.* 39.7; Brakke, "A New Fragment," 57.

[52] *Ep. fest.* 39.10-11.

[53] *Ep. fest.* 39. 12, 32; Brakke, "A New Fragment," 65.

[54] *Ep. fest.* 39.22; Brakke, "A New Fragment," 61–2.

[55] *Ep. fest.* 39. 15, 21.

(the orthodox bishop), and articulating a standard of interpretation (the church's doctrine of the incarnate Word).[56]

Therefore, even while Athanasius articulates his canon in a manner reminiscent of Eusebius' catalogue, he also seeks to undermine the very kind of scholastically oriented Christianity that Eusebius represents. Whereas Eusebius saw himself as participating in a debate that included the opinions of previous writers and would continue well after the completion of his own work, Athanasius sought to bring an end to that debate and to limit the influence of the form of Christianity in which it prevailed since Athanasius regarded it is a breeding ground for heresy. In this manner, Athanasius provides another example of a fourth-century writer who imposes his own concerns about scripture on his predecessors even as he utilizes their work. In the case of Athanasius, this includes the creation of the very idea of canon as a closed list of authoritative writings, a category that had not previously been applied to Christian scriptures as far as the extant evidence suggests. Yet Athanasius presents this innovation as though he is only giving an orderly account of the tradition that has been passed on to him, as though the church had always had a canon of sacred scripture and that any teacher who chooses to teach from another source is intentionally abandoning the most reliable source of truth. Although Athanasius may not have been immediately successful in his attempts to short-circuit debates about the boundaries of Christian scriptures in his own day, his campaign has surely been influential to the extent that it has become the challenge of historians and biblical scholars to imagine a world in which notions of scripture and canon are not intimately intertwined.

Rufinus of Aquileia

If in Athanasius we observed an individual who was indirectly responding to someone *like* Eusebius and the scholastically oriented Christianity that he represented, in Rufinus we have someone who worked directly with Eusebius' writings. Rufinus' translation of the *Ecclesiastical History* into Latin as well as his translation of Origen's *Homilies in Joshua* provide striking examples of a fourth-century Christian who infused his own concerns about canon into the material of earlier writers while his own *Commentary on the Apostles' Creed* exhibits a transformation of bibliographic method reminiscent of Athanasius' *Festal Letter*. Rufinus' treatment of Hebrews in each of these works serves to illustrate the degree to which he has "updated" his source materials in order to conform them to a growing consensus among educated Christian theologians regarding authoritative scriptures in the late fourth century.

Rufinus' own catalogue in his *Commentary on the Apostles' Creed* exhibits the same key characteristics already observed in Eusebius and Athanasius, a similar threefold division that is presented as a mere reporting of the tradition that has been handed down to him. After listing the twenty-seven writings of the New Testament, he states, "These are the writings which the Fathers included in the canon, and on which they

---

[56] David Brakke, "Canon Formation and Social Conflict in Fourth-Century Egypt: Athanasius of Alexandria's Thirty-Ninth 'Festal Letter,'" *Harvard Theological Review* 87, no. 4 (1994): 417.

desired the affirmations of our faith to be based."[57] One may note here the similarities to Athanasius in particular in that Rufinus utilizes the term "canon" to describe this closed, definitive list, the contents of which matches Athanasius'. Furthermore, it is the "Fathers" who included these works in the canon, as though the category of canon had existed for them as it does for Rufinus. Similarly, Rufinus presents his other two categories—ecclesiastical and apocryphal—as designations of his predecessors.

> At the same time we should appreciate that there are certain other books which our predecessors designated "ecclesiastical" rather than "canonical" ... They desired that all these should be read in the churches, but that appeal should not be made to them on points of faith. The other writings they designated "apocryphal," refusing to allow them to be read out in church. Such, then, is the traditional canon handed down to us by the Fathers.[58]

The content of Rufinus' "ecclesiastical" category differs slightly from that of Athanasius but his definition of the category is remarkably similar; these are works that can be read but which should not serve as a source of doctrine.[59] Rufinus does not specify which works belong in the "apocryphal" category but, as with Athanasius, they are works that should not be read at all.[60] Thus, Rufinus' catalogue of scriptures exhibits

---

[57] "Noui uero quattuor euangelia: Mathaei Marci Lucae Johannis. Actus Apostolum, quos descripsit Lucas. Pauli apostoli epistulae quattuordecim; Petri apostoli epistulae duae; Iacobi fratris Domini et apostoli una; Iudae una; Iohannis tres; Apocalypsis Iohannis. Haec sunt quae patres intra canonem concluserunt et ex quibus fidei nostrae adsertiones constare uoluerunt" (*Symb*. 37–8; Gallagher and Meade, *Biblical Canon Lists*, 218–19). "In the New there are four Gospels, those of Matthew Mark, Luke, and John; the Acts of the Apostles, composed by Luke; fourteen epistles by the apostle Paul; two by the apostle Peter; one by James, brother of the Lord and Apostle; one by Jude; three by John; the Apocalypse of John" (Rufinus, *A Commentary on the Apostles' Creed*, trans. J. N. D. Kelly, Ancient Christian Writers [Westminster, MD: Newman Press, 1955], 73).

[58] "Sciendum tamen est quod et alii libri sunt, qui non canonici sed ecclesiastici a maioribus appellati sunt, Quae omnia legi quidem in ecclesiis uoluerunt, non tamen proferri ad auctoritatem ex his fidei confirmandam. Ceteras uero scripturas apochryphas nominarunt, quas in ecclesia legi noluerunt. Haec nobis a patribus" (*Symb*. 38; Gallagher and Meade, *Biblical Canon Lists*, 218–20; Rufinus, *A Commentary on the Apostles' Creed*, 73).

[59] *Symb*. 38; Gallagher and Meade, *Biblical Canon Lists*, 219:

> Sapientia, quae dicitur Solomonis, et alia Sapientia, quae dicitur filii Sirach: qui liber apud latinos hoc ipso generali uocabulo Ecclesiasticus appellatur, quo uocabulo non auctor libelli, sed scripturae qualitas cognominata est. Eiusdem ordinis est libellus Tobiae et Iudith, et Machabeaorum libri. In Nouo uero Testamento libellus qui dicitur Pastoris siue Hermae, et is qui appellatur Duae Viae, uel Iudicium secundum Petrum.

> Thus there is the Wisdom of Solomon, as we call it; and another Wisdom, ascribed to the son of Sirach. This latter is known by the general title Ecclesiasticus among Latin-speaking people, the description pointing, not to the author of the book, but to the character of the writing. The Book of Tobias belongs to the same class, as do Judith and books of the Maccabees. In the New Testament we have the little work known as The Book of the Shepherd, or Hermas, and the book which is named The Two Ways, and The Judgment of Peter. (Rufinus, *A Commentary on the Apostles' Creed*. Kelly, 73)

[60] Gallagher notes that this is the only place in Rufinus' own writings where he uses this term. Edmon Gallagher, "Writings Labeled 'Apocrypha' in Latin Patristic Sources," in *Sacra Scriptura: How "Non-Canonical" Texts Functioned in Early Judaism and Early Christianity*, ed. James H. Charlesworth and Lee Martin McDonald (New York: T&T Clark, 2014), 6.

rhetoric similar to that of Eusebius while also exhibiting the transformation of that rhetoric into more clearly defined categories of canon characteristic of Athanasius.

Rufinus' practice of transforming Eusebius' categories is even more evident in his translation of the *Ecclesiastical History* into Latin, particularly in his translation of Eusebius' catalogue of Christian scriptures in 3.25.[61] Whereas Eusebius had utilized the rhetoric of bibliographic methodology, Rufinus subtly transforms this into a catalogue concerning which writings had been in doubt with regard to their canonical status. So, for example, the works that Eusebius had termed "accepted" or "recognized" Rufinus describes as "the writings which have never been held in any doubt at all." Eusebius' "disputed" category becomes those "writings which a number of people have considered doubtful," and those that Eusebius labeled both "disputed" and "spurious" Rufinus calls "extremely doubtful." Finally, the writings that Eusebius labels "heretical" Rufinus declares "are nowhere mentioned or recorded in any of the writings of those of old."[62] On the surface, one might regard this as a reasonably faithful representation of Eusebius' thought. After all, earlier analysis demonstrated that Eusebius had utilized the language of bibliographic methodology in order to make claims about the recognized status of Christian writings. Rufinus has, in a certain respect, followed in Eusebius' footsteps. His primary concern is with the canonical status of these writings, and he has chosen to cut to the heart of the matter in his translation. What was a complex interplay between authorship, acceptance, and orthodoxy in Eusebius has been flattened into a simple accounting of how much doubt existed as to whether or not a work should be regarded as canonical. Rufinus has, in essence, simplified Eusebius' very complex categories.

On the other hand, it is clear that Rufinus has transformed Eusebius in a manner that was oriented by Rufinus' own opinions about Christian scriptures more so than Eusebius'. Just as the Revelation of John played a pivotal role in understanding

---

[61] Rufinus, *History of the Church*, trans. Philip R. Amidon, Fathers of the Church (Washington, DC: Catholic University of America Press, 2016), 124–5:

> Since, then, we have reached this point, let us list the complete canon of the New Testament, and first of all let us yoke the heavenly chariot of all of the gospels with its team of four, to which the Acts of the Apostles should be joined. After these should be added Paul's letters; the first letter of John should follow those; and the first of Peter's likewise. These are the writings which have never been held in any doubt at all. Next come the writings which a number of people have considered doubtful: the Revelation of John, concerning which we will give the opinions of each of the people of old in their proper places; the letter of James, and also of Jude; the second letter of Peter and the second and third of John, whether these may be shown to be of the evangelist himself or of someone else of the same name. After these works come the writing which is called the Acts of Paul, the short work known as the Shepherd's, and the Revelation of Peter, all of which are considered extremely doubtful. A letter of Barnabas and the Teaching of the Apostles, as it is called, are also in circulation. Some people also join with these works the gospel which is called "According to the Hebrews" and which is especially popular among those Hebrews who appear to accept Christ; but it is opposed in the church.

Rufinus' "freedom" in his translations has long been noted. J. E. L. Oulton, "Rufinus' Translation of the Church History of Eusebius," *JTS* 30 (1929): 150–74. For a comparison of Eusebius' Greek and Rufinus' Latin, see Edmon Gallagher, "Origen via Rufinus on the New Testament Canon," *New Testament Studies* 62 (2016): 468.

[62] Gallagher, "Origen via Rufinus," 466.

Eusebius' categories, it is once again crucial in understanding Rufinus' transformation of those categories. Whereas Eusebius said Revelation could either be located among the accepted works or the spurious ones, Rufinus has placed it squarely among the very works with which Eusebius did *not* associate it: James, Jude, 2 Peter, and 2–3 John. This surely makes sense from Rufinus' perspective since he is concerned with the work's canonical status much more so than the bibliographic methods utilized by Eusebius. If Revelation was either accepted or spurious, as Eusebius said, then surely, Rufinus apparently reasoned, this means its status was doubted by some. Rufinus probably found Eusebius' categories, and his treatment of Revelation in particular, as confounding as many modern scholars have.[63] So he "fixed" them and made them say what Rufinus' own understanding of canon indicated Eusebius must have meant. Rufinus has not only translated Eusebius' catalogue of scriptures but also essentially "updated" it to reflect the canonical "advancements" to which Rufinus was accustomed.

Rufinus' treatment of Hebrews' takes its place alongside Revelation as one of the works that most clearly demonstrates Rufinus' transformation of his source material, especially in his translation of Eusebius' presentations of Clement and Origen. In *Hist. eccl.* 6.13-14 Eusebius enumerates the wide array of writings that Clement utilized and commented upon, designating the Wisdom of Solomon, the Wisdom of Sirach, and the epistles of Hebrews, Barnabas, Clement, and Jude as disputed (ἀντιλεγόμενα) writings. Rufinus changes the designation of these works from "disputed" to those books "which many people do not accept" and he removes Hebrews from the list. This translation decision is akin to those in 3.25 where Rufinus sought to bring closure to Eusebius' open-ended categories in order to reflect the growing consensus regarding accepted scriptures toward the end of the fourth century. Whereas Eusebius, working more closely within the parameters of bibliographic method, did not hesitate to report disagreements about Hebrews' status, Rufinus registers no such doubt about Hebrews. His transformation of this category toward the even more negative designation of books "which many people do not accept" means that it is no longer an adequate category for Hebrews.[64]

A few lines later (6.14.1), Eusebius presents Clement's opinion that Hebrews was authentically Pauline but translated into Greek by Luke. This statement of Clement's opinion regarding Hebrews' authorship is preceded by another list of disputed

---

[63] And probably for the very same reasons, Rufinus' concept of canon is much more like those of most modern readers than Eusebius' categories. For more on Rufinus' translation practices, see Mark Humphries, "Rufinus's Eusebius: Translation, Continuation, and Edition in the Latin Ecclesiastical History," *Journal of Early Christian Studies* 16, no. 2 (2008): 143–64. Oulton, "Rufinus' Translation of the Church History of Eusebius," 150–74.

[64] Jude was also a part of Rufinus' canon and so he might have liked to omit it from this list as well. However, Eusebius had included Jude among the disputed works in 3.25, and, in his translation of that passage, Rufinus kept Jude in the roughly equivalent category of those works doubted by some. As a result, Rufinus may have felt compelled to let Jude remain here as a matter of internal consistency. Hebrews, on the other hand, though unmentioned in 3.25, is presumed to be included among the letters of Paul that are firmly in Rufinus' category of writings about which there has never been any doubt. "He does use examples from those books too which many people do not accept: the Wisdom which is ascribed to Solomon, and the Wisdom of Sirach, which the Latins call Ecclesiasticus. He also includes examples from Barnabas and Clement, and uses too the Letter of Jude" (Rufinus, *Hist.* 6.13.6. Amidon, 249).

writings upon which Clement comments similar to the list in 6.13.[65] The effect of this juxtaposition is that Clement's discussion of Hebrews is an extension of the list of disputed writings. Clement's acknowledgment of questions concerning Hebrews' authorship while ultimately defending its Pauline authorship justifies Eusebius' designation of Hebrews as "disputed" in 6.13 even though he had included it among the fourteen accepted letters of Paul in 6.25. Rufinus reduces this list of disputed writings to include only the *Apocalypse of Peter* and designates it as "apocryphal" rather than disputed.[66] Hebrews is effectively dissociated from the *Apocalypse of Peter* by this arrangement; Clement's comments about Hebrews have little connection to the observation that Clement utilized the apocryphal work.

Among Rufinus' various alterations of Eusebius' catalogues of Christian scriptures, his transformation of Eusebius' presentation of Origen in *Hist. eccl.* 6.25 is arguably the most substantial. In the analysis of Eusebius' catalogues above, the degree to which Eusebius created a catalogue of scriptures for Origen was already noted insofar as Eusebius had to compile excerpts from various writings of Origen just to come to a very incomplete list of the writings he utilized. Rufinus takes Eusebius' facade to another level, polishing his catalogue of Origen's scriptures to give the appearance of a canon list written by Origen himself. Rufinus' translation of Eusebius actually introduces Origen's list as his writing "about the New Testament canon." Eusebius does actually use the word "canon" here but he does so referring to the church's tradition that there are only four Gospels. It is the rule of the church's tradition that Origen is defending, not a closed list of authoritative works.[67] Rufinus also enhances the canon-like appearance of Eusebius' catalogue by removing most of the titles to the specific works of Origen that Eusebius references. Only the first one, the reference to Origen's commentary on Matthew, remains, giving the list the appearance of deriving from

---

[65] The list also includes Jude, the Catholic Epistles, *Barnabas*, and the *Apocalypse of Peter*. Rufinus changes both Eusebius' category and its content, altering "disputed" to "apocryphal" and leaving only the *Apocalypse of Peter* in this category. Jude, the Catholic Epistles, and *Barnabas* are simply omitted from the text. Gallagher, "Origen via Rufinus," 470; "Writings Labeled 'Apocrypha,'" 6.

[66] "In the books of the Hypotyposeis or 'outlines,' he expounds together all of the divine scripture in succinct discourses, to put the matter briefly. In them he has not omitted even those writings which some consider apocryphal, such as the *Apocalypse of Peter*. About the Letter to the Hebrews ..." (Rufinus, *Hist.* 6.14.1-2. Amidon, 250).

[67] "Ταῦτα μὲν οὖν ἐν τῷ προειρημένῳ τίθησι συγγράμματι· ἐν δὲ τῷ πρώτῳ τῶν εἰς τὸ κατὰ Ματθαῖον, τὸν ἐκκλησιαστικὸν φυλάττων κανόνα, μόνα τέσσαρα εἰδέναι εὐαγγέλια μαρτύρεται, ὡδέ πως γράφων·" (*Hist. eccl.* 6.25.3). "These things he inserts in the above-mentioned treatise. But in the first of his [Commentaries] on the Gospel according to Matthew, defending the canon of the Church, he gives his testimony that he knows only four Gospels, writing somewhat as follows" (Oulton, LCL 265:75).

> At the introduction to Origen's Old Testament canon list, Eusebius' word κατάλογος comes across into Latin as canon. On one occasion, Rufinus translates Eusebius' term κανῶν with the Latin term canon, but whereas Eusebius used the word not of a catalogue of books but of a "rule," namely, "the Church's tradition of accepting only four Gospels," Rufinus makes clear that he is speaking about the canon Novi Testamenti. Rufinus also inserts the word where there is no corresponding term in Greek; for instance, at the end of Origen's list of Old Testament books, where Rufinus adds: "With these books concludes the canon of the divine volumes" ... These appearances of the word canon generally give the impression of more established boundaries of scripture, which is appropriate for the era of Rufinus' revision. (Gallagher, "Origen via Rufinus," 466)

a single work of Origen as though Origen himself had created it. Similarly, whereas Eusebius' presentation of Origen's opinion about Paul is interrupted by his thoughts about Peter's writings, Rufinus moves the comments about Peter to the end of the passage so that all of the material on Paul is treated together, thereby creating a greater resemblance to the canon lists that existed in Rufinus' lifetime.

Rufinus' treatment of Hebrews is once again particularly illustrative of his transformative translation decisions. Whereas Eusebius has Origen say of Paul that he "did not so much as write to all the churches that he taught; and even to those to which he wrote he sent but a few lines,"[68] Rufinus' Origen definitively declares that he wrote fourteen letters, thereby including Hebrews.[69] Furthermore, where Eusebius has Origen openly voice his doubts about the Pauline authorship of Hebrews, Rufinus has Origen state, "What I say, though, is what my elders have handed down to me, that it *is quite clearly Paul's, and all of our elders accepted it as Paul's letter*."[70] Rufinus also transforms Origen's suggestions of Clement or Luke as Hebrews' author into a matter of mere wording, conflating Origen's ideas with others reported by Eusebius that perhaps one of these individuals served as Paul's translator.[71]

Rufinus' translation of Origen's *Hom. Jes. Nav.* 7.1 exhibits a similar treatment of Hebrews and another probable example of the infusion of Rufinus' concerns into his translation of an earlier work:

Matthew first sounded the priestly trumpet in his Gospel; Mark also; Luke and John each played their own priestly trumpets. Even Peter cries out with trumpets in two of his epistles; also James and Jude. In addition, John also sounds the trumpet through his epistles, and Luke, as he describes the Acts of the Apostles. And now that last one comes, the one who said, "I think God displays us apostles last," and in fourteen of his epistles, thundering with trumpets, he casts down the walls of Jericho and all the devices of idolatry and dogmas of philosophers all the way to the foundations.[72]

---

[68] οὐδὲ πάσαις ἔγραψεν αἷς ἐδίδαξεν ἐκκλησίαις, ἀλλὰ καὶ αἷς ἔγραψεν, ὀλίγους στίχους ἐπέστειλεν (Oulton, LCL 265:76).

[69] "The tendency of Rufinus' glosses on *Hist. eccl.* 6.25 is to make it appear that Origen has a much more positive attitude toward Hebrews, 2 Peter, 2 and 3 John than he actually does." Robbins, "'Peri Ton Endiathekon Graphon,'" 95.

[70] Rufinus, *Hist.* 6.25.13. Amidon, 263. Emphasis added.

[71] Rufinus, *Hist.* 6.25.14. Amidon, 263:

But if you ask me from whom this wording comes, God knows for sure; the opinion which we have heard, though, is as follows: some used to say that it was from Clement, the disciple of the apostles and bishop of Rome, that the letter received the elegance of its Greek, but not its thought; others attributed this to Luke, who wrote the gospel and the Acts of the Apostles.

[72] Gallagher and Meade, *Biblical Canon Lists*, 91–2:

Sacerdotali tuba primus in Evangelio suo Matthaeus increpuit; Marcus quoque, Lucas et Iohannes suis singuli tubis sacerdotalibus cecinerunt; Petrus etiam duabus epistolarum suarum personat tubis; Iacobus quoque et Iudas. Addit nihilominus adhuc et Iohannes tuba canere per epistolas suas et Lucas Apostolorum gesta describens. Novissimus autem ille veniens, qui dixit: "Puto autem, nos Deus apostolos novissimos ostendit" et in quatuordecim epistolarum suarum fulminans tubis muros Hiericho et omnes idolatriae machinas et philosphorum dogmata usque ad fundamenta deiecit.

No Greek version of this work is extant, so it is impossible to compare Rufinus' translation with his *Vorlage* as we have done in the case of his translations of Eusebius. As a result, only tentative claims can be made about the extent to which either Rufinus or Origen is responsible for this list. Nevertheless, due to general skepticism about Rufinus' translation practices, many scholars have been inclined to see this passage as a complete fabrication on the part of Rufinus.[73] If that is the case, this passage provides yet another example of Rufinus' canonical presuppositions guiding his translation practices, presenting Origen as though he operated out of a definitive list of scriptures that perfectly matched Rufinus' own list. Even if this list really were present in Origen's writings, the presence of a mere list of New Testament authors in a homily of Origen's does not indicate an attempt to create a closed canon of scripture, an idea that would be largely contrary to Origen's use of scripture in any case.[74]

Rufinus has provided further evidence that creating lists of Christian scriptures was a concern of fourth-century theologians, which they retrojected on to the works of earlier writers. He has proved to be an outstanding example of someone who allowed the concerns of his own time to direct the utilization of his predecessors, even to the point of altering their works in order to fit his own categories of thought. Rufinus' alterations of his source materials are especially evident in his treatment of Hebrews as earlier writers like Eusebius and Origen expressed ambiguity regarding Hebrews' Pauline authorship in a manner consistent with bibliographic methodology. Rufinus transformed the opinion of these earlier writers with regard to Hebrews in his translations of their works in order to bring them into harmony with the opinions prevalent among highly educated Christian theologians in the late fourth century.

---

[73] In light of Rufinus' many alterations already considered above, my own assessment is that Rufinus is likely to have exercised similar freedom in his translation of Origen's *Homilies in Joshua*. However, given that none of the examples previously considered have been complete fabrications on Rufinus' part, it does not seem unreasonable to think that there may have been some kernel of what Rufinus presents here in Origen's original work. On the other hand, it has already been observed how thoroughly Rufinus transformed Eusebius' presentation of Origen in *Hist. eccl.* 6.25. If Rufinus has exercised similar freedom in transforming Origen's *Hom. Jes. Nav.* 7.1, then there may be only a faint resemblance between Origen's writing and Rufinus' translation of it. Given the demonstrated unreliability of Rufinus as a translator and the absence of any *Vorlage* to which to compare his work in this instance, I am not inclined to draw any definitive conclusions about the authenticity of this particular list nor does the thesis of this chapter necessitate that I do so. Everett R. Kalin, "Re-Examining New Testament Canon History: 1. The Canon of Origen," *Currents in Theology and Mission* 17 (1990): 274–82. For an opposing view, see Gallagher, "Origen via Rufinus."

[74] Gallagher, "Origen via Rufinus," 475–6:

> This list does not clearly represent Origen's attempt to produce an exclusive canon list, just as *Hom. Num.* 27.1.3. does not represent Origen's attempt to limit the Scriptural books without obscurities (i.e. those easy to understand) to Esther, Judith, Tobit and Wisdom of Solomon. The passage from *Hom. Jes. Nav.* 7.1 might not carry the connotations of Athanasius' list from 367, in which the Alexandrian bishop very explicitly excluded all books not on his list. In other words, Origen did not necessarily know a definitive canon of Christian Scripture. After all, at least one book that Origen consistently regarded as an authentic composition of an apostle—the Apocalypse of John—apparently found no place in the list originally.

The Muratorian Fragment

The Muratorian Fragment, a Latin catalogue of Christian writings consisting of eighty-five lines, was first published by Ludivico Antonio Muratori in 1740.[75] It was inscribed in a seventh- or eighth-century codex along with works by Ambrose of Milan, Eucherius of Lyon, and John Chrysostom as well as five early Christian creeds.[76] The provenance of this list of Christian writings has been extensively debated; the most common assessments are that it was written in the West in the second century or in the East in the fourth century. The omission of Hebrews from the Fragment has often functioned as a pillar of the argument for the Fragment's second-century Western provenance since scholarly reconstructions of Hebrews' reception have typically asserted that Hebrews was broadly rejected at an early stage in the West. A reevaluation of the evidence regarding Hebrews' reception, however, suggests that the omission of Hebrews from this list of Christian writings is consistent with other characteristics of the Fragment when it is understood as a fourth-century Roman document posing as a list from the second century, a provenance further supported by the similarities between the Fragment and the use of bibliographic method exhibited by the other fourth-century writers considered in this chapter.[77]

The Fragment has traditionally been regarded as a second-century Roman production due primarily to the reference in lines 74–76 that the Shepherd of Hermas was written *nuperrime temporibus nostris ... sedente cathedra urbis Romae ecclesia Pio*.[78] That the Fragment was composed shortly after the writing of the Shepherd was largely the consensus of scholarship until it was challenged by Albert Sundberg in 1965.[79] Geoffrey Hahneman built on the work of Sundberg and further complicated

---

[75] Eckhard J. Schnabel, "The Muratorian Fragment: The State of Research," *Journal of the Evangelical Theological Society* 57, no. 2 (2014): 231.

[76] Gallagher and Meade, *Biblical Canon Lists*, 175. Additionally, "Excerpts from the Muratorian Fragment were discovered in three manuscripts from the 11th century and in one manuscript from the 12th century, all containing the *corpus Paulinum* belonging to the Benedictine monastery on Monte Cassino" (Schnabel, "The Muratorian Fragment," 234).

[77] A comprehensive argument concerning the provenance of the Fragment is well beyond the scope of the current work. My primary goals are (1) to demonstrate that the typical scholarly reconstruction of Hebrews' broad rejection in the West is insufficiently nuanced and therefore should not play the decisive role in determining the Fragment's provenance as it often has, and (2) that a fourth-century Roman provenance for the Fragment serves to highlight similarities between the Fragment and the other writings considered in this chapter.

[78] "... very recently in our times ... while bishop Pius was occupying the chair of the church of the city of Rome" (Schnabel, "The Muratorian Fragment," 240).

[79] Sundberg argued that the Fragment was a fourth-century list of Eastern provenance, suggesting that *nuperrime temporibus nostris* could mean only that in comparison to the other works mentioned in the Fragment the Shepherd was written "most recently" (not necessarily close in time to the author but more so than the works mentioned) and that "in our time" could mean in the non-apostolic age that the writer inhabited as opposed to the apostolic one in which the authoritative works of the list were written (Sundberg, "Canon Muratori," 9–11). Sundberg relies on a similar phrase in Irenaeus to make this point in which Irenaeus says that Revelation was written "in our generation." Ferguson argues against this parallel: "Irenaeus says 'almost'; his point was to bring it [Revelation] near his own lifetime and not to put it in apostolic times, as a contrast between apostolic times and subsequent times would demand. He was not trying to make a point about the lateness of the Apocalypse" (Everett Ferguson, "Canon Muratori: Date Provenance," *Studia Patristica* 17 (1982): 678). Sundberg's thesis was later defended and expanded by Geoffrey Hahneman, who further demonstrates the tenuous nature of the evidence for a second-century date while also

the Fragment's relationship to the time period of the Shepherd by noting that the Shepherd was probably written near the beginning of the second century whereas Pius was bishop in the middle of the second century.[80] Hahneman also states that the Fragment's encouragement of the private use of the Shepherd but discouragement of its public reading "can be easily correlated with fourth-century eastern traditions, but not with late second- or early third-century references."[81] Additionally, the legend that Hermas and Pius were brothers was not cited by any other Christian writers prior to the fourth century.[82] Furthermore, Osiek argues that because Pius is a Latin name whereas Hermas is a Greek one, it is possible but improbable that they would be brothers. She adds, "The [Muratorian] Canon's reference to Hermas may be the device of a later document to make it seem earlier."[83] Finally, William Horbury has further problematized the Fragment's relationship to the Shepherd by arguing that the Fragment intends to *positively receive* both the Shepherd and the Wisdom of Solomon as *antilegomena*. If Horbury is correct, this would further complicate the Fraternity Legend in that it would suggest a later date for a work it intends to receive.[84]

Clare K. Rothschild has drawn on these many complications regarding the Fragment's chronological relationship to the Shepherd to suggest that the Fragment "represents a fictitious attempt to provide a venerable second-century precedent for a later position on canon."[85] This claim is further supported by the catalogue of

---

arguing that the catalogue found in the Fragment is much more akin to lists of the fourth century than anything known from the second. Geoffrey Mark Hahneman, *The Muratorian Fragment and the Development of the Canon* (Oxford: Clarendon Press, 1992); Geoffrey Mark Hahneman, "The Muratorian Fragment and the Origins of the New Testament Canon," in *The Canon Debate*, ed. Lee Martin McDonald and James A. Sanders (Peabody, MA: Hendrickson, 2002), 405–17.

[80] Hahneman, *Muratorian Fragment*, 71; Carolyn Osiek, *Shepherd of Hermas: A Commentary* (Minneapolis, MN: Fortress Press, 1999), 20; Clare K. Rothschild, "The Muratorian Fragment as Roman Fake," *Novum Testamentum* 60 (2018): 71.

[81] Hahneman, "Origins of the New Testament Canon," 410.

[82] Hahneman, *Muratorian Fragment*, 53–61:

> To demonstrate the problems set in motion by its appropriation in the Fragment, Hahneman discusses other occurrences of the tradition. It occurs in three (likely) fourth-century witnesses: the Liberian Catalogue, the *Carmen adversus Marcionitas* and the *Letter of Pius to Justus of Vienne*. Collectively these witnesses support emergence of the legend no earlier than the fourth-century. It is not attested by Irenaeus, Origen, or Clement of Alexandria; and in Carolyn Osiek's opinion, if Eusebius had known the Fraternity Legend, he would have mentioned it.

Osiek, *Shepherd of Hermas*, 19. Rothschild, "The Muratorian Fragment as Roman Fake," 72.

[83] Osiek, 18. Rothschild, "The Muratorian Fragment as Roman Fake," 73.

[84] Rothschild, "The Muratorian Fragment as Roman Fake," 74:

> Horbury points out that Athanasius, Rufinus, Epiphanius, Cyril of Jerusalem, Jerome, and the Stichometry of Nicephorus group *antilegomena* of both testaments at the end of their lists of received texts. What is more, Athanasius, Rufinus, Epiphanius, and Jerome all classify Wisdom as first of the "outside" books, and Athanasius, Rufinus, and Jerome all categorize the Shepherd as an *antilegomenon*. Rufinus also includes the "Judgment according to Peter," possibly identical to Peter's apocalypse. In short, the case for the Fragment's *inclusion* of the Shepherd as *antilegomenon* is strong.

William Horbury, "The Wisdom of Solomon in the Muratorian Fragment," *Journal of Theological Studies* 45, no. 1 (1994): 149–59.

[85] Rothschild, "The Muratorian Fragment as Roman Fake," 55–82. Also noteworthy in recent scholarship on the Fragment is Jonathan J. Armstrong, "Victorinus of Pettau as the Author of the Canon Muratori," *Vigiliae Christianae* 62, no. 1 (2008): 1–34.

heresies at the end of the Fragment. This section of the Fragment suffers from extensive corruption, particularly the references to Arsinous and Miltiades.[86] More certain, however, is the use of the term "Cataphrygians" in the final line of the Fragment, a term that does not appear as a nickname for the Montanists in Greek or Latin until the fourth century.[87] The catalogue also refers to the Epistle to the Laodiceans, a work not attested until the fourth century.[88]

The omission of Hebrews plays an important role in one's interpretation of this document as well. Hebrews' omission from the Fragment has often been seen as evidence of the Fragment's traditional dating to the second century since the typical reconstruction of Hebrews' reception claimed that Hebrews was rejected throughout the West at this early stage but accepted by the fourth century. This, however, has as much to do with geography as chronology since Hahneman argued that the Fragment's provenance was both fourth century *and* Eastern. Since Hebrews is typically considered to have enjoyed broad acceptance at an early stage in the East, its omission from the Fragment has made an Eastern provenance unthinkable for many.[89] If one locates the Fragment in fourth-century Rome, however, the omission of Hebrews is not an obstacle but what one might expect given the available evidence. Among his reports about Hebrews' reception, Eusebius writes,

---

[86] Arsinous is an unknown figure. It is not clear if the Fragment reads Mitiades or Miltiades. The former may be a reference to an early leader of Montanists, the latter a reference to an individual who opposed Valentinians. Miltiades is the reading supported by the Benedictine prologues but it would obviously be problematic among a list of heretics. Rothschild, "The Muratorian Fragment as Roman Fake," 75.

[87] Ibid., 76. Ferguson and Schnabel both argue that the term is an interpolation of the Latin translator and not part of the original Greek document. Ferguson, "Canon Muratori," 681. Schnabel, "The Muratorian Fragment," 250.

[88] As one final collection of evidence, Rothschild offers merely a list of traditions that are later than the second century but represented in the Fragment nonetheless: order of the Gospels, tradition of Luke as doctor and companion of Paul (l. 3-5), tradition that neither Paul nor Luke saw Jesus in the flesh (ll. 6-8), legend about the authorship of the Fourth Gospel (ll. 10-16), *regula fidei* (ll. 19-26), "Reminiscence of Jerome's Latin Vulgate," reference to Acts as treating "all" the apostles (ll. 34-39), Echo of Hermas, *Mand.* 5.1 (ll. 67-68), suggestion that Wisdom was written by Philo (ll. 68-70), inclusion of the *Apocalypse of Peter* (ll. 71-72), reference to Miltiades the Montanist (l. 81; cf. Eusebius, *Hist. eccl.* 5.17.5), and designation "prophets and apostles" (ll. 79-80). Rothschild offers four possible historical contexts for a fourth-century document posing as one from the second century:

1. The drive toward unification in the Church in the fourth century may have contributed to the Fragment's composition.
2. The Fragment was composed to trace the history of beliefs deemed heresy at a later date to their beginning in the second century.
3. As book production became more important to the Christian mission, the Fragment addressed a need to regulate what was published.
4. The later church, concerned with the earliest days of the episcopate, traced it back to Pius under whom its authority is first manifested. On this final point, Rothschild notes that this concern may extend well beyond the fourth century to the eighth century when the codex that contains the Fragment was copied. Rothschild, "The Muratorian Fragment as Roman Fake," 77-8, 80-2.

[89] "The exclusion of the Epistle to the Hebrews would have been considered a 'heresy' in the East in the fourth century" (Schnabel, "The Muratorian Fragment," 249). Bruce M. Metzger, *The Canon of the New Testament: Its Origin, Development, and Significance* (New York: Oxford University Press, 1987), 193.

And there has reached us also a Dialogue of Gaius, a very learned person (which was set a-going at Rome in the time of Zephyrinus), with Proclus the champion of the heresy of the Phrygians. In which, when curbing the recklessness and audacity of his opponents in composing new Scriptures, he mentions only thirteen epistles of the holy Apostle, not numbering the Epistle to the Hebrews with the rest; seeing that even to this day among the Romans there are some who do not consider it to be the Apostle's.[90]

Eusebius locates the single definitive rejection of Hebrews' Pauline authorship specifically in Rome.[91] Questions concerning Hebrews' authorship may very well have endured in Rome into the fourth century, especially if Eusebius' knowledge of these questions is any indication of their persistence. On the other hand, Justin Martyr made use of Hebrews centuries earlier, and Eusebius' report about Gaius likely indicates that Hebrews was still widely enough known in Rome that Gaius felt the need to challenge it.[92] Furthermore, surviving manuscripts of Paul's letters suggest that Greek editions of the Pauline corpus included Hebrews while Latin editions did not, a situation that may have prompted further confusion about Hebrews' status in fourth-century Rome.[93]

Given the conflicting opinions regarding Hebrews that were likely prevalent in Rome in the fourth century, the author of the Fragment may have found that the easiest solution was simply not to mention Hebrews at all. Of course, one may wonder why the author did not just categorize Hebrews alongside the disputed works of the *Apocalypse of Peter* and the Shepherd. However, the dispute regarding these works is about their being read publicly in church, not their authorship. The author of the Fragment does not actually employ a category specifically for a work that is generally accepted but the authorship of which is disputed. Indeed, any writing the Fragment labels a forgery is also considered heretical. A document like the Muratorian Fragment, organized as it is around the concept of authorship, essentially has no place for the Epistle to the Hebrews, a work that was too highly regarded to be labeled heretical but also did not have an established tradition of authorship in fourth-century Rome.[94]

---

[90] *Hist. eccl.* 6.20 (Oulton, LCL 265:67):

Ἦλθεν δὲ εἰς ἡμᾶς καὶ Γαΐου, λογιωτάτου ἀνδρός, διάλογος, ἐπὶ Ῥώμης κατὰ Ζεφυρῖνον πρὸς Πρόκλον τῆς κατὰ Φρύγας αἱρέσεως ὑπερμαχοῦντα κεκινημένος· ἐν ᾧ τῶν δι' ἐναντίας τὴν περὶ τὸ συντάττειν καινὰς γραφὰς προπέτειάν τε καὶ τόλμαν ἐπιστομίζων, τῶν τοῦ ἱεροῦ ἀποστόλου δεκατριῶν μόνων ἐπιστολῶν μνημονεύει, τὴν πρὸς Ἑβραίους μὴ συναριθμήσας ταῖς λοιπαῖς, ἐπεὶ καὶ εἰς δεῦρο παρὰ Ῥωμαίων τισὶν οὐ νομίζεται τοῦ ἀποστόλου τυγχάνειν

[91] Additionally, it may be noteworthy that both Eusebius' report and the Fragment express a concern about the (Cata)Phrygians.

[92] The closing of Hebrews (13:24) includes a greeting from "those in Italy," perhaps suggesting that the epistle had some connection to Rome. The subscription to Hebrews in Codex Alexandrinus also describes it as having been written from Rome.

[93] The evidence for Justin Martyr's use of Hebrews is discussed at length in Chapter 3 and the evidence regarding its relationship to the Pauline corpus in Chapters 4 and 5.

[94] Of course, one must also account for the omission of James, 1–2 Peter, and 3 John while Jude and 1–2 John are included. However, this odd combination presents an obstacle for any provenance one might suggest since it is "a combination that is unparalleled in the collections or lists of canonical books." Schnabel, "The Muratorian Fragment," 249. There are some parallels with the Cheltenham canon, a Latin stichometric list known from ninth- and tenth-century manuscripts and dated to 365 in North Africa, which omits Hebrews, James, and Jude. It counts three letters of John and two of

If the Muratorian Fragment was composed in the fourth century in an attempt to portray itself as a second-century list of Christian scriptures, it provides yet another example of a fourth-century writer imposing their concerns about which Christian scriptures were acceptable on an earlier time, in this case, even to the point of forging a document to justify those concerns. The similarities of the Fragment to the other works considered in this chapter may also serve to bolster the interpretation of the Fragment as a fourth-century document. First, one may observe the similarities between the Fragment and the bibliographic methods outlined above. The Fragment is clearly concerned with authorship in the sense that it carefully attaches each work to a named author. For several of these authors, it even provides a brief biographical sketch of how the author came to write the work that bears their name. The Fragment also separates authentic works from spurious ones, categorizing Laodiceans and Alexandrians as letters forged in Paul's name. In addition to separating works into categories of authentic and spurious, it appears to offer a disputed category as well. Although it does not use that specific terminology, it notes a debate about whether or not the *Apocalypse of Peter* and the Shepherd should be read in church. This highlights the second important point of similarity between the Fragment and the other works considered in this chapter: even while it utilizes familiar bibliographic categories, it translates those categories according to its own concerns. The dispute over the disputed works is not primarily about their authorship but about whether or not they should be read in church. Forgeries are only composed by heretics thereby aligning authorship and orthodoxy in a manner reminiscent of Athanasius and Rufinus. Ultimately, the catalogue is about what writings can and "cannot be received into the catholic church."[95] These characteristics, as well as the omission of Hebrews, are consistent with an understanding of the Fragment as a fourth-century composition posing as second-century list of Christian scriptures.

Jerome and Augustine

The opinions of Jerome and Augustine are often identified as a critical turning point for Hebrews' reception in the West, but a close examination of the evidence suggests that rather than signaling a marked change in attitude toward Hebrews, the opinions of Jerome and Augustine actually bear a remarkable resemblance to those of their predecessors. Likewise, the manner in which they report those opinions are also consistent with the translation of traditional bibliographic methods in a manner that suits fourth-century concerns about canon.

Peter, but under each of these lines there is a notation reading "una sola," perhaps suggesting there was some debate about the authenticity of 2–3 John and 2 Peter. Gallagher, *Biblical Canon Lists*, 189–91.

[95] "… ra quae in catholicam eclesiam recepi non …" l. 66 (Schnabel, "The Muratorian Fragment," 238. It should be noted that the Fragment does not utilize the language of canon found in other fourth-century documents, or even Eusebius' term "recognized." However, this may be simply an accident of the Fragment's surviving condition as the opening lines are missing and it is often in these opening lines that the nature of the catalogue to follow was introduced.

Jerome provides a list of Christian scriptures in *Epist.* 53, the New Testament portion of which includes no more or less than the twenty-seven works of Athanasius' collection. In his description of the collection of Pauline letters, he writes, "The apostle Paul writes to seven churches – for an eighth, that to the Hebrews, is not generally counted in with the others."[96] It is not entirely clear if Jerome means that Hebrews is not included among the seven because its authorship is doubted or because it has not traditionally been included in the sevenfold organization of churches to which Paul wrote. However, Jerome's knowledge of debates about Hebrews' authorship is certain from other portions of his writings. In *viris illustribus*, Jerome repeats the ideas concerning the authorship of Hebrews from Eusebius' reports about Pantaenus and Clement.[97] In *Epist.* 129, he states,

> The Epistle which is inscribed to the Hebrews is received not only by the churches of the East but also by all Church writers of the Greek language before our days, as of Paul the apostle, though many think that it is from Barnabas or Clement. And it makes no difference whose it is, since it is from a churchman, and is celebrated in the daily readings of the Churches. And if the usage of the Latins does not receive it among the canonical Scriptures, neither indeed by the same liberty do the Church of the Greeks receive the Revelation of John. And yet we receive both, in that we follow by no means the habit of today, but the authority of ancient writers, who for the most part quote each of them, not as they are sometimes to do the apocrypha, and even also as they rarely use the examples of secular books, but as canonical and churchly.[98]

---

[96] "Paulus apostolus ad septem scribit ecclesias—octaua enim ad Hebraeos a plerisque extra numerum ponitur—, Timotheum instruit ac Titum, Philemonem pro fugitiuo famulo deprecatur. super quo tacere melius puto quam pauca dicere" (*Epist.* 53.9.3; Gallagher, *Biblical Canon Lists*, 209).

[97] Patrick W. Skehan, "St. Jerome and the Canon of the Holy Scriptures," in *A Monument to St. Jerome: Essays On Some Aspects of His Life, Work, and Influence*, ed. Xavier Murphy (New York: Sheed and Ward, 1952), 267:

> Paul ... wrote nine letters to seven churches ... and to his disciples, two to Timothy, one to Titus, one to Philemon. But the epistle known as "to the Hebrews" is believed not to be his, because of its divergent style and diction. (Here Jerome enumerates Barnabas, Luke, Clement, and Paul himself writing anonymously, as possible authors. Pursuing this last possibility, he adds -) Himself a Hebrew, he had written fluently in Hebrew, his own language; in consequence, what had been eloquently written in the Hebrew was rendered more eloquently into Greek. This they allege to be the reason why the Epistle is seemingly different from the other epistles of Paul. There is also on record an Epistle to the Laodiceans, but it is rejected by everybody.

[98] *Epist.* 129.3; Gallagher and Meade, *Biblical Canon Lists*, 214; Metzger, *Canon and the New Testament*, 236; Skehan, "St. Jerome and the Canon," 269–70:

> Illud nostris dicendum est, hanc epistulam, quae scribitur ad Hebraeos, non solum ab ecclesiis orientis sed ab omnibus retro ecclesiae graeci sermonis scriptoribus quasi Pauli apostoli suscipi, licet plerique eam uel Barnabae uel Clementis arbitrentur, et nihil interesse, cuius sit, cum ecclesiastici uiri sit et cotidie ecclesiarum lectione celebretur. quodsi eam latinorum consuetudo non recipit inter scripturas canonicas, nec graecorum quidem ecclesiae Apocalypsin Iohannis eadem libertate suscipiunt, et tamen nos utramque suscipimus nequaquam huius temporis consuetudinem sed ueterum scriptorum auctoritatem sequentes, qui plerumque utriusque abutuntur testimoniis, non ut interdum de apocryphis facere solent—quippe et gentilium litterarum raro utantur exemplis—, sed quasi canonicis et ecclesiasticis.

Jerome here exhibits the same utilization of established bibliographic methods as observed in the works of previous authors. He notes that there are disputes over the authorship of Hebrews and he reports a sampling of the opinions of his predecessors on the matter. However, his concern is not primarily with authorship but with whether or not Hebrews and Revelation should be received among the canonical scriptures. Jerome says that "we receive both" but is adamant that the reason for doing so is the "authority of ancient writers" who quote them and who themselves used these works as "canonical and churchly." Of course, it is impossible for "ancient authors" to have quoted anything as "canonical" since such a concept did not exist until close to Jerome's own lifetime. Like several of his intellectual peers, Jerome has transformed traditional bibliography into a method for discerning canonical works from noncanonical ones and thereby imposed his own concept of canon on previous authors as though it was a concept they shared.

Augustine is also aware of Hebrews' disputed authorship and is apparently unconcerned by it. He accepts Hebrews "because of the authority of the eastern churches, which expressly place it among the canonical scriptures."[99] In his canon list in *Doctr. chr.* 2.8.13.29, Augustine even lists Hebrews as one of the fourteen epistles of Paul.[100] In accepting Hebrews even while registering conflicting opinions about its authorship, Augustine's opinion about Hebrews is like many of his predecessors.

What is most interesting about Augustine's comments on Christian scriptures for the present argument is his articulation of criteria for discerning the canonicity of a writing:

> In the matter of canonical Scriptures he should follow the authority of the great majority of catholic churches, including of course those that were found worthy to have apostolic seats and receive apostolic letters. He will apply this principle to the canonical Scriptures: to prefer those accepted by all catholic churches to those which some do not accept. As for those not universally accepted, he should prefer those accepted by a majority of churches, and by the more authoritative ones, to those supported by fewer churches, or by churches of lesser authority. Should he find that some Scriptures are accepted by the majority of churches, but others by the more authoritative ones (though in fact he could not possibly find this situation), I think that they should be considered to have equal authority.[101]

---

[99] *Pecc. merit.*1.50.
[100] "quattuordecim epistolis apostoli Pauli: ad Romanos, ad Corinthios duabus, ad Galatas, ad Ephesios, ad Philippenses, ad Thessalonicenses duabus, ad Colossenses, ad Timotheum duabus, ad Titum, ad Philemonem, ad Hebraeos" ["fourteen letters of the apostle Paul (Romans, Corinthians (two), Galatians, Ephesians, Philippians, Thessalonians (two), Colossians, Timothy (two), Titus, Philemon, Hebrews)"] (Gallagher and Meade, *Biblical Canon Lists*, 229).
[101] *Doctr. chr.* 2.8.12.24-25; Gallagher and Meade, *Biblical Canon Lists*, 227:

> Tenebit igitur hunc modum in scripturis canonicis, ut eas quae ab omnibus accipiuntur ecclesiis catholicis praeponat eis quas quidam non accipiunt. In eis vero quae non accipiuntur ab omnibus, praeponat eas quas plures gravioresque accipiunt, eis quas pauciores minorisque auctoritatis ecclesiae tenent. Si autem alias invenerit a pluribus, alias a gravioribus haberi, quamquam hoc invenire non possit, aequalis tamen auctoritatis eas habendas puto.

Augustine's criteria for determining the canonicity of Christian writings represent a certain culmination in the translation of bibliographic methods utilized for determining authorship into a means for asserting the authority of certain works by fourth-century theologians. Although it is not a perfectly linear progression, a certain trajectory may be discerned in which the concern for authorship, most prevalent in earlier writings, gradually gave way to acceptance among the churches as the primary method for determining canonicity. It would be too much to claim that this transformation is irreversibly complete in Augustine since debates over the authorship of New Testament writings did not cease in his lifetime. Nevertheless, the nearly complete absence of authorship as a concern in Augustine's criteria is remarkable given the other discourses considered in this chapter. The only remnant of it is that those churches that hold apostolic seats and letters are to be given more weight in their opinions. Otherwise the matter of canonical scriptures is settled entirely by the opinions of the churches. Whereas previously the authority of a work was determined by a mix of concerns about authorship, orthodoxy, and acceptance, in the theology of Augustine the former two are essentially determined by the latter.

Conclusions

Hebrews serves as a particularly illuminating case study among the writings included in lists enumerating the Christian scriptures in late antiquity insofar as Hebrews' complex reception history highlights the different criteria that were utilized in their creation. The lists of Jerome and Augustine have commonly been regarded as especially decisive in the case of Hebrews; their opinions are often considered a major turning point in Hebrews' reception in the West. Close examination of their comments on Hebrews in the context of other fourth- and fifth-century discourses has revealed, however, that their opinions about the epistle are actually quite similar to the opinions expressed by their predecessors. Theologians and church leaders of late antiquity regularly utilized established bibliographic methods to impose their own desire for a clearer delineation of Christian scriptures upon the works of their predecessors as though these earlier writers shared this concern. Although many of these fourth- and fifth-century sources give the appearance of canon lists or catalogues of scripture in their presentation of earlier material, detailed analysis of these texts suggests that those instances are indeed only an appearance and not reality. Therefore, the method of evaluating the citation practices of Christian writers prior to the fourth century to determine the parameters of their "canon" is essentially to accept a fourth-century framework while attempting to understand the second or third century, a practice that will naturally obscure one's view of those centuries and the interaction with Christian scriptures practiced within them. The citation practices of these patristic writers must be evaluated in their own context, apart from concerns of canon, if one seeks to understand the full variety of ways in which early Christians were interacting with their scriptures. The citation habits of these second- and third-century writers are the subject of the next chapter.

3

Quoting Hebrews: Patristic Citations of Hebrews in the Second and Third Centuries

Introduction

The catalogues of authoritative scriptures discussed in the previous chapter are the exception rather than the rule when it comes to early Christian interactions with the Epistle to the Hebrews. The vast majority of those interactions offer very little explicit commentary regarding the authority invested in this document and demonstrate no concern to determine its "canonical" status. Exercising their rhetorical training, patristic writers used many writings to a variety of ends in their arguments, often without explicit indications about the relationship between the authority or acceptance of that document and the end to which it was employed. Hebrews is no exception to this rule as second- and third-century Christian writers frequently quoted or alluded to its text alongside many other quotations from various sources in a manner consistent with the "inartificial proofs" discussed in Greek and Latin rhetorical handbooks. The utility of the text of Hebrews to an author's rhetorical aims appears to be the critical factor in Hebrews' reception among patristic authors prior to the fourth century. Rather than explicitly sorting works by their authoritative status, these writers negotiated the traditions of authorship and utility they had received in order to authorize documents to very specific ends. Even in the rare discussions that include explicit statements about Hebrews' authority, second- and third-century writers demonstrate a range of opinions about Hebrews' utility and authorship that are far more nuanced than a simple "in or out" mentality.[1]

---

[1] One may argue that this principle of utility remains a critical factor in Hebrews' reception even into the fourth century and beyond. Indeed, Hebrews plays no small role in the Christological controversies of those later centuries. The present chapter focuses on the utilization of Hebrews in the second and third centuries primarily for two reasons. The first is a very practical one; this limitation provides a manageable scope of evidence with which to contend given the sheer abundance of scriptural quotations in patristic material. The *Biblia Patristica* offers 7,765 total quotations or allusions to Hebrews within its database. Limiting the search to the second and third centuries brings this number down to 1,421. Second, the quotations of Hebrews in the second and third centuries are the ones most often cited in studies that seek to weigh Hebrews' acceptance or rejection prior to its ascension to canonical status in the fourth century. This methodology is fraught with difficulty, I argue, insofar as it attempts to discern the authority or acceptance of a document beyond the immediate rhetorical context in which it is employed.

The most common interpretation of Hebrews' reception has been that it was accepted at an early stage in the East while it was either neglected or rejected in the West until the fourth century when it achieved canonical status. Such a reading is typically founded upon the repeated quotations of Hebrews by Clement and Origen as well as Hebrews' prominent position in P^{46} in contrast to its relative neglect among Christian writers in the West. Although it is true that Hebrews may not have enjoyed the same level of favor among other localities that it did in Alexandria, a blanket claim of Hebrews' rejection in the West minimizes the appearance of text from Hebrews in the writings of Clement of Rome, Justin Martyr, and Tertullian as insignificant while elevating the significance of its supposed rejection by a single presbyter as reported by Eusebius.

In addition to these generalizations about East and West, this view is informed by a dichotomy of total acceptance or rejection as the only options available with regard to a document's reception. That is, Clement and Origen must have "accepted" Hebrews since they quoted it frequently while authors in the West "rejected" it since they used it so sparingly. A closer look at the relevance of Hebrews to these writers suggests a much more varied landscape of reception than a flat binary of acceptance or rejection. Patristic citations of Hebrews in the second and third centuries suggest a reception of the epistle that is best understood along a spectrum of utility relative to each writer's rhetorical goals rather than an orientation toward wholesale acceptance or rejection. Of course, authority and utility are not mutually exclusive categories since the usefulness of a text to one's argument often assumes it will be in some way persuasive for one's audience. The contention of this chapter is, however, that any implication of authority or acceptance inherent in the quotation of a work may be best understood in the context of ancient rhetorical and compositional practice rather than being forced into separate containers labeled "acceptance" or "rejection."

Expressions of Utility in Ancient Compositional Practice

Expressions of this principle of utility may be modeled along three different but related axes, so to speak: a utility of selection, interpretation, and attribution of authorship. By utility of selection, I mean that ancient authors demonstrate a concern for a text's benefit to their own argument as they select which texts to include in their own writings. Likewise, ancient writers interpret the texts that they do select in the manner they find most useful or beneficial to their audience. Finally, the attribution of authorship to a text often functions to authorize a text for a specific rhetorical purpose. In many instances, these three axes can be seen working together in nuanced and varied ways among different authors as they employ various sources in order to construct their own arguments.

Although ancient writers offered varied and numerous instructions about how to compose written works and construct persuasive arguments carefully, there are unfortunately few instances of ancient writers specifically discussing their citation of other sources in composing their own works. Perhaps this is because there was no agreed-upon methodology concerning the quotation of sources in composition. On the one hand, Pliny the Elder counts it a point of pride as well as a demonstration of his "honorable modesty" that he has carefully documented the sources he referenced in his *Natural History*. He likens other writers who fail to follow his practice to those who would "prefer being detected in a theft to repaying a loan."² Cicero similarly likens borrowing from another source without acknowledging the debt to an act of theft.³ Dionysius provides a list of some of his most important sources at the beginning of his *Roman Antiquities*, noting that he received some information "orally from men of the greatest learning ... and the rest I gathered from histories written by the approved Roman authors," and frequently mentions his sources by name throughout his work.⁴ Many other writers, however, recorded no such qualms when it came to a failure to cite sources. On the contrary, it appears to have been common practice to read or listen to other works read aloud more so with an eye to the inspiration of one's own work than out of any concern for faithfully reproducing or crediting one's prior source.⁵ Seneca even disparages those who "slip into the department of the philologist or the scholar" in that they "hunt out archaic or far-fetched words and eccentric metaphors and figures of speech" rather than recognizing that the goal of philosophy is to "seek

---

² Pliny, Nat. 21–23, trans. H. Rackham, LCL 330 (Cambridge, MA: Harvard University Press, 1938), 14–15:

> scito enim conferentem auctores me deprehendisse a iuratissimis et proximis veteres transcriptos ad verbum neque nominatos, non illa Vergiliana virtute, ut certarent, non Tulliana simplicitate, qui de re publica Platonis se comitem profitetur, in consolatione filiae "Crantorem," inquit, "sequor," item Panaetium de officiis, quae volumina ediscenda, non modo in manibus cotidie habenda nosti. obnoxii profecto animi et infelicis ingenii est deprehendi in furto malle quam mutuum reddere, cum praesertim sors fiat ex usura. [For you must know that when collating authorities I have found that the most professedly reliable and modern writers have copied the old authors word for word, without acknowledgement, not in that valorous spirit of Virgil, for the purpose of rivalry, nor with the candour of Cicero who in his Republic declares himself a companion of Plato, and in his Consolation to his daughter says "I follow Crantor," and similarly as to Panaetius in his De Officiis—volumes that you know to be worth having in one's hands every day, nay even learning by heart. Surely it marks a mean spirit and an unfortunate disposition to prefer being detected in a theft to repaying a loan—especially as interest creates capital.]

³ *Brutus* 75–76.

⁴ "καὶ τὰ μὲν παρὰ τῶν λογιωτάτων ἀνδρῶν, οἷς εἰς ὁμιλίαν ἦλθον, διδαχῇ παραλαβών, τὰ δ' ἐκ τῶν ἱστοριῶν ἀναλεξάμενος, ἃς οἱ πρὸς αὐτῶν ἐπαινούμενοι Ῥωμαίων συνέγραψαν" (Dionysius of Halicarnassus, Roman Antiquities 1.8, trans. Earnest Cary, LCL 319 [Cambridge, MA: Harvard University Press, 1937], 22–5).

⁵ Ovid complains bitterly about the pain of trying to write while being away from his own library:

> Misfortunes have broken my talent whose source was even aforetime unproductive and whose stream was meagre. But such as it was, with none to exercise it, it has shrunken and is lost, dried up by long neglect. Not here have I an abundance of books to stimulate and nourish me: in their stead is the rattle of bows and arms. There is nobody in this land, should I read my verse, of whose intelligent ear I might avail myself, there is no place to which I may withdraw. The guard on the wall and a closed gate keep back the hostile Getae. Often I am at a loss for a word, a name, a place, and there is none who can inform me. Oft when I attempt some utterance—shameful confession!—words fail me. (Ovid, Tristia 3.14.37, trans. A. L. Wheeler, LCL 151 [Cambridge, MA: Harvard University Press, 1924], 155)

precepts which will help us, utterances of courage and spirit which may at once be turned into facts."[6]

Despite this diversity of opinion about the importance of acknowledging one's sources, a certain commonality does emerge among these various writers: the selection of specific texts from among a larger array of sources based on the usefulness of the text to one's own argument. Commonly known as "inartificial" or "atechnic" proofs, such proofs were drawn from previously existing sources. Aristotle contrasted these proofs that were "already in existence, such as witnesses, tortures, contracts, and the like" with the artificial proofs that "can be constructed by system and by our own efforts. Thus we have only to make use of the former, whereas we must invent the latter."[7]

Authors commonly employed this rhetorical pattern by writing down certain passages of other works they wished to retrieve later or, in some cases, to simply make a mental note of the relevant details with little concern for latter attribution or accurate reproduction.[8] Once this collection of material was arranged, either mentally or in writing, the author could set about assimilating the relevant pieces of the collection into their own work. Lucian provides an apt description of this process in his instruction for composing a work of history:

> As to the facts themselves, he should not assemble them at random, but only after much laborious and painstaking investigation. He should for preference be an eyewitness, but, if not, listen to those who tell the more impartial story, those whom one would suppose least likely to subtract from the facts or add to them out of favour or malice. When this happens let him show shrewdness and skill in putting together the more credible story. When he has collected all or most of the facts let him first make them into a series of notes, a body of material as yet with no beauty or continuity. Then, after arranging them into order, let him give it beauty and enhance it with the charms of expression, figure, and rhythm.[9]

---

[6] "Sed ne et ipse, dum aliud ago, in philologum aut grammaticum delabar, illud admoneo, auditionem philosophorum lectionemque ad propositum beatae vitae trahendam, non ut verba prisca aut ficta captemus et translationes inprobas figurasque dicendi, sed ut profutura praecepta et magnificas voces et animosas, quae mox in rem transferantur" (Seneca, Epist. 108.35-37, trans. R. M. Gummere, LCL 77 [Cambridge, MA: Harvard University Press, 1925], 252–3).

[7] Aristotle, Rhet. 1.2.2, trans. J. H. Freese, LCL 193 (Cambridge, MA: Harvard University Press, 1926), 15. See also Cicero, De. Or. 2.116; Rowan A. Greer and Margaret Mary Mitchell, Belly-Myther of Endor: Interpretations of 1 Kingdoms 28 in the Early Church (Atlanta: Society of Biblical Literature, 2007), 76; Margaret Mary Mitchell, "Rhetorical Handbooks in Service of Biblical Exegesis: Eustathius of Antioch Takes Origen Back to School," in The New Testament and Early Christian Literature in Greco-Roman Context: Studies in Honor of David E. Aune, Supplements to Novum Testamentum 122, ed. John Fotopoulos (Boston: Brill, 2006), 350; G. H. Wikramanayake, "A Note on the Pisteis in Aristotle's Rhetoric," American Journal of Philology 82, no. 2 (1961): 194.

[8] Sean Alexander Gurd, Work in Progress: Literary Revision as Social Performance in Ancient Rome (New York: Oxford University Press, 2011), 10–11; Karen King, "What Is an Author?: Ancient Author Function in the Apocryphon of John and the Apocalypse of John," in Scribal Practices and Social Structures among Jesus Adherents: Essays in Honour of John S. Kloppenborg, ed. William E. Arnal et al. (Leuven: Peeters, 2016), 32.

[9] Lucian, Quom. Hist. 47–8, trans. K. Kilburn, LCL 430 (Cambridge, MA: Harvard University Press, 1959), 61:

Lucian requires a basic threshold of credibility for one's sources while also expressing the expectation that those sources will be arranged and molded to the present author's own purposes. Dio Cassius represents a similar selection process more succinctly when he states, "Although I have read pretty nearly everything about them that has been written by anybody, I have not included it all in my history, but only what I have seen fit to select."[10] Ancient authors exhibit a high degree of comfort adapting their sources in a manner that was most beneficial to their own work.

The selection of a text based on its benefit to a given argument is matched by an interpretation of the text that is oriented toward usefulness to the author and benefit to the assumed audience. Ancient writers were not confined to a particular method of interpretation, whether literal or allegorical, but were trained to read and interpret texts with an eye to the plain meaning of the text as well as the spirit or intent of its author. Cicero states, "The task of the public speaker is to discuss capably those matters which law and custom have fixed for the uses of citizenship, and to secure as far as possible the agreement of his hearers."[11] In case he has not made the point bluntly enough, he goes on to say, "From the discussion of the facts themselves we shall render the hearer well-disposed by extolling our own cause with praise and by contemptuously disparaging that of our adversaries."[12]

One accomplishes this contemptuous disparaging of one's opponents by making the text work for one's own argument. If the plain reading of the text is in one's favor, then the task is easy enough. Attention only has to be drawn to the careful crafting of the text itself; how the author has taken care to leave out nothing that he intended and that any interpretation of the text to the contrary is a fanciful and intentional misrepresentation of what the author so carefully sought to safeguard with written words. On the other hand, if the plain reading of the text appears to be opposed to one's argument, then the proper task is to draw attention to the clear intent of the author and how obvious it is that the plain reading of what has been written is insufficient and

---

Τὰ δὲ πράγματα αὐτὰ οὐχ ὡς ἔτυχε συνακτέον, ἀλλὰ φιλοπόνως καὶ ταλαιπώρως πολλάκις περὶ τῶν αὐτῶν ἀνακρίναντα, καὶ μάλιστα μὲν παρόντα καὶ ἐφορῶντα, εἰ δὲ μή, τοῖς ἀδεκαστότερον ἐξηγουμένοις προσέχοντα καὶ οὓς εἰκάσειεν ἄν τις ἥκιστα πρὸς χάριν ἢ ἀπέχθειαν ἀφαιρήσειν ἢ προσθήσειν τοῖς γεγονόσιν. κἀνταῦθα ἤδη καὶ στοχαστικός τις καὶ συνθετικὸς τοῦ πιθανωτέρου ἔστω. καὶ ἐπειδὰν ἀθροίσῃ ἅπαντα ἢ τὰ πλεῖστα, πρῶτα μὲν ὑπόμνημά τι συνυφαινέτω αὐτῶν καὶ σῶμα ποιείτω ἀκαλλὲς ἔτι καὶ ἀδιάρθρωτον· εἶτα ἐπιθεὶς τὴν τάξιν ἐπαγέτω τὸ κάλλος καὶ χρωννύτω τῇ λέξει καὶ σχηματιζέτω καὶ ῥυθμιζέτω.

[10] "Ἀνέγνων μὲν πάντα ὡς εἰπεῖν τὰ περὶ αὐτῶν τισι γεγραμμένα, συνέγραψα δὲ οὐ πάντα ἀλλ᾿ ὅσα ἐξέκρινα" (Dio Cassius, Rom. Hist. 1.1, trans. E. Cary, LCL 32 [Cambridge, MA: Harvard University Press, 1914], 3).

[11] "Oratoris officium est de iis rebus posse dicere quae res ad usum civilem moribus et legibus constitutae sunt, cum adsensione auditorum quoad eius fieri poterit" (Cicero, Rhet ad Herr. 1.2.1, trans. H. Caplan, LCL 403 [Cambridge, MA: Harvard University Press, 1954], 5); Geoffrey D. Dunn, "Tertullian's Scriptural Exegesis in de Praescriptione Haereticorum," Journal of Early Christian Studies 14, no. 2 (June 12, 2006): 141–55; Kathy Eden, Hermeneutics and the Rhetorical Tradition: Chapters in the Ancient Legacy & Its Humanist Reception, Yale Studies in Hermeneutics (New Haven, CT: Yale University Press, 1997); Margaret Mary Mitchell, Paul, the Corinthians, and the Birth of Christian Hermeneutics (New York: Cambridge University Press, 2012).

[12] "Ab rebus ipsis benivolum efficiemus auditorem si nostram causam laudando extollemus, adversariorum per contemptionem deprimemus" (Cicero, Rhet ad Herr., 1.5.8 [Caplan, LCL 403:17]).

could not possibly have been what the author intended.[13] The well-trained rhetorician is not characterized by strict adherence to either the spirit or the letter as the proper hermeneutical approach but by mastery of both approaches in an attempt to produce the interpretation that is most useful or beneficial to the present cause.

Finally, in addition to a work being selected and interpreted by virtue of its utility to a writer's present purposes, the attribution of authorship to a work was also characterized by utility. Karen King notes, "Works receive attribution only when it is useful to perform certain kinds of discursive work with regard to some present social enterprise."[14] This discursive work could exist in a variety of forms, but one of the most common functions of authorship attribution is, of course, to authorize the work itself by connecting it to a credible source. The previous chapter outlined the importance of authorship attribution among Greek and Roman bibliographers. Questions about a work's authorship could often lead to the relegation of that work to the end of a particular author's corpus of writings or removal of the work from the corpus entirely, eventually resulting in a diminished valuation of the work. Also noted were the ways in which fourth- and fifth-century theologians utilized these same bibliographic methods with regard to Christian scriptures, specifically to authorize texts as "accepted" or "canonical." Although second- and third-century theologians do not create these same categories, attributions of apostolic authorship or association (or lack thereof) do authorize the utilization of Hebrews in different ways for each patristic writer. That is not to say that these patristic writers have completely fabricated claims of authorship for Hebrews or the other documents they employ. These writers have received certain traditions about Hebrews' authorship that they employ for their own specific rhetorical aims.

In summary, the quotation of or allusion to a prior work in ancient writings was characterized by a principle of utility. Writers cited the material that was most beneficial for their present argument, they interpreted it in a manner they regarded as most beneficial for their audience, and the authorship attributed to the work (or lack of such attribution) was similarly employed in this same task. The guiding principle in the quotation of an earlier writing within one's own work was not primarily an assessment of that writing's authority or acceptance but the utility of the writing to the present author's own argument. Therefore, the utilization of Hebrews by patristic writers is best understood as an assessment of the document's usefulness to arguments these writers wish to make in negotiation with local traditions regarding the work rather than an assessment of its broad authority or acceptance beyond the author's present rhetorical aims. Furthermore, quotations of Hebrews by writers of the second and third centuries do not exhibit a simple dichotomous attitude toward Hebrews as either useful or not but are characterized by a spectrum of utility along which different writers may be plotted as they found Hebrews useful to varying degrees and ends.

---

[13] Ibid., 2.9.13–2.10.14.
[14] King, "What Is an Author?," 41.

The Diverse Utilization of Hebrews among Patristic Writers

Although there are over 1,400 recorded references to Hebrews in the second and third centuries, the vast majority of these can be attributed primarily to four writers: Justin Martyr, Tertullian, Clement of Alexandria, and Origen. Origen quotes Hebrews the most frequently by a large margin with over one thousand citations credited to him alone. Clement is credited with just over one hundred, while Tertullian and Justin Martyr are variously credited with citations numbering in the thirties and teens, respectively. These numbers alone begin to suggest that second- and third-century theologians found Hebrews useful to varying degrees. The landscape of Hebrews' reception becomes still more nuanced when consideration is given to the ends to which these quotations are utilized in their respective contexts. Origen repeatedly utilizes Hebrews to justify his spiritual reading of scripture, while Clement is fond of citing Hebrews to justify his use of philosophical works as sources of knowledge alongside of scripture; both depend heavily on the Pauline authorship of Hebrews in order to make these claims. Tertullian, on the other hand, attributes the epistle to Barnabas. Although Tertullian does not concur with the Alexandrian attribution of Pauline authorship, his attribution of the text's authorship to an associate of the apostle functions similarly. Tertullian discusses the authorship of Hebrews on only one occasion, and, when he does, his attribution is designed to buttress his own argument. Apart from this single instance, Tertullian's use of Hebrews bears considerable resemblance to that of Justin Martyr; Justin appears to know Hebrews and to find it useful, but he never cites it by title or author. None of these writers concern themselves with the question of acceptance or rejection. Instead, they exhibit nuance and complexity in their selection of passages from Hebrews, their interpretation of those passages, their opinions about Hebrews' authorship, and the relationship between all three.

Justin Martyr

Among the second- and third-century theologians whose writings exhibit discernible references to Hebrews, Justin utilizes the epistle the least frequently.[15] Furthermore, Justin never references Hebrews as his source, attributes its authorship to any individual, or makes any explicit statements about how widely accepted he believes it to be relative to other works. This treatment of the epistle by Justin has often been combined with other, later reports of controversy over Hebrews in Rome in order to construct a scholarly picture of Hebrews' neglect in the West prior to the fourth century. Much of this evidence, however, postdates Justin's writings, including the *Dialogue*

---

[15] The *Biblia Patristica* lists thirteen references to Hebrews for Justin Martyr though this estimation fluctuates among secondary literature depending on what is numbered as an allusion to Hebrews as opposed to mere references to the same LXX passages referenced by Hebrews. Eleven and five references are also listed for Hippolytus and Cyprian, respectively, but many, if not all of these, are such weak allusions to Hebrews or verses quoted by Hebrews that any influence is not clearly discernible.

with Trypho, which alludes to Hebrews on a number of occasions. The rhetorical aims of the *Dialogue* also provide a context that explains why Justin failed to leverage the authority of Hebrews in any explicit way. Justin commonly utilizes Hebrews as a source of inauthentic proofs, borrowing from particular collections of scriptural texts already listed in the epistle or in Testimonia Collections (TCs) and employing both in his arguments with "Jews" about the proper interpretation of the Septuagint. Therefore, Justin's reception of Hebrews serves to illuminate the difficulties inherent in generalizing about a document's authority or acceptance beyond the immediate rhetorical context in which it is employed.

Justin's writings are often taken as evidence that Hebrews was known, but not regarded as scripture, particularly in Rome, a point that is commonly supplemented by other Roman evidence. The Shepherd of Hermas, a document also thought to be of Roman provenance, is one such frequently cited piece of evidence for Hebrews' poor reception in the city. The possibility of a second repentance offered by the Shepherd in *Vis.* 2.2.4-5, a teaching thought to be in conflict with Heb 6:4-6, is typically regarded as an indication that Hebrews was not well received there. Eusebius' report about Gaius, bishop of Rome in the late third century, is often added to these in arguments concerning Hebrews' rejection at Rome.[16] Eusebius' report concerning Hebrews' supposed rejection is, however, limited on several fronts. It is attributed to a single presbyter due to specific concerns about the Phrygian heresy, and it is described only as a rejection of the document's Pauline authorship, not the document itself. Likewise, it is not clear that the offering of second repentance by the Shepherd is a direct response to the teaching of Hebrews.[17] The Shepherd does not reference Hebrews or give any indication of literary dependence upon it, and the two documents are not directly juxtaposed until decades later, when Tertullian, writing in North Africa rather than Rome, employs them both. Therefore, the evidence for Hebrews' rejection in Rome is actually quite limited and comes from a later date than Justin's own use of the epistle. Of course, it is possible that these later instances represent broad and long-standing conflict over the epistle in the imperial city but Justin himself registers no such conflict. On the contrary, his utilization of Hebrews resembles that of 1 Clement before him: a borrowing of both Hebrews' ideas and its citations of the Septuagint without identifying it as a source.[18]

---

[16] *Hist. eccl.* 6.20. (Oulton, LCL 265:67):

> And there has reached us also a Dialogue of Gaius, a very learned person (which was set a-going at Rome in the time of Zephyrinus), with Proclus the champion of the heresy of the Phrygians. In which, when curbing the recklessness and audacity of his opponents in composing new Scriptures, he mentions only thirteen epistles of the holy Apostle, not numbering the Epistle to the Hebrews with the rest; seeing that even to this day among the Romans there are some who do not consider it to be the Apostle's.

[17] Indeed, it is not even clear that the Shepherd wholly contradicts Heb 6:4–6 though there is obviously some tension around the issue of second repentance. In *Man.* 4.3.1-7, the Shepherd actually agrees with Hebrews concerning the impossibility of second repentance for those who have been baptized. The offering of second repentance in *Vis.* 2.2.4-5 occurs in an eschatological context, which makes its relationship to the impossibility of renewal in Hebrews unclear. Carolyn Osiek, Shepherd of Hermas: A Commentary (Minneapolis, MN: Fortress Press, 1999), 29, 54–57, 109–16.

[18] First Clement 36:2–6 quotes Heb 1:3–4 while also citing several of the same passages of the LXX cited in the rest of Heb 1:

Justin's references to Hebrews are almost entirely contained within the *Dialogue*.[19] As a result, his rhetorical aim in the *Dialogue* of demonstrating the truth of Christianity to his Jewish opponent through the use of Jewish scriptures provides important context for Justin's utilization of Hebrews. It would make little sense for Justin to identify a Christian writing as his source or demonstrate any concern for that text's authorship or authenticity as such concerns would carry little rhetorical weight.[20] Rather than leveraging the authority of Christian writings, Justin treats these writings as a source for inartificial proofs, mining them for particular readings of scripture that he might utilize in his arguments with Trypho. It is no surprise then that Justin makes regular use of TCs, lists of Jewish scripture citations arranged together to support particular Christian understandings of those scriptures, as these collections are perfectly suited for the kind of arguments Justin wishes to construct. Justin utilizes Christian writings, Hebrews included, in a manner akin to these TCs, by reusing their own interpretations of multiple scriptural texts.[21]

Justin's utilization of Hebrews may be observed in *Dial.* 33.2-4 where he states,

If your ears were not so dull, or your hearts so hardened, you would see that the words refer to our Jesus. For, by the words, "The Lord hath sworn, and He will

ὃς ὢν ἀπαύγασμα τῆς μεγαλωσύνης αὐτοῦ, τοσούτῳ μείζων ἐστὶν ἀγγέλων, ὅσῳ διαφορώτερον ὄνομα κεκληρονόμηκεν. γέγραπται γὰρ οὕτως· ὁ ποιῶν τοὺς ἀγγέλους αὐτοῦ πνεύματα καὶ τοὺς λειτουργοὺς αὐτοῦ πυρὸς φλόγα. ἐπὶ δὲ τῷ υἱῷ αὐτοῦ οὕτως εἶπεν ὁ δεσπότης· υἱός μου εἶ σύ, ἐγὼ σήμερον γεγέννηκά σε· αἴτησαι παρ᾽ ἐμοῦ, καὶ δώσω σοι ἔθνη τὴν κληρονομίαν σου καὶ τὴν κατάσχεσίν σου τὰ πέρατα τῆς γῆς. καὶ πάλιν λέγει πρὸς αὐτόν· κάθου ἐκ δεξιῶν μου, ἕως ἂν θῶ τοὺς ἐχθρούς σου ὑποπόδιον τῶν ποδῶν σου. τίνες οὖν οἱ ἐχθροί; οἱ φαῦλοι καὶ ἀντιτασσόμενοι τῷ θελήματι αὐτοῦ. ["*who, being the brightness of his majesty, is by so much greater than angels as he has inherited a more excellent name.*" For it is written thus, "*Who makes his angels spirits, and his ministers a flame of fire.*" But of his Son the Master said thus, "*You are my son; Today have I begotten thee. Ask of me and I will give you the heathen for your inheritance, and the ends of the earth for your possession.*" And again he says to him, "*Sit at my right hand until I make your enemies a footstool for thy feet.*' Who then are the enemies? Those who are wicked and oppose his will."] (Harold W. Attridge, Hebrews: A Commentary on the Epistle to the Hebrews [Philadelphia: Fortress Press, 1989], 6)

---

[19] The only two exceptions are *1 Apol.* 1.12 and 61, both of which may be considered questionable allusions to the text of Hebrews.

[20] Cosgrove argues that Christians are the real audience of the *Dialogue* and that the absence of explicit references to Christian writings actually indicates the insignificance of those writings to Justin. I agree that Christians are the target audience of Justin's debate with Trypho. Nevertheless, the premise of this literary fiction is still the proper interpretation of Jewish scripture. Even to an intelligent Christian audience, I suspect that repeated references to Christian writings would undermine the pretense that the truth of Christianity can be proved from the Jewish scriptures themselves. Charles H. Cosgrove, "Justin Martyr and the Emerging Canon," *Vigiliae Christianae* 36 (1982): 209–32.

[21] See, for example, the similarity of Justin's argument in *Dial.* 23.4 to Rom 4 and *Dial.* 95.1 and 96.1 to Gal 3:10–13. Justin's use of the Gospels is slightly different though it still fits within this general scheme. Justin frequently quotes sayings of Jesus from the "memoirs of the apostles" in *Dial.* 99–107 as fulfillments of Hebrew scripture. He seems to have very little concern for the gospels as distinct literary entities. Like the TC and Paul's writings, they are a source for demonstrating Jesus' fulfillment of prophecy. Craig D. Allert, Revelation, Truth, Canon, and Interpretation: Studies in Justin Martyr's Dialogue with Trypho, Supplements to Vigiliae Christianae 64 (Boston: Brill, 2002), 237; Cosgrove, "Justin Martyr and the Emerging Canon," 224.

not repent; Thou art a priest forever according to the order of Melchisedech," God, because of your lack of faith, swore that Jesus is the High Priest according to the order of Melchisedech. For, as Melchisedech was the priest of the Most High (as Moses tells us), and as he was the priest of the uncircumcised, and blessed the circumcised Abraham who offered him tithes, so has God announced that His eternal Priest, called Lord by the Holy Spirit, should be the priest of the uncircumcised. Those circumcised persons who approach Him with faith in their hearts and a prayer on their lips for His blessings will be welcomed and blessed by Him.[22]

Here we have not only the application of Ps 110:4 to Jesus in a way that is unique to Hebrews prior to Justin.[23] There is also an emphasis on Abraham's payment of tithes to Melchizedek as found in Heb 7. Finally, when Justin says this everlasting priest is "called also by the Holy Spirit 'Lord,'" he is referring once again to Ps 110:1 and thus connecting vv. 1 and 4 of Ps 110 in precisely the same way that Hebrews does.[24]

Justin did not limit his mining of Hebrews—or any Christian text—to scriptural proofs but could also utilize these writings as an example to follow in Christian interpretations of Septuagint texts. A Christian reading of a particular verse of Jewish scripture in a writing like Hebrews could be extrapolated to the rest of the passage in which the verse was found. Justin extrapolates the Christological reading of Ps 110:1 common throughout many New Testament writings, for example, to interpret the rest of Ps 110 at the end of *Dial*. 33. There he says with reference to Christ,

Those circumcised persons who approach Him with faith in their hearts and a prayer on their lips for His blessings will be welcomed and blessed by Him. The concluding words of the Psalm, "He shall drink of the torrent in the way," and, "Therefore shall He lift up the head," prove that Christ was to be first humble man, and later He was to be exalted.[25]

Justin's use of the final verse of Ps 110 to speak of Jesus' first lowly appearance and a later glorious one follows the "two advents" pattern. Martin Albl identifies this same pattern in other TCs utilized by the *Epistle of Barnabas*, Irenaeus, and Tertullian.[26] Justin has combined here patterns of interpretation found in both Hebrews and TCs and melded them together to forge a new interpretation of Ps 110:7.

A similar expansion of Hebrews and a corresponding TC is present in *Dial*. 56. Justin quotes Pss 110:1 and 45:7–8, both of which are also quoted in Heb 1, but it is

---

[22] Justin, Dial. 33.2-4, trans. Thomas Falls (Washington, DC: Catholic University of America Press, 2003), 197. See also *Dial*. 19.1 where Justin intertwines Ps 110.4 and Gen 14:18–20 in a manner reminiscent of Hebrews. Oskar Skarsaune, The Proof from Prophecy: A Study in Justin Martyr's Proof-Text Tradition: Text-Type, Provenance, Theological Profile (Leiden: Brill, 1987), 107.
[23] Skarsaune, *Proof from Prophecy*, 127.
[24] For other examples of Justin's utilization of Hebrews, see *Dial*. 31.1, 67.9, 96.1, and 113.5.
[25] Justin, *Dial*. 33.2-4. Falls, 197.
[26] Allert, *Revelation, Truth, Canon, and Interpretation*, 231. Martin C. Albl, And Scripture Cannot Be Broken: The Form and Function of the Early Christian Testimonia Collections, Supplements to Novum Testamentum 96 (Boston: Brill, 1999), 128–31.

Gen 19:24 that takes center stage. Oskar Skarsaune observes that these three verses belong together "in a cluster of testimonies proving that Scripture knows two Gods or two Lords: Genesis 19:24 two Lords; Psalm 110:1 two Lords, Psalm 45:7f two Gods."[27] Justin, however, does much more than merely quote these verses. *Dial.* 56 is a lengthy commentary on Gen 18–19 in which three angels visit Abraham at the oaks of Mamre and later destroy Sodom and Gomorrah. He utilizes this passage to argue that one of the angels who appeared to Abraham is, in fact, the Lord of the other two angels and that this Lord is not the same Lord who rained fire down from heaven. Justin has added considerable exegetical work of his own in order to expand upon these verses that appeared alongside of each other with little intervening commentary in Hebrews and a TC.

Justin's utilization of Hebrews, or any Christian writing for that matter, is patterned after the rhetorical use of inartificial proofs insofar as Hebrews provides a useful collection of Christian interpretations for scriptural texts in Justin's *Dialogue with Trypho*. He shows no interest in matters of authorship or any concern for the document's standing among Christian communities. It would be a mistake, however, to assume that this meant that Justin did not "accept" Hebrews. On the contrary, Hebrews' arguments and use of scriptural texts influenced his own. Likewise, Justin's failure to comment on these matters does not suggest that Hebrews had no standing or tradition concerning authorship in Rome or the West at large; such concerns served no purpose for Justin's immediate rhetorical aims. Justin was simply not interested in investing specific Christian writings with the status of "scriptures." His utilization of Hebrews demonstrates the inadequacy of categorizing the document's reception within the binary of "acceptance" or "rejection" as well as the problematic nature of generalizing an author's reception beyond his immediate rhetorical context. Evaluating Justin's use of Hebrews or any Christian writing through the fourth-century category of canon by asking which writings were among those Justin considered authoritative only serves to skew one's understanding of a writer who showed very little concern for this type of authority when utilizing Christian texts. Justin "accepted" Hebrews for the specific ends to which he desired to employ it—as a source of proofs for his claims about Jesus—and his use of the epistle signifies neither more nor less than its utility toward those ends.

Tertullian of Carthage

Tertullian's reception of Hebrews bears considerable resemblance to Justin Martyr's with one notable exception: his attribution of the document's authorship to Barnabas. Tertullian attributes the epistle to Barnabas only once in his writings, however, and does so in service to the very specific goal of refuting any doctrine of second repentance. Aside from this single instance, Tertullian never mentions the epistle or its author by name among the approximately thirty-five times he echoes its text. Much like Justin Martyr, whom Tertullian also utilized as a source for his own writings, Tertullian's

---

[27] Skarsaune, *Proof from Prophecy*, 209.

frequent failure to credit Hebrews as his source is likely a by-product of the literary framework in which these references commonly appear, namely, arguments about the proper interpretation of the Septuagint. Far from being marginalized on the basis of a suspicion about authorship or origin, Hebrews was an important source for both Justin and Tertullian, akin to TCs, in their arguments that the Jewish scriptures are "about" Jesus. Therefore, Tertullian's use of the epistle represents a complex negotiation between local traditions regarding Hebrews' authorship, the utility of Hebrews to Tertullian's own theological position, and his expectations about what will be persuasive to his target audience.

De pudicitia 20.2 includes Tertullian's only explicit reference to Hebrews by its title and author. Prior to this passage, Tertullian has outlined the teaching and example of the apostles with regard to modesty. He now adds a reference to Hebrews as the testimony of an associate of the apostles:

> For there exists also a letter, entitled "by Barnabas to the Hebrews," by a man sufficiently authorized by God, since Paul put him besides himself in observance of abstention: "For is it only I and Barnabas who have no power to forebear working?" At any rate, this Letter of Barnabas is better received by the churches than that apocryphal "Shepherd of the adulterers."[28]

Tertullian's attribution of authorship to Barnabas is probably not his own invention but a reflection of the tradition he received in North Africa, perhaps even indicating a title tag on the manuscript utilized by Tertullian, which may have read *Barnabae ad Hebraeos*.[29] This tradition of authorship is likely reflected in Tertullian's arrangement of *De pudicitia* as well. Tertullian begins his argument with examples from the Gospels and then moves on to Paul's letters, the epistles of John, and Revelation. Only after he has treated these apostolic sources does he move to the "sub-apostolic" work of Hebrews, which is only apostolic by association.[30] Nevertheless, Tertullian is doing more than merely reporting a tradition concerning Hebrews' authorship. He is leveraging that tradition in order to raise the authority of Hebrews relative to the Shepherd, a work he wishes to denigrate. In addition to his attribution of Hebrews' authorship to an associate of the apostles, Tertullian also describes Hebrews as being more broadly received than the Shepherd.[31] The reason for Tertullian's concern regarding Hebrews'

---

[28] "Extat enim et Barnabae titulus ad Hebraeos, a Deo satis auctoritati uiri, ut quem Paulus iuxta se constituerit in abstinentiae tenore: aut ego solus et Barnabas non habemus operandi potestatem? Et utique receptior apud ecclesias epistola Barnabae illo apocrypho Pastore moechorum'" (*Pud.* 20.2. [CCSL 2, 1324]; E.A. de Boer, "Tertullian on 'Barnabas' Letter to the Hebrews' in De Pudicitia 20.1–5," *Vigiliae Christianae* 68, no. 3 [2014]: 244).

[29] de Boer, "Tertullian on 'Barnabas' Letter to the Hebrews,'" 247–9.

[30] Matthew V. Novenson, "The Pauline Epistles in Tertullian's Bible," *Scottish Journal of Theology* 68, no. 4 (2015): 474.

[31] Tertullian's claim that Hebrews is better received by the churches than the Shepherd may be evidence for the relatively early and widespread public reading of Hebrews. On the other hand, the denigration of the Shepherd and elevation of Hebrews serve Tertullian's rhetorical aims in this passage. As a result, it is difficult to estimate how accurately his statement reflects the actual reception of either document.

authority, specifically as it relates to the Shepherd, becomes clear just a few sentences later when Tertullian quotes Heb 6:4 as evidence for the impossibility of a second repentance. Tertullian's concern all along has been to show that anyone who learned directly from the apostles would never accept the second repentance offered by the Shepherd. Tertullian highlights local traditions concerning Hebrews' authorship and acceptance in order to leverage them in his quotation of this single verse as a part of his argument against the possibility of a second repentance. For him, the attribution to Barnabas strengthens rather than undermines the book's authority.

Although this is Tertullian's only reference to the authorship of Hebrews, it is not the only instance where arguments about the authenticity of a text are leveraged toward a particular end. In *Bapt.* 17.5, Tertullian declares that no one should look to Thecla as an example for women to preach and baptize since the person who wrote the so-called *Acts of Paul* admitted that the work was composed "to add of his own to Paul's reputation."[32] Conversely, Tertullian defends the epistles he views as authentically Pauline by citing a tradition that the churches to which Paul wrote act as guardians of the text of Paul's epistles:

> Go through the apostolic churches, where the very thrones of the apostles at this very day preside over their own districts, where their own genuine letters are read, which speak their words and bring the presence of each before our minds. If Achaia is nearest to you, you have Corinth. If you are not far from Macedonia, you have Philippi. If you can travel into Asia, you have Ephesus. Or if you are near to Italy, you have Rome, where we too have an authority close at hand.[33]

Tertullian distinguishes himself from Justin Martyr in these specific expressions of concern over the authenticity of Christian texts. Such a distinction is likely a corollary of the differing rhetorical goals for which these authors composed their works. Whereas the rhetoric of Justin's *Dialogue* must maintain the rhetorical fiction of debate with a Jewish opponent, the writings by Tertullian cited above address very specifically Christian concerns with a Christian audience in mind. As a result, the authenticity of Christian writings is of much greater consequence to Tertullian's rhetorical aims.

Tertullian demonstrates no such concern for the authenticity of Hebrews elsewhere in his writings, despite his many citations of the epistle. Like Justin Martyr, Tertullian regularly borrows concepts or particular readings of the Septuagint from the epistle

---

[32] Novenson, "Pauline Epistles in Tertullian's Bible," 475.
[33] *Praescr.* 36.1-2; T. H. Bindley, trans., *Tertullian: On the Testimony of the Soul and On the Prescription of Heretics* (London: SPCK, 1914), 84:
> Age iam, qui uoles curiositatem melius exercere in negotio salutis tuae, percurre ecclesias apostolicas apud quas ipsae adhuc cathedrae apostolorum suis locis president, apud quae ipsae authenticate litterae eorum recitantur sonantes uocem et repraesentantes faciem uniuscuiusque. Proxima est tibi Achaia, habes Corinthum. Si non longe es a Macedonia, habes Philippos; si potes in Asiam tendere, habes Ephesum; si autem Italiae adiaces, habes Roman unde nobis quoque auctoritas praesto est.

without acknowledging that he is doing so.³⁴ There are also several places in Tertullian's writings where he constructs his argument from a combination of sources. In the conclusion of *Adversus Judaeos*, for example, Tertullian utilizes Hebrews, Justin Martyr's *Dial.* 31.3, and a TC that shares many of the same passages from the LXX quoted by Hebrews. *Adversus Judaeos* 14 includes two references to Ps 8:5 and one to Ps 2:7 as well as lengthy discussions of Jesus' priesthood and Lev 16:27, all of which play a prominent role in Hebrews as well.³⁵ Tertullian's argument in this work is largely built on the idea that the scriptures predicted two advents for the Christ, that he would come once in humility and then a second time in glory. Tertullian's conclusion to this argument appears to depend at least in part on a "two advents" TC, which was also known by the author of the *Epistle of Barnabas*, Justin Martyr, and Irenaeus. In addition to Lev 16:27 and the reference to Jesus' priesthood, this passage from Tertullian also shares Isa 53:2-3,7-8; 8:14; 28:16; Ps 118:22; and Dan 2:34 as common sources with the authors just mentioned.³⁶ Furthermore, Tertullian's references to Lev 16:27 and Jesus' priesthood are more akin to the TC than to Hebrews. Whereas Hebrews likens Jesus only to the animals that are slaughtered during the Day of Atonement ritual (the bull and *one* of the goats), Tertullian and the TC on which he draws both utilize the *two* goats of the ritual as a symbol of Jesus' two advents. Likewise, Tertullian's discussion of Jesus' priesthood is not framed by a reference to Ps 110:4, as it is in Hebrews, but by a reference to Zech 3:1-5, a passage utilized by the *Epistle of Barnabas*, Justin Martyr, and Irenaeus in their "two advents" arguments. On the other hand, Tertullian utilizes Pss 2:7 and 8:5, both of which are quoted in Heb 1-2 and are absent from the "two advents" TC.³⁷ Additionally, Tertullian's use of Ps 8:5 bears resemblance to its use in Heb 2:5-9 in that both portray Jesus as one who was "made a little lower than the angels" in his first advent but who is subsequently "crowned with glory and honor."³⁸ Finally, Tertullian depends directly on Justin Martyr for his quotation of Dan 7:13 rather than on Justin's testimonia source.³⁹ This suggests that Tertullian's conclusion

---

[34] Many of these instances are only brief allusions to Hebrews like the one found in *Adv. Jud.* 9.19 where Tertullian describes the divine word as being doubly sharpened by the old law as well as the new law of Christ, echoing the image of the word of God as double-edged sword found in Heb 4:12. For other examples, see *Mon.* 7.8; *Carn. Chr.* 5.10; *Marc.* 5.14. The legend of Isaiah being sawn in two, which was important to Origen, appears to be known by Tertullian as well. Although he does not legitimate the legend by Hebrews' authority, he does assume that the reference in Hebrews is about Isaiah. See *Scorp.* 8.3; *Pat.* 14.1.

[35] *Adv. Jud.* 14; Heb 1-2.

[36] Albl, *Scripture Cannot Be Broken*, 128-31.

[37] Both of these verses are frequently quoted with Ps 110:1 in early Christian writings as they are in Hebrews. Yet Hebrews is the only instance up through the time of Justin Martyr in which all three Psalms (2, 8, 110) are quoted together. Psalm 110:1 is quoted with Ps 8:5-6 in 1 Cor 15:25-27; Rom 8:34; 1 Pet 3:22; Heb 1:3-2:8; Eph 1:20-23; Mark 12:36; Matt 22:44; and Polycarp *Phil* 2:1; and with Ps 2:7 in Heb 1:3-13; 1 Clem. 36:2-6; and *Proof* 49. Tertullian does quote all three Psalms together in *Adv. Marc.* 5.9, and here also, as in the passage above, Tertullian employs these texts quoted by Hebrews with a number of other verses from Hebrew scripture to similar rhetorical ends.

[38] There is a slight difference, however, in their respective interpretations of when this "crowning" occurs. Tertullian appears to regard it as a future event upon Jesus' return while Hebrews regards it as having happened now that Jesus has ascended to heaven and is seated at the right hand of God.

[39] For another example of Tertullian's dependence on Justin's interpretation of scriptural texts, see Justin's *Dial.* 32-34, 83, 121, and Tertullian's *Adv. Marc.* 5.9.9-13.

to *Adversus Judaeos* has been informed by the "two advents" TC and Justin Martyr's *Dialogue* as well as Hebrews and that his reading of Hebrews has been somewhat shaped by his other two sources.

Tertullian's common practice of omitting any specific citation of Hebrews as his source can be explained by the rhetorical context in which those references are employed. Tertullian frequently utilizes Hebrews in the midst of arguments about the proper interpretation of Hebrew scripture in which Christian writings like Hebrews would not have been viewed as admissible evidence. Tertullian's failure to leverage the authority of Hebrews in these instances is an indication not of his failure to accept the document but of his rhetorical aims. Indeed, Tertullian's decision to utilize Hebrews at all in a context where this utilization pays such limited rhetorical dividends may be an indication of just how influential Hebrews proved to be. On the other hand, Tertullian's single defense of Hebrews' authority also serves a very specific rhetorical purpose. He seeks to elevate it above the Shepherd solely for the purpose of refuting its teaching on second repentance. Were it not for the few verses in Hebrews 6 that were beneficial to Tertullian in this particular argument, it is easy to imagine that Tertullian might never have found it necessary to make any explicit statements about Hebrews' authorship or acceptance. In that case we would be left only with the many instances in which he consistently fails to call attention to the document itself or any traditions about the document that might give it more weight. His utilization of Hebrews would be similar to the TCs with which he intertwines its influence, a source of proofs that he might utilize for his own rhetorical aims.

Tertullian's reception of Hebrews illustrates the difficulties inherent in attempting to infer a document's acceptance or authority beyond the immediate rhetorical ends to which it is employed. That is not to say that nothing of interest can be learned from Tertullian's utilization of Hebrews. His knowledge of the document indicates its presence in North Africa in the late second century, and it is likely that his attribution of the document's authorship to Barnabas reflects a local tradition regarding the epistle. The relative importance of these various factors influences the way in which Hebrews is employed in differing rhetorical contexts. These factors converge in Tertullian's utilization of Hebrews and serve to complicate the reception of the epistle beyond a simple dichotomy inasmuch as Tertullian both utilizes the document and defends its authoritative source even as he frequently fails to leverage that authority in his use of Hebrews.

Clement of Alexandria

Clement of Alexandria quotes Hebrews more than twice as many times as Justin and Tertullian combined. In contrast to these authors, he does not simply borrow ideas from the epistle or imitate its readings of the Jewish scriptures. Clement frequently acknowledges that he is borrowing from another source, most commonly crediting the words he quotes to "the apostle" since he regarded the epistle as having been written by Paul. Furthermore, Clement leverages this attribution of Pauline authorship to lend authority to his quotation of Hebrews in a way that Justin and Tertullian do not. All of these factors have often led scholars to conclude that Clement "accepted" Hebrews among the writings he considered authoritative. It is not Hebrews as a written work, however, that is the most important point of authority for Clement. It is the person of Paul as a trustworthy witness to the church's *gnosis* concerning the *logos* upon which Clement seeks to draw. Texts themselves are not safeguards of truth in Clement's theology but a cipher through which the voice of the *logos* speaks. True *gnosis* is handed down from the witness of the apostles and carried through the teachings of the church in a manner that even apostolic writings cannot accomplish. As a result, the place of any text in the theology of Clement, Hebrews included, is inherently utilitarian insofar as its value is determined by the degree to which the voice of the *logos* can be clearly heard through it and thereby direct one toward true *gnosis*. Therefore, the characterization of Clement's reception of Hebrews merely as one of "acceptance" fails to ask precisely what such acceptance signifies about the place of Hebrews in Clement's theology. Although Hebrews may be grouped among some of the texts that Clement found most beneficial, there is no set of authoritative texts in Clement's theology that fully capture the *logos*.

Clement held that knowledge of the divine *logos* could be obtained through a variety of sources. He likens these various sources of knowledge to tributaries that feed into a larger river. "There is only one way of truth," Clement declares, "but different paths from different places join it."[40] Among these many tributaries, however, two major branches of the river may be identified: the scriptures and Greek philosophy. Among the scriptures, Clement distinguishes between those that belong to the old covenant and those of the new, though he does not delineate a precise set of writings that belong to each.[41] The more important point for Clement is that Greek philosophy and the scriptures of the old covenant both serve as a tutor to lead one to Christ, the law for Jews and philosophy for Greeks.[42] Christians, however, come to know the divine *logos* in a "new and spiritual" way that is superior to either the law or philosophy.[43]

Clement frequently cites Hebrews to support this idea that knowledge of the *logos* can be found in various sources. Nearly a tenth of all Clement's references to the epistle are from Heb 1:1, which states, "God spoke to our ancestors in many and various ways." Clement repeatedly utilizes this verse along with quotations from other scriptures to support his idea that knowledge can be gained from various sources. *Stromateis* 1.27 is a representative example:

> The Apostle had good reason to call God's wisdom "variegated," "working in many forms and many ways" through technical skill, scientific knowledge, faith, prophecy; it shows us its power to our benefit, because "all wisdom comes from the Lord and is with him to all eternity," as the wisdom of Jesus puts it.[44]

---

[40] Clement of Alexandria, Strom. 1.5, trans. John Ferguson (Washington, DC: Catholic University of America Press, 1991), 42.
[41] Judith L. Kovacs, "Introduction. Clement as Scriptural Exegete: Overview and History of Research," in Clement's Biblical Exegesis, ed. Veronika Cernuskova, Judith L. Kovacs, and Jana Platova (Boston: Brill, 2016), 5.
[42] *Strom.* 1.5.
[43] *Strom.* 6.5.
[44] Clement, *Strom.* 1.4. Ferguson, 41. See also *Strom.* 5.6; 6.7, 10; 7.16.

Given this approach, it is no surprise that Clement draws on a wide variety of sources; the influence of 348 different authors have been detected among his works.[45] He utilizes Philo, Plato, and Homer with an especially high degree of frequency while also commonly making use of Euripides, Chrysippus, Hesiod, and Herodutus.[46] Clement regularly places these sources directly alongside quotations of Christian writings, even intertwining these various sources together as though they were one. In his *Exhortation to the Greeks*, for example, Clement weaves quotations from the Odyssey into an imaginary conversation with John the Baptist based on John 1:19–23.[47] David Dawson elucidates the significance of this intertwining of sources for Clement's' theology:

> Clement does not allude to Homer simply because of his apologetic desire to make Christianity appealing to his educated, urbane Alexandrian readership. He inserts these Homeric echoes into his reworking of a scriptural passage for the much-larger and far-reaching purpose of suggesting that the words of Homer belong with the language of scripture at least as an equal partner. In fact, by using Homeric diction in place of the Jews' questions put to the Baptist (who for Clement is the immediate precursor of Jesus, the incarnate divine *logos*), Clement illustrates his revisionary claim that the divine *logos* in the form of philosophy was a pedagogue leading the Greeks to Christ, just as the law led the Hebrews. Both pedagogues are ultimately the same *logos* that leads pupils to acknowledge its final and complete manifestation as Jesus of Nazareth.[48]

---

[45] Clement, *Strom.* 1.5. Ferguson, 4.
[46] Van den Hoek provides the following citation statistics: Philo 279, 9 columns; Plato 618, 15.5 columns; Homer 243, 6 columns; Euripides 117, 3.5 columns; Chrysippus 4 columns; Hesiod 1 column; Herodotus 2 columns; Matthew 11 columns; Luke 7.5 columns; Mark 3 columns; John 5 columns; Acts 1.5 columns; and Paul 1273, 27 columns. Annewies Van Den Hoek, "Techniques of Quotation in Clement of Alexandria: A View of Ancient Literary Working Methods," *Vigiliae Christianae* 50, no. 3 (1996): 237.
[47] Clement of Alexandria, Protr. 1.9.1, trans. G. W. Butterwork, LCL 92 (Cambridge, MA: Harvard University Press, 1919), 23:

> ἢ γὰρ οὐχὶ καὶ Ἰωάννης ἐπὶ σωτηρίαν παρακαλεῖ καὶ τὸ πᾶν γίνεται φωνὴ προτρεπτική; πυθώμεθα τοίνυν αὐτοῦ· 'τίς πόθεν εἶς ἀνδρῶν;' Ἠλίας μὲν οὐκ ἐρεῖ, Χριστὸς δὲ εἶναι ἀρνήσεται· φωνὴ δὲ ὁμολογήσει ἐν ἐρήμῳ βοῶσα. τίς οὖν ἔστιν Ἰωάννης; ὡς τύπῳ λαβεῖν, ἐξέστω εἰπεῖν, φωνὴ τοῦ λόγου προτρεπτικὴ ἐν ἐρήμῳ βοῶσα. τί βοᾷς, ὦ φωνή; "εἰπὲ καὶ ἡμῖν." "εὐθείας ποιεῖτε τὰς ὁδοὺς κυρίου." πρόδρομος Ἰωάννης καὶ ἡ φωνὴ πρόδρομος τοῦ λόγου, φωνὴ παρακλητική, προετοιμάζουσα εἰς σωτηρίαν, φωνὴ προτρέπουσα εἰς κληρονομίαν οὐρανῶν· δι᾽ ἣν ἡ στεῖρα καὶ ἔρημος ἄγονος οὐκέτι. [Do you not know that John also invites us to salvation and becomes wholly a voice of exhortation? Let us then inquire of him. "*Who and whence art thou?*" will say he is not Elijah; he will deny that he is Christ; but he will confess, "a voice crying in the desert." Who then is John? Allow us to say, in a figure, that he is a voice of the Word, raising his cry of exhortation in the desert. What dost thou cry, O voice? "*Tell us also.*" "Make straight the ways of the Lord." John is a forerunner, and the voice is a forerunner of the Word. It is a voice of encouragement that makes ready for the coming salvation, a voice that exhorts to a heavenly inheritance; and by reason of this voice, the barren and desolate is fruitless no longer.]

Italics indicate quotes from the Odyssey.
[48] David Dawson, Allegorical Readers and Cultural Revision in Ancient Alexandria (Berkeley: University of California Press, 1992), 200.

Even as Clement finds utility in a wide range of texts and regularly places those texts directly alongside of Christian writings, it is still those texts that are subsumed into Clement's understanding of the Christian narrative rather than the other way around. In whatever text one might hear the voice of the *logos*, that voice always directs one to Jesus as the ultimate expression of the *logos*. This principle is evident in two more instances of Clement's references to Hebrews. The first is in *Strom*. 1.11 where he claims that "the philosophers too are children, if they have not been brought to maturity by Christ."[49] He then quotes Gal 4:30 along with Heb 4:13–14 as warrant for this division between those who are only children in their understanding of wisdom and the mature who have a genuine grasp of truth. These verses from Hebrews are employed to similar ends in *Strom*. 5.10, though in this case philosophy is not the object of Clement's critique but his other favorite pedagogue, the Jewish scriptures. The mature reader is the one who knows that some truths remained hidden in the scriptures of the old covenant and were only more recently revealed to the apostles. In both instances, Clement used the child/adult dichotomy of Heb 4:13–14 to portray Greek philosophy and Hebrew scriptures as mere tutors that prepare one for Christ.

The many works that Clement references may be located along a spectrum of utility. Works that were attributed to apostles, especially the Gospels and Paul's Epistles, may be counted as the most significant for Clement. Still prominent but a step below these are the scriptures of the old covenant and Greek philosophical writings as tutors who lead one to Christ. Beyond these, virtually any writing is a potential cipher for the voice of the *logos* if one has the *gnosis* with which to discern that voice. Although some of these works are clearly regarded by Clement as more beneficial than others, if one were to ask which of these texts Clement regarded as "in" and which were "out," no clear answers emerge. Despite the prominence of the apostolic writings, those writings are only a vehicle for the *gnosis* handed down through the church's teaching—a somewhat inferior vehicle at that. Therefore, the reception of Hebrews by Clement may be characterized as that of a prominent text among the many that Clement utilizes, more prominent than Greek philosophical or Hebrew scriptural texts, but still only a text, an instrument by which one might hear the voice of the *logos*.

Origen of Alexandria

Given their proximity to one another and their shared influences, it is no surprise that the handling of Hebrews by Clement and Origen display a high degree of resemblance. Both of these writers utilize Hebrews to various ends but chief among these for each writer is their use of Hebrews to articulate the place of Christian scriptures in their overall theological project. Like Clement before him, Origen also frequently urged his readers to a higher, spiritual understanding of the scriptures beyond the literal, bodily reading, commonly referencing Hebrews to do so. Despite these significant similarities, the place of Hebrews in the respective hermeneutics of Clement and Origen do diverge in significant ways. Whereas Clement regards scripture as the best of many

---

[49] Clement, *Strom*. 1.11. Ferguson, 62.

expressions of the *logos* that one comes to know primarily through the *gnosis* of the church, Origen treats Hebrews and the rest of the Pauline corpus as an authorization for his own scriptural hermeneutic. It is the person of Paul as one who passed down the church's *gnosis* that is important for Clement, but it is the interpretive method that Paul exhibited in his letters that is most important to Origen. Origen's theology is founded in textuality in a manner that Clement's is not. As a result, the Pauline authorship of Hebrews serves a specific function for Origen insofar as it legitimates Hebrews, along with the other Pauline Epistles, as an interpretive model worth imitating.

When it comes to the relative utility of Hebrews to second- and third-century theologians, Origen firmly anchors one end of the spectrum. In addition to the significant role that Hebrews plays in Origen's overall interpretive project, he also cites the epistle far more frequently than any other second- or third-century writer, accounting for 1,078 of the 1,421 references to Hebrews in these centuries. However, even as Hebrews plays this important role for Origen, it would be simplistic to categorize his utilization of the epistle merely as "acceptance" since both Origen's quotations of the epistle and his explicit statements about the other writings he quotes locate Hebrews as one work among many that Origen found valuable to varying degrees. Rather than placing Hebrews on the "accepted" side of a clearly demarcated line separating it from the works Origen rejects, Hebrews exists along a spectrum of writings that Origen found more or less beneficial.

Origen employs Hebrews to a variety of ends. His frequent quotation of Heb 1:3–4 in order to build a case for Christ's divinity or his use of Heb 1:14 to defend the existence of angels are representative examples.[50] Often these quotations appear alongside many other quotations from a variety of sources utilized to the same end. The source of these quotations is sometimes indicated as the Epistle to the Hebrews, but more often they are introduced as the words of "the apostle" who is sometimes specifically identified as Paul. However, there are some instances in which Origen quotes the work without identifying Hebrews or Paul as the source.

Origen's most frequent use of Hebrews, however, is to justify his interpretive approach to scripture. Origen outlines this method in the fourth book of *De Principiis*. The meaning of scripture may be divided into three parts just as there are three parts to a person; body, soul, and spirit. The body corresponds to a literal reading of scripture, which Origen regards as the lowest and least edifying understanding of scripture. In some instances, Origen even characterizes the literal reading of scripture as indefensible. That is why one must move on to the higher, spiritual reading where the real truth of scripture is found. The middle category of soul is left considerably underdeveloped by Origen though he does utilize it to characterize those who have made some progress beyond the mere literal level but have not yet achieved a truly spiritual reading.[51]

Origen frequently quotes Hebrews as a means to support this distinctive hermeneutic. He is particularly fond of Heb 10:1, which speaks of the law as having

---

[50] *Princ.* 1.2.5; 1.5.1; 4.1.28; *Cels.* 5.4; 8.12.
[51] Origen, Homilies on Leviticus 1–16, trans. Gary Wayne Barkley (Washington, DC: Catholic University of America Press, 2005), 14–20.

only a shadow of the good things to come rather than the true realities that are found in Christ. This is, in fact, the verse that Origen cites from Hebrews more than any other, fifty-seven times in total.[52] *Homiliae in Leviticum* 8, in which Origen discusses the purifications for various leprosies in Lev 13–14, provides a representative example of his use of this verse. After treating the passage on the literal, bodily level by outlining the six types of leprosy found there, Origen states that it seems to him that these different leprosies represent different kinds of sins. He begins to outline what those types of sin might be but then declares that a single sermon will not allow him to continue. Instead, he appeals to his audience to follow the path set out by Paul in Hebrews:

> Therefore, to the best of our ability, as much as it is fitting to be brought forth in our midst, let us pursue the path of understanding which the Apostle Paul opens to us when he says, "The Law has the shadow of the good things to come, not the very image of the things." And according to this, he proclaims that the writings which appear in the Law about calves are not to be understood about "the calves whose concern may not be for God" but about Apostles. In which surely by a consequent reason we are taught also that these things which are written about lepers may be "a shadow" having the image of truth found in other things. Therefore, let us first apply ourselves to this "shadow" of Scripture, if it appears good, and then let us seek its truth.[53]

This passage is employed again, along with two other passages from Hebrews, in *Hom. Lev.* 10. Origen declares that it is the church that rightly receives the Law of Moses as symbols and signs of what was to come. He likens the Law of Moses to the practice of making a clay model of a coin or statue before fashioning the final work out of metal. Likewise, the law is a type or shadow of what was ultimately fulfilled in Christ. In the same homily, Origen also utilizes Hebrews' theology of Jesus' High Priesthood, quoting Heb 10:4 and 13:12. Origen concludes the opening section of this homily by referring to another of his most frequently utilized passages from the epistle, Heb 5:12–14. He argues that those who are enraptured by the "forms" of the law rather than the realities are those who are feeding on milk.[54]

In both of Origen's homilies discussed above, he also frequently recalls verses from letters attributed to Paul to the very same ends as these verses from Hebrews. Immediately before the above quote from *Hom. Lev.* 8, Origen mentions those who have had the veil removed from their reading of the Old Testament, an allusion to 2 Cor

---

[52] For a few examples, see *Princ.* 2.7; 3.6.8; 4.1.13; 4.1.24; *Comm. Matt.* 11.12.
[53] Origen, *Hom. Lev.* 8.5. Barkley, 161.
[54] Origen, *Hom. Lev.* 10.1. This is Origen's third-most frequently cited passage from Hebrews (42x). He often employs Heb 5:12–14 as a justification for seeking higher spiritual truth in scripture. In response to Celsus' complaint that Christians do not seek to present their message to wise men but only to play tricks on those who are simple, Origen quotes Heb 5:13–14 to argue that some require teaching in the form of "milk" while others are certainly capable of receiving and presenting the higher, spiritual "meat" of the gospel. Similarly, Origen utilizes these verses to argue that there are two kinds of wisdom, human and divine. See *Cels.* 3.53; 6.13. Origen's second-most frequently cited passage from Hebrews (12:22–23 – 49x), is frequently used as a justification for interpreting the land promises to Abraham as a promise to Christians about heaven.

3:14. He also quotes 1 Cor 9:9 where Paul says that the law about muzzling a threshing ox is not really about the ox but is written "for our sake." Likewise, in *Hom. Lev.* 10, he intersperses references to 1 Cor 10:11, Eph 5:2, and Rom 14:1 among his references to Hebrews. Thus Origen's use of Hebrews among the other letters he believed to be authored by Paul is not unlike Justin and Tertullian's utilization of Hebrews; they all quote Hebrews in a manner similar to their use of TCs. Origen has compiled a list of verses from Paul as inartificial proofs to support his argument.

There is, however, a substantial difference between Origen and these two earlier writers. Justin and Tertullian cited the verses from the Septuagint that Hebrews cited and even imitated Hebrews' interpretation of those verses in many instances, but it was not the norm for either of these authors to leverage the authority of Hebrews or its assumed author in those citations (save the single exception in Tertullian's writings). Origen, on the other hand, cites Paul specifically as justification for his interpretive method. Origen's threefold hermeneutic, in fact, appears to have derived directly from Paul, specifically 1 Cor 2. Origen's introduction of his "perfect" or "spiritual" category with a direct quote from 1 Cor 2:6 suggests this Pauline passage as the source of Origen's hermeneutic. The virtual neglect of the "soul" category in 1 Cor 2 and its corresponding underdeveloped state in Origen's own hermeneutic similarly suggest that Origen derived his threefold interpretive method directly from 1 Corinthians.[55] Therefore, when Origen utilizes Hebrews to support his spiritual reading of scripture, he is not merely quoting a few favorite verses from Hebrews. He sees himself as imitating the very hermeneutic of the apostle Paul and since Origen regards Hebrews as a part of that corpus, it provides ample opportunities for imitation.

The importance of Hebrews' Pauline authorship for Origen also appears in his correspondence with Africanus who questioned the authenticity of the story of Susanna. A significant piece of Origen's defense of the work's authenticity involves accusations against "the Jews" of editing the parts of writings that they found embarrassing. Origen offers as one such example the tradition that the prophet Isaiah had been sawn in two. Although this tradition could not be found in any of "their public books," Origen regards it as "guaranteed by the Epistle to the Hebrews."[56] Shortly thereafter, Origen acknowledges that one may not find this argument persuasive since he knows that there are some who do not think the epistle is Paul's. Unfortunately, Origen states that he must leave his arguments concerning Pauline authorship for another time. Nevertheless, what Origen has written suggests the importance of Hebrews' Pauline authorship not only for the authorization of Hebrews but for other stories to which it attests as well.

Origen's use of Hebrews to authorize both his own interpretive method and the legitimacy of Susanna suggest a greater significance of Pauline authorship to Origen than the impression one might receive from Eusebius' report on the matter. In *Hist. eccl.* 6.25, Eusebius presents Origen as the dispassionate scholar who sees that the style of Hebrews is not like Paul's but concludes that the thoughts are similar enough; perhaps, then, they were recalled by a student of Paul. Origen is so disinterested in the

---

[55] Mitchell, *Paul, the Corinthians*, 53–4.
[56] *Ep. Afr.* 9.

matter of authorship that he concludes that, if anyone attributes the letter to Paul, they should be commended for doing so even though only God knows who wrote it. Of course, it is possible that Eusebius had access to an opinion of Origen that was at some variance with those he expressed elsewhere and is now lost. Nevertheless, the writings of Origen that do survive suggest not a scholar who is distant and dispassionate with regard to the Pauline authorship of Hebrews but one for whom Pauline authorship informed and legitimated his use of the epistle.

Origen's extensive citations of Hebrews and his attribution of Pauline authorship to the document suggest a place of prominence for the epistle in Origen's library. Nevertheless, consideration of the other works Origen employed shows that library to be rather large. In addition to the thirty-nine books of the Jewish Scriptures, Origen quotes eleven other documents not found in modern editions of these scriptures.[57] He also cites several Christian writings in addition to the twenty-seven that came to form the New Testament: the *Gospel of the Hebrews*, the *Gospel of Peter*, the *Preaching of Peter*, the Shepherd, 1 Clement, the *Epistle of Barnabas*, and the *Acts of Paul*.[58] He also drew on numerous philosophical writings, most prominently those of Philo.[59]

Yet within this wide-ranging use of texts, Origen placed greater emphasis on some works than others. Even while Origen made use of a wide range of Gospels, he surely privileged Matthew, Mark, Luke and John. In his *Hom. Luc.* 1:14, he claims that when Luke says that many before him have "tried" to compose an account like his, the implication is that those other attempts failed because these writers did not write with the aid of the Holy Spirit as did the writers of those four Gospels that have been "chosen from among these gospels and passed on to the churches."[60] In one of his more emphatic statements about the status of particular Christian writings, Origen claims, "The Church has four Gospels. Heretics have many."[61]

The Law of Moses apparently held a position somewhat akin to the Gospels for Origen while the epistles and Acts derived their authority from the law and the prophets. In his *Commentary on John*, Origen states,

> One would not go wrong, then, in saying that of the Scriptures which are in circulation in all the churches of God and which are believed to be divine, the law of Moses is the firstling, but the gospel is the firstfruits. For the perfect Word has blossomed forth after all the fruits of the prophets up to the time of the Lord Jesus. But if someone should object, because of the idea inherent in the explanation of firstfruits, and say that the Acts and the Epistles of the apostles were brought forth after the Gospels, and that the statement that the gospel is the firstfruits of all Scripture would not still prevail in accordance with our previous explanation of

---

[57] They are the Epistle of Jeremiah, Baruch, Tobit, Judith, 1 and 2 Maccabees, Sirach, the Wisdom of Solomon, and the three expansions of Daniel in the Septuagint. Ronald E. Heine, Origen: Scholarship in the Service of the Church (Oxford: Oxford University Press, 2010), 68.
[58] Ibid., 46–7, 79–80.
[59] Ibid., 31.
[60] Origen, Homilies on Luke: Fragments on Luke, trans. Joseph T. Lienhard (Washington, DC: Catholic University of America Press, 2009), 5.
[61] Ibid., 5.

firstfruits, we would surely have to say that you have in the Epistles which are in circulation the understanding of wise men who have been aided by Christ, who need the testimonies contained in the words of the law and Prophets in order to be believed. Consequently, we must say that the apostolic writings are wise and trustworthy and most beneficial; they are not, to be sure, on a par with, "Thus says the Lord almighty."[62]

Origen does not provide a systematic or complete hierarchy of scriptures in this passage, but what he does articulate about the relationships between various writings is rather fascinating. Given the importance of the Pauline Epistles to Origen's hermeneutic observed above, it may be somewhat shocking to modern ears to find that Origen thinks that the epistles "need the testimonies of the law and the Prophets in order to believed" and that even though they "are wise and trustworthy and most beneficial" they are not "on par with, 'Thus says the Lord almighty.' "

In addition to this distinction between the Gospels and epistles, one may also note the disparity in the number of quotations from Origen's other sources. Although Origen quotes from a wide range of works, his use of many of these writings pales in comparison to his use of the Gospels and epistles. First John and 1 Peter are referenced 462 and 385 times, respectively, a ratio one might expect for works of their size. However, James and 2 Peter both have fewer than one hundred references each while 2 John and 3 John have only eleven and four, respectively. He cites the Shepherd only six times, even though he says it is inspired, and 1 Clement and the *Epistle of Barnabas* only once each, even though he may have regarded their authors as associates of Paul.[63] Origen's references to the *Gospel of the Hebrews* further complicate any notion of a simple hierarchy among the works which Origen cites. He quotes the *Gospel of the Hebrews* only three times, prefacing it with "if one accepts" each time, but he also allowed the work to influence his own Christology.[64] In his *Commentary on the Gospel of John*, Origen quotes a line from the *Gospel of the Hebrews* in which the Holy Spirit is referenced as the mother of Jesus.[65] Rather than reject this idea, Origen supports it

---

[62] Origen, Commentary on the Gospel according to John *1:14–15*, trans. Ronald E. Heine, Fathers of the Church 80 (Washington, DC: Catholic University of America Press, 1989), 35:

> Τῶν τοίνυν φερομενον γραφῶν και εν πασαις ἐκκλησίαις θεοῦ πεπιστευμένων εἶναι θείων, οὐκ ἂν ἁμάρτοι τις λέγων πρωτογέννημα μὲν τὸν Μωσέως νόμον, ἀπαρχὴν δὲ τὸ εὐαγγέλιον. Μετὰ γὰρ τοὺς πάντας τῶν προφητῶν καρποὺς τοὺς μέχρι τοῦ κυρίου Ἰησοῦ ὁ τέλειος ἐζλάστησε λόγος. Ἐὰν δὲ τις ἀνθυποφέρη δια τὴν ἔννοιαν τῆς ἀναπτύξεως τῶν ἀπαρχῶν φάσκων μετὰ τὰ εὐαγγέλια τὰς πράξεις καὶ τὰς ἐπιστολὰς φέρεσθαι τῶν ἀποστόλων καὶ κατὰ τοῦτο μὴ ἂν ἔτι σώζεσθαι τὸ προαποδεδομένον περὶ ἀπαρχῆς, τὸ ἀπαρχὴν πάσης γραφῆς εἶναι τὸ εὐαγγέλιον, λεκτέον ἤτοι νοῦν εἶναι σοφῶν ἐν Χριστῷ ὠφελημένων ἐν ταῖς φερομέωαις ἐπιστολαῖς, δεομένων, ἵνα πιστεύωνται, μαρτυριῶν τῶν ἐν τοῖς νομικοῖς καὶ προφητικοῖς λόγοις κειμένων. ὥστε σοφὰ μὲν καὶ <εὔ>πιστα λέγειν καὶ σφόδρα ἐπιτετευγμένα τὰ ἀποστολικά, οὐ μὴν παραπλήσια τῷ "Τάδε λέγει κύριος παντοκράτωρ."

[63] Heine, *Scholarship*, 46, 82; *Princ.* 2.3.6; 3.2.4.

[64] Heine, *Scholarship*, 79–80.

[65] "But if someone accepts the Gospel according to the Hebrews, where the Savior himself says, 'My mother, the Holy Spirit, took me just now by one of my hairs and carried me off to the great mountain Tabor,' he will question how the 'mother' of Christ can be 'the Holy Spirit' which was made through the Word" (Origen, *Comm. Jo.* 2.15.87. Heine, 117).

with Jesus' claim from the fourfold Gospels that anyone who does the will of the Father is his "brother and sister and mother," reasoning that this statement is also applicable to the Holy Spirit.[66] Even the combination of limited citations and explicit hesitancy about a work's acceptance, therefore, did not mean that Origen did not value the work in question.

If a line were to be drawn separating the works that Origen "accepted" from the ones he did not, one wonders where among this list of works that line would fall. It seems fair to say that Origen regarded the Septuagint and the Gospels as divine proclamation. In the case of every other work that Origen utilizes, however, the question is quite a bit more complicated. Indeed, the question nearly ceases to make any sense at all. The more appropriate inquiry might be to ask for what or as what exactly these various other works were accepted. Without explicit statements from Origen about the nature of these works, those answers are difficult to discern and certainly require much more than a mere counting of references. The evidence reviewed here suggests that Origen's reception of Hebrews existed within a complex network of relationships between the many writings Origen cites, a network that involved varying degrees of utility, attributions of authorship, and ideas about each work's broader acceptance that are not necessarily predictive of one another. "Acceptance" is, therefore, too simple a term to offer an adequate picture of Hebrews' reception among Origen's writings. The Epistle to the Hebrews was received by Origen as an epistle of Paul and thus may be regarded among the works that were most useful and influential for Origen, though perhaps not at the level of divine proclamation found in the law and the Gospels.

Conclusions

Any plausible reconstruction of the reception of the Epistle to the Hebrews cannot be separated from the rhetorical aims of the works in which it is employed. Each of the authors surveyed above utilize Hebrews to very particular ends. Justin Martyr mines Hebrews, along with other Christian writings and TCs, as a resource for Christian interpretations of the Septuagint while demonstrating no concern to identify or authenticate Hebrews as his source since doing so would carry little rhetorical weight. Tertullian's use of Hebrews is similar to Justin's except in the single instance that defending Hebrews' apostolic association and relatively broad acceptance serve Tertullian's rhetorical aims in his arguments concerning Christian modesty. Clement frequently invokes Hebrews' Pauline authorship specifically so that he may highlight the potential of all texts as conduits for the voice of the *logos* who has spoken in many and various ways. Origen similarly employs the attribution of Pauline authorship to Hebrews in order to justify his own interpretive method, which he claims is an

---

[66] Matt 12:50; Mark 3:35. "In other words, Origen regarded this statement from the Gospel of the Hebrews as authoritative and, rather than rejecting it as heretical or somehow external to apostolic teaching, he made one of its teachings foundational to his Christological framework" (Jennifer Knust and Tommy Wasserman, To Cast the First Stone: The Transmission of a Gospel Story [Princeton, NJ: Princeton University Press, 2018], 62).

imitation of Paul's. Each of these writers follows the principles of ancient citation and composition in which they were trained: a document is quoted, interpreted, and attributed to a particular author in a manner that serves the rhetorical goal of the present writer.

That is not to say that patristic citations of Hebrews were arbitrary or that claims about its authorship were wholly fabricated. The four authors surveyed above likely reflect certain local traditions about the interpretation and authorship of Hebrews that existed prior to their own writing; traditions that had to be negotiated in their own utilization of the epistle. Nevertheless, these authors knew how to employ (or omit) those traditions in a manner that was most beneficial for their own rhetorical aims. As a result, claims concerning Hebrews' broad acceptance or rejection are not easily extrapolated from such rhetorically specific contexts. Furthermore, resisting the temptation to view Hebrews' reception through such extrapolations provides an opportunity to envision the early reception of Christian scriptures as a richly colorful and varied landscape. If the binary, black-and-white question of whether Hebrews was "in" or "out" of categories that did not yet exist may be set aside, then the various hues of Hebrews' reception as a document among many others that early Christian writers found beneficial may emerge.

4

Editing Paul: Hebrews among Editions of the Pauline Corpus

Introduction

P. Amherst 1.3 (P¹²) is exceptional among ancient manuscripts that contain text from the Epistle to the Hebrews, most notably because of how little of the text of the epistle it contains. This single leaf of a papyrus role was first utilized by a Christian in Rome to write a letter to associates in Egypt concerning financial matters.[1] It was only later that most of Heb 1:1 was written above the second column of this three-column letter. On the verso of the papyrus, two versions of Gen 1:1–5 are found: that of the Septuagint and Aquila.[2] The juxtaposition of these various texts on a single papyrus begs for an interpretation: the lack of an immediately apparent explanation for the relationship between these texts invites one to imagine who the human agents were who arranged these texts as they did and what context guided such an arrangement?[3] Did the recipients

---

[1] Bernard P. Grenfell and Arthur S. Hunt, *The Amherst Papyri: Part I* (London: H. Frowde, 1900), 28. P¹² is one of only four manuscripts containing New Testament texts on a papyrus roll as opposed to a codex. P¹³, another manuscript that includes Hebrews and will be discussed more below, also enjoys this distinction. All four rolls have been reused in some manner. Kurt and Barbara Aland, *The Text of the New Testament: An Introduction to the Critical Editions and to the Theory and Practice of Modern Textual Criticism*, 2nd ed. (Grand Rapids, MI: Eerdmans, 1989), 102; Eldon Jay Epp, "Issues in the Interrelation of New Testament Textual Criticism and Canon," in *The Canon Debate*, ed. Lee Martin McDonald and James A. Sanders (Peabody, MA: Hendrickson, 2002), 485–515. For the early Christian preference for the codex, see Harry Y. Gamble, *Books and Readers in the Early Church: A History of Early Christian Texts* (New Haven: Yale University Press, 1995); E. G. Turner, *The Typology of the Early Codex*, Haney Foundation Series 18 (Philadelphia: University of Pennsylvania Press, 1977).

[2] A date was originally included in the letter but the year has been lost. Grenfell and Hunt date the letter to the second half of the third century and the text of Hebrews to the late third, or more likely, the early fourth century. The Genesis text is described by Grenfell and Hunt as written in a "more cursive hand" than the text of Hebrews, though Clark suggests both may have been written by the same hand. Grenfell and Hunt, *Amherst Papyri*, 30. Kenneth Clark, *A Descriptive Catalogue of Greek New Testament Manuscripts in America* (Chicago: University of Chicago Press, 1937), 170.

[3] "Texts are bound up in the lived lives of the human actors who copied them, used them, and wore them out … these textual objects materialized the investments of a particular set of ancient religious actors" (Jennifer Knust, "Miscellany Manuscripts and the Christian Canonical Imaginary," in *Ritual Matters: Material Remains and Ancient Religion*, ed. Jennifer Knust and Claudia Moser [Ann Arbor: University of Michigan Press, 2017], 114). "The basic thesis of materiality studies is that we can view 'objects,' in principle man-made objects, including architecture, art, and landscape, but also certain elements of the natural world, 'as though' they were agents. Such a move reveals the inherent

of this letter find at a later date that they merely required a scrap of papyrus on which to scribble some verses of scripture? Perhaps someone with text-critical interests wanted to compare different versions of Genesis. Or it may be that the beginnings of Hebrews and Genesis function as incipits on an amulet, thereby locating the later use of the papyrus in some sort of ritual context.[4] It is not my aim to determine which of these scenarios provides the proper context for understanding this particular papyrus as much as it is to highlight the way the arrangement of various texts in relation to one another is itself a vehicle for meaning. Indeed, the arrangement of texts within a given medium may be such a potent vehicle of meaning that it can actually transform the genre and value of the text. For example, perhaps reuse transformed the text of a letter into something less valuable than the papyrus on which it was composed, a letter that came to be regarded as mere rubbish, on the one hand, or into a powerful amulet, on the other. P^{12} illustrates the degree to which the meaning of a text is intertwined with its own material manifestation, its arrangement relative to other texts in that material manifestation, and the social settings that these invite us to imagine. Those imagined social settings in turn significantly shape the interpretation modern readers ascribe to these ancient texts and the artifacts that preserve them.

Although P^{12} is helpful for thinking about the juxtaposition of Hebrews among other texts, it is in many respects not representative of the reception and reproduction of Hebrews in the Greek and Latin manuscript tradition as that tradition has come down to us. It is the only extant manuscript in which any text of Hebrews is known not to have been reproduced as part of an edition of Paul's letters. Of course, several of the manuscripts that include Hebrews are too fragmentary to enable scholars to

---

reflexivity of the relation object-human" (Richard L. Gordon, "'Straightening the Paths': Inductive Divination, Materiality, and Imagination in the Greco Roman Period," in *Ritual Matters*, 120). Responding to Knust's analysis of the "Dishna Papers" in the same volume, Frankfurter writes,

> Their potency, their agency to drive people and shape action, takes place not in antiquity (or at least not recognizably) but in modernity. It is scholars today who find themselves compelled by the codices themselves to theorize them as indexes of an original creative agency: the esoteric or canonical value of the book, the theological program uniting the assemblage, a distantly recognizable literate book collector whose interests were broad-ranging. Their object agency lies both in the confusion they impose on modern scholars and the assumptions they trigger of an original textual value (like the mortuary guide) or programmatic assemblage. That is to say, the agency of things still affects us in the here and now: not only the gift certificate that makes us go to the store or the car that needs to get inspected but, in this case, historical artifacts that impel us to attend to them, to invent narratives to minimize their jarring anomalies, and to "abduct" (in Gell's terminology) from their discovery and contents an original agency: a conscientious compiler with a specific theological program. (David Frankfurter, "Ritual Matters: Afterword," in *Ritual Matters*, 149)

See also Bruno Latour, *Reassembling the Social: An Introduction to Actor-Network-Theory* (New York: Oxford University Press, 2005); D. F. McKenzie, *Bibliography and the Sociology of Texts* (New York: Cambridge University Press, 1999); Peter L. Shillingsburg, "Text as Matter, Concept, and Action," *Studies in Bibliography* 44 (1991): 31–82.

4   Joseph Emanuel Sanzo, *Scriptural Incipits on Amulets from Late Antique Egypt: Text, Typology, and Theory* (Tübingen: Mohr Siebeck, 2014), 100–1, 138, 144–7, 160. Although the use of these particular verses would be outside the norm for scriptural amulets that typically utilize verses from the Gospels or Psalms. Theodore de Bruyn, *Making Amulets Christian: Artefacts, Scribes, and Contexts* (Oxford: Oxford University Press, 2017), 140.

determine if they included all of Hebrews or other writings along with Hebrews.[5] However, no complete or nearly complete manuscripts of Hebrews survive that include signs of production apart from editions of Paul's letters. Indeed, the vast majority of manuscripts that include Hebrews attest to a close relationship between the epistle and the *corpus Paulinum*. Therefore, Hebrews' reception in the Greek and Latin manuscript tradition of the third through sixth centuries suggests that the letter was perceived to be part of a collection and not a single work. An evaluation of Hebrews' reception among these manuscripts in terms of its canonical status, in other words, serves to obfuscate the available evidence that suggests that the primary criterion in Hebrews' reproduction was the status of its relationship to editions of Paul's letters. Careful consideration of Hebrews' reception in the context of ancient editorial practices reveals a consistent inclusion of Hebrews within the Pauline corpus among Greek manuscripts, while Latin manuscripts reflect hesitancy, though not outright rejection, concerning Hebrews' place among a larger corpus of Paul's letters. It is this hesitancy concerning the place of Hebrews within the Pauline corpus, I argue, and not questions about its canonical status that led to Hebrews' position after Philemon in the majority of the manuscript tradition.

Creating an Edition in Antiquity

P^{12} is by no means what one might consider an edition; nonetheless, this peculiar copy is useful for illustrating the manner in which editions situated and interpreted texts. As a hermeneutical vehicle, the juxtaposition of the various texts on a single sheet of papyrus requires a reconstruction of the social context that produced it; so also does the juxtaposition of various texts attributed to Paul in a single edition. The creation of an edition of an author's works is never an ideologically neutral endeavor since it involves a series of choices on the part of an editor choices about which works to include in the edition, how to arrange them, and how to edit the text of the works themselves. These choices inherent in the creation of an edition render it more than a mere collection of texts; it is a specific interpretation of the texts it contains.[6]

---

[5] These fragmentary manuscripts include P^{17}, P^{79}, P^{89}, P^{114}, and P^{116}. The extant fragments of P^{13} also contain only Hebrews, but evidence that will be discussed later suggests other works were included in this codex.

[6] Mary Beard, "Ciceronian Correspondence: Making a Book Out of Letters," in *Classics in Progress: Essays on Ancient Greece and Rome*, ed. T. P. Wiseman (New York: Oxford University Press, 2006), 120. Scherbenske states it well when he says that

> editors' conceptions regarding textual authenticity were shaped by their interpretations and that, as a result, editions transmitted hermeneutics. In the transmission and alteration of the text, the selection and arrangement of the content, and deployment of paratexts (such as prologues, bioi, hypotheses, kephalaia), editors tacitly (and sometimes explicitly) presented the reader with an interpretation of the accompanying edition. An edition was thus the product of interpretation and, in turn, sought to shape subsequent interpretation. (Eric W Scherbenske, *Canonizing Paul: Ancient Editorial Practice and the Corpus Paulinum* [New York: Oxford University Press, 2013], 15)

Authorship was operative in the creation of editions in a manner akin to the function of authorship in the bibliographic and citation practices discussed in previous chapters.[7] In their attempts to properly catalogue the works of various authors, ancient bibliographers like Callimachus and Diogenes Laertius reported the judgments of their predecessors and made their own judgments about the kind of work a given author could have possibly written. If the style or thought of a work was judged to be inconsistent with the bibliographer's image of a particular author, then the work could be labeled as spurious. A bibliographer's determination regarding a work's authenticity could in turn shape the subsequent reception of the work in question. Ancient writers made similar judgments about a work's authenticity and trustworthiness in their citations of earlier works, simultaneously negotiating traditions of authorship that they had received, and in turn employed their judgments about authorship to serve their own rhetorical goals. In the case of both bibliographic method and citation practices, previous traditions about authorship were evaluated and employed to specific ends in the context of that evaluation that would in turn shape subsequent evaluations of the work.

Authorship served a similar function in the work of an ancient editor since the choice of which works to include in an authorial edition would be among the editor's primary tasks. The creation of such editions in antiquity were frequently organized around a particular authorial construct, the editor's ideas about what this particular author would have written that could itself be shaped by prior editions of the author's works. Decisions about the inclusion or exclusion of particular works from an edition would themselves become hermeneutical vehicles for the editor's own authorial construct since it not only informed the choice to include or exclude a given work from a collected corpus but also would shape the authorial construct of those who received the edition that had been created. The inclusion of a single work in an author's corpus might significantly alter the way an author was viewed by those who received this particular edition of the author's works.[8] Thrasyllus' edition of Plato's writings provides an instructive example as he included sections of the *Epistles* to which no one prior to him had referred and the authenticity of which had been questioned. These sections emphasized the esoteric qualities of Plato's teaching, a theme of Platonic philosophy that Thrasyllus himself desired to highlight, suggesting that Thrasyllus edited the Platonic corpus in accordance with this own understanding of Plato. Tarrant has argued that "Thrasyllus' judgement, it seems, was not the impartial judgment of an Alexandrian scholar, but the inevitably coloured judgment of a philosopher with his own convictions."[9] His judgments about which writings to include in his edition of

---

[7] Michel Foucault, *Language, Counter-Memory, Practice: Selected Essays and Interviews* (Ithaca, NY: Cornell University Press, 1977); Karen King, "What Is an Author?: Ancient Author Function in the *Apocryphon of John* and the Apocalypse of John," in *Scribal Practices and Social Structures among Jesus Adherents: Essays in Honour of John S. Kloppenborg*, ed. William E. Arnal et al. (Leuven: Peeters, 2016), 15–42.

[8] Beard illustrates this point with a modern example. The decision of editors to include Virginia's Woolf's suicide note as the final "letter" in an edition of her correspondence had a significant impact on the collection as a whole. Of course, in this example, the issue is not the question of authorship but of genre. Beard, "Ciceronian Correspondence," 120.

[9] "Thrasyllus has turned out to have had quite an extensive effect upon the way the Platonic corpus has been handed down. The tetralogies have also had a considerable effect upon which works of

Plato's works also had a significant impact on the subsequent reception of the Platonic corpus.

The question of authorship could also impact the arrangement of the works included in a corpus. In many instances, ancient editors chose to include works in an edition even if they had a questionable connection to the author rather than exclude them completely. Such works of questionable authenticity were often placed at the end of the corpus, a position that could significantly alter the subsequent reception of these works despite their inclusion.[10] Once spurious works were separated from authentic ones, however, the editor still had to decide how to arrange the remaining texts of the corpus. Several principles of arrangement were available to an editor: alphabetical, chronological, topical, pedagogical, or, in many instances, some combination of these.[11] Whatever principle of arrangement the editor chose, it typically served to reinforce an important component of the editor's authorial construct. A topical or pedagogical arrangement, for example, might guide the reader through a writer's works in the "correct" order that would lead to the proper interpretation. Thrasyllus' edition of the Platonic corpus invited the reader to begin with works concerned with the purification of the soul before proceeding to works involving logic, ethics, and politics.[12] Albinus criticized this arrangement in his own interpretation of Plato, arguing that Plato's teaching had no beginning or end but was like a perfect circle.[13] The edition of Aristotle arranged by Andronikos as reflected in the *pinax* of Ptolemaios exhibits overlapping principles of organization: Aristotle's most famous works were placed first while the rest were arranged either alphabetically or by genre.[14] In each of these editions, the ordering of works within a corpus was an opportunity for an editor to shape the interpretations of those works as well as the image of the author responsible for them.[15]

Plato are assumed to be genuine or spurious over the ages" (Harold Tarrant, *Thrasyllan Platonism* [Ithaca, NY: Cornell University Press, 1993], 178).

[10] Scherbenske, *Canonizing Paul*, 46:

> This separation of inauthentic works by placing them at the end of catalogs parallels implicit judgments made by their placement in actual manuscripts. Galen offers numerous examples of inauthentic writings appended to the end of books. In his *De Placitis Hippocratis et Platonis* Galen disparages teachings found at the end of *On the Nature of Man* because they are clearly false and thus surely not Hippocratic. Galen claims that the person interpolating or revising (διασκευάζων) these teachings placed them at the end in order to escape detection. In fact, Galen attempts to justify his rejection of Hippocratic teachings and opinions he deemed inauthentic by appealing to a work's susceptibility to tampering at its end. Coincidentally, Blum suggests that Callimachus may have included pseudepigrapha at the end of his lists of writings in the Pinakes.

[11] Ibid., 48.
[12] Jaap Mansfeld, *Prolegomena: Questions to Be Settled before the Study of an Author, or a Text* (New York: Brill, 1994), 71.
[13] Scherbenske, *Canonizing Paul*, 50.
[14] Rudolf Blum, *Kallimachos: The Alexandrian Library and the Origins of Bibliography* (Madison: University of Wisconsin Press, 1991), 194–5.
[15] Scherbenske, *Canonizing Paul*, 54–5:

> The role of the editor in selecting and ordering an author's writings was no less significant for shaping the interpretation of the author than for changing the text itself ... Ordering tracts to lead the neophyte pedagogically through an author's body of work starts with an understanding and interpretation of the author's life and thought. Because of the connection between an author's life and writings, many isagogical patterns began with a bios of the

Many of the principles guiding the arrangement of editions generally were also applicable specifically to editions of letter collections. Editors of these collections could also follow several different organizing principles, sometimes following more than one simultaneously. When multiple criteria are employed in a single corpus, a loosely defined hierarchy is often discernible among these principles. A collection as a whole might be organized by topic, for example, while the letters within this single topic subcollection might be organized by addressee and those arranged around the same addressee might be organized by yet another principle.[16] Book 4 of Cicero's *ad Familiares* provides a representative example of this pattern of arrangement as it consists entirely of correspondence between Cicero and holders of high office. The letters within this book are separated according to addressee, and the letters to each addressee are arranged chronologically though the book as a whole is not.[17] The hierarchy of these criteria, however, was often not a firm one insofar as the lesser criteria may shift in importance within the organization of subcollections.[18] In addition to the important organizing principles of addressee and topic, a distinction between public and private letters was also present in several ancient letter collections.[19] Questions concerning the clarity of this demarcation have been raised since even private letters were often read aloud and thereby acquired somewhat

author that served as a moral exemplum for displaying to the student how the philosopher embodied his or her philosophy in life.

[16] Gibson notes that there is not one grand, unifying theory to explain the organizing principle of letter collection, but there is one principle that is notably absent from most ancient letter collections: chronology. Ancient editors of letters rarely show any interest in arranging letters chronologically as a means for reconstructing the life of the letter writer. Furthermore, when chronology is employed as an organizational criterion, it is typically a secondary or tertiary one (letters first arranged by addressee may show signs of chronological ordering within this initial arrangement), which is often abandoned in favor of more pressing criteria. Roy Gibson, "On the Nature of Ancient Letter Collections," *Journal of Roman Studies* 102 (2012): 56–78. Beard notes the contrast between ancient and modern editions of Cicero's correspondence, the latter of which are all organized by chronology. Beard, "Ciceronian Correspondence," 114.

[17] Gibson, "Ancient Letter Collections," 64–5.

[18] Gibson also offers editions of Fronto and Symmachus as examples of overlapping criteria of organization (ibid., 64–6). Fronto:

Owing to the complications of the transmission process, uncertainty hangs over the exact number of letters in some books of the collection, and their exact placement ... Nor can we be sure that the broad order of the collection as we have it represents an order that was canonical in antiquity. Be that as it may, it is clear that the consolidation of various letters into topic-based groupings has now been formalized with the explicit provision of appropriate titles by an ancient editor. Thus, for example, four letters written to Marcus Aurelius after his accession, all united by the emperor's retreat to the seaside resort of Alsium, are grouped under the title *de Feriis Alsiensibus*.

Symmachus: "The first seven books of the letters are ordered by correspondent, with each correspondent group kept strictly separate from its neighbors, albeit without strong internal chronology for any given group." Bronwen Neil, "Continuities and Changes in the Practice of Letter-collecting from Cicero to Late Antiquity," in *Collecting Early Christian Letters: From the Apostle Paul to Late Antiquity*, ed. Bronwen Neil and Pauline Allen (Cambridge: Cambridge University Press, 2015), 5.

[19] Cicero maintained a distinction between public and private letters and Pliny's collection of letters were divided on this principle. It was also a principle imitated in several letter collections of late antiquity. Neil, "Continuities and Changes," 6.

of a public nature.[20] However strong such a distinction may have been in the original composition of the letter, it was obviously transcended when "private" letters were prepared for public consumption by their inclusion in an edition. Irrespective of the original intent of their composition, once letters have been collected together in an edition, they take on the quality of a certain public performance.[21] Their genre has, in fact, been transformed from mere correspondence to "literary collection."[22]

This summary of ancient editorial practice highlights the creation of an edition as an inherently interpretive practice. Decisions concerning the inclusion or exclusion of certain texts as well as the arrangement of those texts that are included in the edition communicate the editor's authorial construct while also informing the authorial construct of those who receive the edition. These same decisions are also likely to have a lasting impact on the reception of individual works themselves, the inclusion of a work within an author's corpus solidifying its association with that author, while its exclusion or placement at the end of a collection could permanently call that association into question or even cause the work to fall out of circulation. Furthermore, the creation of an edition, perhaps most powerfully so in the collection of letters, represents a transformation of genre insofar as the works collected in a single corpus now draw their meaning from the others works with which they are juxtaposed. These insights illuminate the reception of the Epistle to the Hebrews in the Greek and Latin manuscripts of the third through sixth centuries as the editors of Paul's letters sought to negotiate the relationship between Hebrews and the rest of the Pauline corpus.

---

[20] Ibid., 11–12.
[21] Gibson, "Ancient Letter Collections," 74:

> Within the correspondence of Cicero, the devotion of an entire book to letters of recommendation has clear didactic uses. The seventy-nine letters of the book are in fact rather hard going as a unit if read for any purpose other than how to compose one's own recommendation in a variety of (sometimes tricky) circumstances. Furthermore, if one wishes to know how to write appropriately to a father, fellow senator, son-in-law, or son, then Books 1, 2, 6 and 7 respectively of Symmachus provide copy-book examples for a late antique audience. Churchmen eager to know how best to write to a fellow bishop will find Sidonius' Books 6–7 of particular interest—and so on. In sum, ancient letter collections may be understood as a field of "significant performance," where the writer's skill in managing social and familial relationship (dealing with others right, and comporting oneself right in such dealings) is put on public display and held up for imitation. The reader's interest is assumed to lie more in observing the ability of the letter-writer to conduct social relations with his family and the most powerful men of the time in an appropriate manner, and to lie less in following his life story. … At any rate, the organization of correspondence by (type of) addressee or by theme allows these social abilities to emerge with particular clarity.

[22] "Whatever their origin in the day-to-day world of real life letter writing, through their collection and publication, through the very editorial practices I have been discussing, through their reading and reception, they were progressively reformulated as a *literary collection*" (Beard, "Ciceronian Correspondence," 124). This transformation also likely occurred with Paul's letters as they were copied and circulated as a collection.

The Reception of Hebrews in Greek Editions of Paul's Letters

The vast majority of Greek manuscripts from the third through sixth centuries that include Hebrews exhibit the influence of editions of Paul's letters on the reception of the epistle. In some instances the influence of editions of the *corpus Paulinum* are rather obvious in that the manuscript in question may be interpreted specifically as a Pauline letter collection beyond any reasonable doubt. In other instances larger collections of scripture bear witness to the inclusion of Paul's letter not as individual works but as a previously established corpus. In manuscripts of Hebrews that are too fragmentary to establish what other works, if any, may have been included alongside the epistle, there is no definitive evidence to suggest that Hebrews was reproduced apart from an edition of Paul. Indeed, even in one of these fragmentary manuscripts of Hebrews, there is evidence that other works of Paul may have originally been included. The manuscripts of the Pauline corpus that have survived in better condition exhibit several of the same organizing principles previously observed in other ancient letter collections. The placement of Hebrews within Greek editions of the *corpus Paulinum* reflect a reception of the epistle as authored by Paul.

P[46]: An Early Edition of Paul's Letters

P[46] is a single quire papyrus codex typically dated to the beginning of the third century originally consisting of 104 leaves (208 pages), 86 leaves of which are now extant.[23] It first came to be known among scholars in the early 1930s when it was purchased by Chester Beatty from an antiquities dealer in Egypt through a third party along with a number of other Greek papyri.[24] The surviving leaves of P[46] contain about two-thirds of Romans, all of Hebrews, 1 and 2 Corinthians, Ephesians, Galatians, Philippians, Colossians, and most of 1 Thessalonians. It is typically dated to the beginning of the third century, making it the earliest surviving collection of any of Paul's letters. The portions of the manuscript that are missing, however, have drawn much of the attention of recent scholarship; the first fourteen and final fourteen pages of the manuscript are no longer extant. There is little debate concerning the contents of the first fourteen pages of the manuscript, which are generally assumed to have contained the first five

---

[23] Eldon Jay Epp, "The Papyrus Manuscripts of the New Testament," in *The Text of the New Testament in Contemporary Research: Essays on the Status Quaestionis, Studies and Documents*, 2nd ed., ed. Bart D. Ehrman and Michael William Holmes (Boston: Brill, 2014), 5.

[24] The other papyri purchased by Beatty include a codex of the four Gospels and Acts; one of Revelation; two codices of Genesis; one containing Numbers and Deuteronomy together; one of Isaiah, Jeremiah, and Ecclesiasticus each; one containing Ezekiel, Susanna, Daniel, and Esther together; and finally a codex containing a letter of Enoch, Melito's *On Passover*, and the Apocryphon of Ezekiel. Unfortunately, it is difficult to attain any kind of certainty regarding the provenance of these finds. Brent Nongbri, *God's Library: The Archaeology of the Earliest Christian Manuscripts* (New Haven, CT: Yale University Press, 2018), 117–18. The University of Michigan also acquired a portion of the Pauline codex though these were eventually sold to Beatty as well. Brent Nongbri, "The Acquisition of the University of Michigan's Portion of the Chester Beatty Biblical Papyri and a New Suggested Provenance," *Archiv Für Papyrusforschung* 60, no. 1 (2014): 93–116.

chapters of Romans.²⁵ The contents of the final fourteen pages of the manuscript, however, remain a mystery.

It seems natural to assume 2 Thessalonians would follow 1 Thessalonians. Some scholars have proposed that the manuscript simply ended there and that it never contained nor was meant to contain the Pastoral Epistles since they would not have fit in the space remaining after 2 Thessalonians.²⁶ Such an arrangement, however, would leave about nine pages blank at the end of the codex.²⁷ Discerning the contents of the final pages of this codex is further complicated by the compression of text in the later part of the manuscript, a phenomenon typically interpreted as an indication that the scribe anticipated a lack of necessary space to complete the copying of whatever the codex was meant to contain. J. Duff has argued that this increased number of letters per page is an indication that the scribe did, in fact, intend to include the Pastorals at the end of his codex.²⁸ Duff's methodology has been questioned by other scholars and, in any case, Duff himself admits that the inclusion of the Pastorals would still have required the addition of more pages at the end of the codex even as the scribe increasingly compressed the text of the epistles.²⁹ This leads Epp to conclude that "as

---

[25] Epp, "Textual Criticism and Canon," 497–502.

[26] Jerome Quinn, "P46, the Pauline Canon," *Catholic Biblical Quarterly* 36, no. 3 (1974): 379–85; Aland and Aland, *Text of the New Testament*, 87. See also Edgar Battad Ebojo, "A Scribe and His Manuscript: An Investigation into the Scribal Habits of Papyrus 46 (P. Chester Beatty II – P. Mich. Inv. 6238)" (PhD diss., University of Birmingham, 2014).

[27] Epp, "Textual Criticism and Canon," 497.

[28] J. Duff, "Papyrus-Codex-46 (P46) and the 'Pastorals': A Misleading Consensus? (Scribal Compression and Miscalculation as Evidence for an Omitted Pastoral Epistle Section in the Pauline Corpus)," *New Testament Studies* 44, no. 4 (1998): 584:

> Not long after the scribe passed the half-way point in the codex, he started fitting more and more text on each page. This is not simply the common phenomenon in which there is a larger writing area on the earlier and later parts of a codex compared to the central part, since the number of letters on each page near the end of the codex far exceeds not only that in the middle of the codex but also that at the beginning. Indeed, in the final section of the codex there are approximately 50% more letters per page than in the middle section.

Duff offers two hypotheses to account for this increase in letters per page, both of them suggesting that the scribe *intended* to include the Pastorals in his codex. The first hypothesis is that the scribe intended to include the Pastorals but realized he would run out of space and so left the final nine pages of the codex blank. The other hypothesis, which Duff prefers, is that the scribe ran out of pages about half way through 2 Timothy and simply added more pages to the end of his codex, a method attested in other manuscripts. Ibid., 586–7.

[29] Parker and Epp have both critiqued Duff's proposal with regard to his letter-per-page calculations and their comparisons. Parker argues that Duff's methodology of calculating is flawed "because he has taken a short cut to calculate this, namely the use of a computerised version of a printed edition 'adjusted to reflect the spelling used in P46.'" Parker asserts that the more exact method would be to count the number of letters per line, which has not been done. D. C. Parker, *An Introduction to the New Testament Manuscripts and Their Texts* (New York: Cambridge University Press, 2008), 253. Epp does not question Duff's calculations but argues that they have been utilized inappropriately. Whereas Duff compares the final pages of the codex to those in the middle in order to illustrate just how much the scribe has strived to include more text, Epp points out that the center pages of a codex would have held fewer letters than those at the beginning and the end in any case. This is the case since the center pages would have stuck out further than those at either end of the codex and thus had to be trimmed in order to make a neat edge. This would have been especially true of a large single quire codex like P⁴⁶. Epp, "Textual Criticism and Canon," 498–9.

yet neither Duff nor anyone else has a feasible answer to what occupied the end of P^{46}."[30]

Although the complete contents of P^{46} cannot be known with certainty, it is nevertheless reasonable to conclude that this codex was intended as an edition of Paul's letters. The final pages of the codex would no more readily fit any non-Pauline writing or combination of writings than Pauline ones.[31] Therefore, the proposal of any non-Pauline work to fill the final pages of the codex only presents more questions than answers. Furthermore, the codex bears points of resemblance to other extant collections of Paul's letters. It begins with Romans as is customary for such collections, and, aside from the unusual placement of Hebrews and the switching of places for Galatians and Ephesians, it follows a relatively standard order throughout. Ephesians' placement before Galatians may be explained by an organizing principle of length while Hebrews' placement may be explained by the principle of length combined with organization by addressee. Hebrews is longer than every letter in the collection except for Romans and 1 Corinthians, but the editor placed Hebrews before 1 Corinthians in order to keep the Corinthian correspondence together.[32] Another mark of this codex as an edition is the titles each of the letters in P^{46} bear, which are typical in Pauline collections, namely, "πρὸς + addressee." This is in contrast to collections of the Catholic Epistles, for example, in which each letter is titled by the name of the supposed author since the work of various authors are contained in the collection. The absence of Paul's name from the title of the letter suggests that the reader already knew the works collected in the edition to be exclusively those of Paul, rendering the addition of his name unnecessary.[33] If this interpretation of P^{46} is correct, it suggests that at least some Christians were interacting with Paul's letters as a collected edition no later than the early third century and that Hebrews was an important part of that edition.

P^{13}: An Amateur Edition of Paul's Letters?

The original contents of the papyrus roll known by New Testament scholars as P^{13} (P.Oxy. IV. 657) are even more uncertain than those of P^{46}. It is an opisthograph; one of seven such rolls reused for Christian texts to have been pulled from the trash heaps of Oxyrhynchus.[34] The recto contains fragments of a Latin epitome of Livy (P. Oxy. IV. 668) while fragments of Hebrews ranging from the fifth chapter to the eleventh

---

[30] Epp, "Textual Criticism and Canon," 502.
[31] Epp considers several combinations of canonical and noncanonical writings but does not regard any of these combinations as satisfactory. Ibid., 501.
[32] David Trobisch, *Paul's Letter Collection: Tracing the Origins* (Minneapolis, MN: Fortress Press, 1994), 20–3.
[33] Although I agree with Trobisch's assessment that these titles attest to a relatively early edition of Paul's letters, I do not follow him in his further conclusion that there was also an early canonical edition of the New Testament. David Trobisch, *The First Edition of the New Testament* (Oxford: Oxford University Press, 2000), 41.
[34] AnneMarie Luijendijk, "Sacred Scriptures as Trash: Biblical Papyri from Oxyrhynchus," *Vigiliae Christianae* 64, no. 3 (2010): 253; Nongbri, *God's Library*, 234.

are found on the verso.³⁵ P. Head and M. Warren have argued that the work of the scribe who copied the Hebrews text should be classified as "non-professional," citing a "distinct lack of discipline in column width and a wide variation in the number of lines per column" as well as the "marked deterioration" of the writing as "letter formation becomes increasingly erratic and the individual letters increase in size, while lines begin to slope up at the end and the lower lines become longer."³⁶

Although no other writings survive in these fragments aside from the text of the epitome and Hebrews, column numbers included on the roll suggest another work came before Hebrews. While it is impossible to know what that work may have been, a rough correspondence between the page numbers of P⁴⁶ and the column numbers of P¹³ offer Romans as a reasonable possibility.³⁷ Given these characteristics of Hebrews' in P¹³, one might reasonably imagine that it was prepared as an edition of Paul's letters for personal use by an amateur scribe, a hypothesis that is, of course, far from certain. The relevant point for the present study, however, is that even in the case of this fairly exceptional papyrus there is still evidence to suggest that this copy of Hebrews existed as part of an edition of Paul's letters.

Evidence for Editions of Paul within Larger Collections

Manuscripts that include all twenty-seven writings of Athanasius' New Testament are exceedingly rare; codices incorporating both testaments within their covers, like Sinaiticus (א 01), Vaticanus (B 03), and Alexandrinus (A 02), even more so.³⁸ Much more common are codices that contain the smaller collections of which the New Testament was composed: collections of Paul's letters, the Gospels, and Acts with the Catholic Epistles. This observation alone may suggest that those who produced these manuscripts were not primarily concerned with the reproduction of scriptures in strict accordance with the idea of a closed canon. Furthermore, the manuscripts

---

³⁵ Heb 2:14–5:5; 10:8–22; 10:29–11:13; and 11:28–12:17. Bernard P. Grenfell and Arthur S. Hunt, *The Oxyrhynchus Papyri. Vol. IV* (London: Egypt Exploration Fund, 1904), 35–7, 90–5.

³⁶ P. Head and M. Warren, "Re-Inking the Pen: Evidence from P. Oxy. 657 (P13) Concerning Unintentional Scribal Errors," *New Testament Studies* 43, no. 3 (1997): 469–70.

³⁷ James R. Royse, "The Early Text of Paul (and Hebrews)" in *The Early Text of the New Testament*, ed. Charles E. Hill and Michael J. Kruger (Oxford: Oxford University Press, 2014), 185:

> The chief clue to the original extent consists of the column numeration, which begins with μζ (= 47) and ends with ξθ (= 69) for the extant columns ... Moreover, the beginning of Hebrews would likely have occurred at column μδ (= 44), so presumably some earlier work(s) of Paul preceded it. Now, on the basis of a rough correspondence between the column numbers of P¹³ and the page numbers of P⁴⁶, Sanders argued that P¹³ like P⁴⁶, attested to a sequence that began with Romans and continued with Hebrews. While this hypothesis can hardly be considered certain, it would seem to be the most likely sequence; otherwise, P¹³ must have contained Hebrews in a unique order. Moreover, as we shall see, there is a close textual affinity between P¹³ and P⁴⁶.

³⁸ Sinaiticus (א 01 London, British Library, Add MS 43725), Vaticanus (B 03 Vatican Library, Vat. gr. 1209), and Alexandrinus (A 02 London, British Library, Royal I D.VIII). Out of the roughly 5,500 Greek manuscripts that contain NT writings, "only 3 uncials (א 01, A 02, C 04) and 56 minuscules (or 57, if 205ᵃᵇˢ is counted separately) contain the whole of the New Testament. In 2 uncials and 147 minuscules only Revelation is lacking because of its canonical history" (Aland and Aland, *Text of the New Testament*, 78).

that most closely approximate a complete canon also contain noncanonical works: the Shepherd and the *Epistle of Barnabas* in Sinaiticus and 1–2 Clement in Alexandrinus, for example. In both instances, these noncanonical works are placed at the end of the collection, the position reserved for works of questionable authenticity in the creation of an edition, and set off by more substantial subscriptions for the works which precede them (Figure 1).[39] This suggests that even these larger collections of scriptures that more closely resembled Athanasius' canon were guided more so by ancient editorial concepts of book production than by an overwhelming concern to conform to Athanasius', or anyone else's, canon.

The paratextual features of these pandect bibles also witness to their character as a collection of these subcollections—an edition of editions, so to speak. Whereas the creators of these editions could have erased the identifying marks of their subcollections in order to create one seamless "New Testament edition," they chose instead to use superscriptions, subscriptions, tailpieces, and blank pages to distinguish one collection from another.[40] These features indicate that the *corpus Paulinum* already existed as an edition in the exemplar(s) of these manuscripts and that Hebrews was included in that edition. Furthermore, the same organizing principles observed above continued to guide the arrangement of Paul's letters even as they were included in the context of a large collection of scriptures. The reception of Hebrews, therefore, remains inseparably linked to editions of the Pauline corpus even in the pandect bibles of the fourth and fifth centuries.

The character of the *corpus Paulinum* as an edition within a larger collection of scriptures is evidenced within Codex Vaticanus primarily by its superscriptions and subscriptions as well as the capitulation of the Pauline corpus. The superscriptions and accompanying artwork in Vaticanus are remarkably consistent throughout the manuscript. The first letter of each work is enlarged and illuminated with blue and red ink.[41] A green bar appears above the first line of each work with a series of three

---

[39] The coronis around the subscription for Revelation, which is followed by 1 Clement, is more ornate than the preceding works in Alexandrinus. For more on these works at the end of Sinaiticus and Alexandrinus, see Dan Batovici, "The Apostolic Fathers in Codex Sinaiticus and Codex Alexandrinus," *Biblica* 97, no. 4 (2016): 581–605. All images of Codex Alexandrinus are courtesy of the British Library. © British Library Board Royal I D.VIII f.133v. https://www.bl.uk/collection-items/codex-alexandrinus.

[40] The Alands note that the existence of these subcollections is also attested by the varying quality of the text in the different collections within Vaticanus and Alexandrinus. The quality of the text of the Pauline epistles is considerably inferior to that of the Gospels in Codex Vaticanus while the reverse is the case in Alexandrinus, suggesting that B and A were copied from manuscripts of varying quality. Aland and Aland, *Text of the New Testament*, 50.

[41] It should be noted, however, that these features were later additions to the manuscript. Despite their origin in a later time period, they suggest knowledge of previously existing editions within this larger collection of scriptures. For more information on the superscriptions and accompanying artwork as later additions, see Contantine Tischendorf, *Novum Testamentum Vaticanum: Post Angeli Maii Aliorumque Imperfectos Labores Ex Ipso Codici* (Leipzig: Giesecke et Devrient, 1867), xxviiii; Grover Payne, "A Textual Analysis, Critical Reconstruction, and Evaluation of the Superscriptions and Subscriptions to the Corpus Paulinum" (PhD diss., Southwestern Baptist Theological Seminary, 2002), 104; Paul Canart, "Le Vaticanus Graecus 1209: notice paleographique et codologique," in *Le Manuscrit B de La Bible (Vaticanus Graecus 1209)*, ed. Patrick Andrist (Lausanne: Editions du Zebre, 2009), 32; Jesse R. Grenz, "Textual

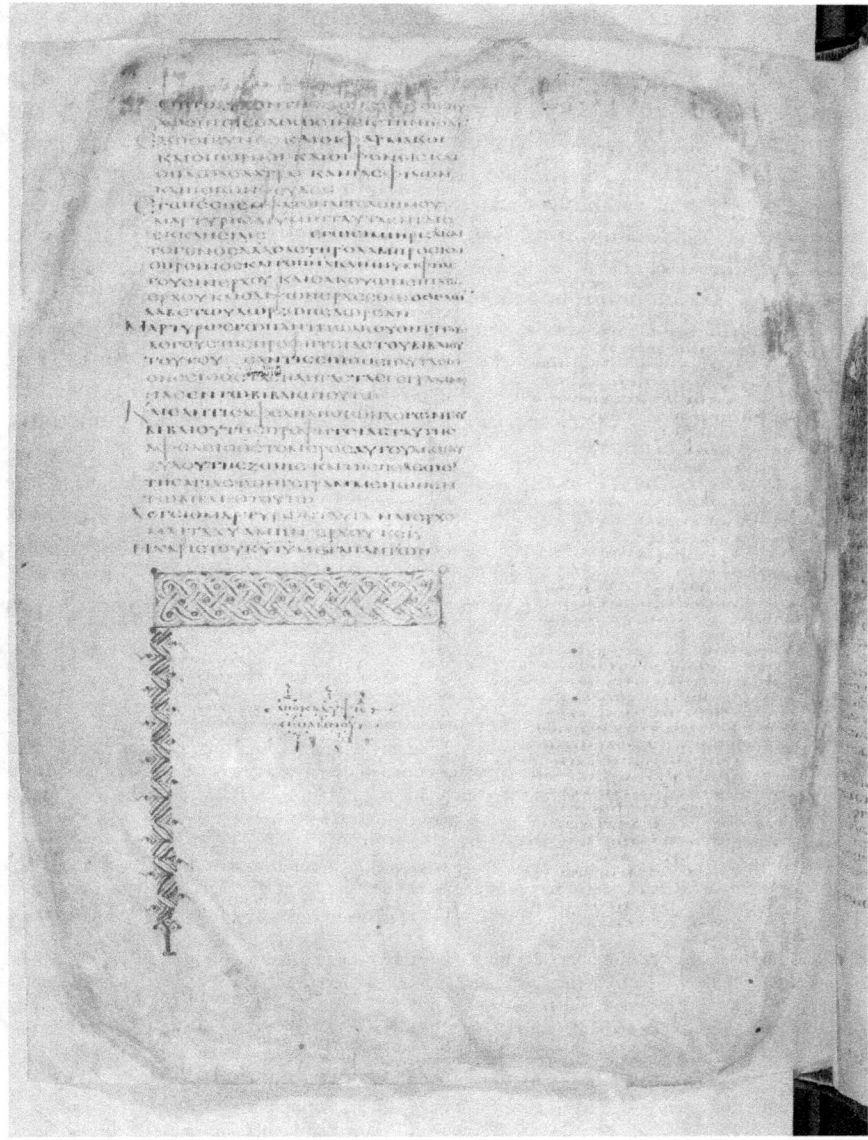

Figure 1 Subscription for Revelation in Codex Alexandrinus. Used with permission of the British Library.

crosses above the bar and the title of the work above the three crosses. Exceptions to this regular pattern appear with Matthew, the first of the Gospels, and Romans,

Divisions in Codex Vaticanus: A Layered Approach to the Delimiters in B (03)," *TC: A Journal of Biblical Textual Criticism* 23 (2018): 8.

the first of Paul's letters. The artwork at the beginning of Romans is more ornate than the artwork at the beginning of the other Pauline letters, replacing the solid green bar with a red bar including green detail. Similar ornate detail is present in the superscription to the Gospel of Matthew, suggesting that these superscriptions mark the beginning of a new collection within the larger collections of works in the manuscript. The subscription to the Gospel of John reinforces this interpretation of the Gospels as an established collection within the larger work. Whereas most subscriptions in Vaticanus are accompanied by a simple coronis, some variation of two intersecting lines that separate the text of the work from its subscription, John's subscription is accompanied by a more substantial coronis than is found after any of the other Gospels, thereby signaling the end of the Gospel collection.[42] Unfortunately, the leaves of Vaticanus after Hebrews 9 are no longer extant, having been replaced by pages inscribed with a later minuscule script, so it remains unknown whether a subscription like that of the Gospel of John might also have been found at the end of the Pauline collection.[43]

In addition to the superscriptions and subscriptions of this manuscript, the capitulation system preserved in Vaticanus also attests to the collection of Paul's letters as an edition. Chapter numbers were added to the Pauline corpus by a later scribe after the production of Vaticanus.[44] These chapter numbers, however, do not start over with each new Pauline letter but rather continue on throughout the Pauline corpus as though

---

[42] For a brief survey of coroni in different manuscripts, see W. Andrew Smith, *A Study of the Gospels in Codex Alexandrinus: Codicology, Paleography, and Scribal Hands* (Leiden: Brill, 2014), 128–30.

[43] It is worth noting that Acts and the Catholic Epistles do not bear the same marks in Codex Vaticanus of having existed as an edition. The superscriptions of these works are all consistent with the superscriptions of other New Testament works aside from Matthew and Romans. There is diversity among the subscriptions and accompanying artwork for these works but none that marks one work as discernibly different from the others. Perhaps this is because Acts and the Catholic Epistles appear between the Gospels and Paul in Vaticanus, the distinctive boundary markers of these collections thereby providing default boundaries for the collection of the Apostolos that appears between them. Or perhaps Acts and the Catholic Epistles were not as well established as a collection as were the Gospels and Paul.

[44] Although these chapter numbers were not produced by the original scribes, Goswell regards them as a fourth-century addition. They also witness to an earlier arrangement of the epistles in which Hebrews was placed between Galatians and Ephesians. Gregory Goswell, "An Early Commentary on the Pauline Corpus: The Capitulation of Codex Vaticanus," *Journal of Greco-Roman Chrsitainity and Judaism* 8 (2011): 51. Bruce M. Metzger notes,

> Although in codex Vaticanus Hebrews follows 2 Thessalonians, the chapter numbers in that manuscript disclose that in an ancestor it occupied a position after Galatians. The chapter numeration of the Pauline Letters begins with Romans and runs continuously through 2 Thessalonians. The Letter to the Galatians concludes with the 58th chapter, whereas the next Epistle, that to the Ephesians, begins with the 70th chapter, and then the numbers continue regularly through Philippians, Colossians, 1 and 2 Thessalonians, ending with the 93rd chapter. Following 2 Thessalonians (as was mentioned above) stands Hebrews, which begins with the 59th chapter, and proceeds with the 60th, 61st, 62nd, 63rd, and 64th chapters, as far as He 9.14, where the manuscript breaks off, the remaining part being lost. Doubtless there were originally eleven chapters in Hebrews (59 to 69). It is clear, therefore, from the sequence of chapter divisions that in an ancestor of codex Vaticanus Hebrews stood after Galatians and before Ephesians, and that the scribe of Vaticanus copied mechanically the chapter numbers even though they no longer were appropriate after Galatians. (*A Textual Commentary on the Greek New Testament*, 2nd ed. [New York: United Bible Societies, 1994], 591)

it were a single work.⁴⁵ This is a treatment unique to the *corpus Paulinum* in Vaticanus as both the Gospels and the Catholic Epistles are given chapter numbers distinctive to each individual work.⁴⁶ Therefore, the paratextual features present in Codex Vaticanus attest to the knowledge and reproduction of Paul's letters as a collection.

Three distinct collections are attested in Codex Alexandrinus; the Gospels, Acts with the Catholic Epistles, and the Pauline corpus.⁴⁷ The Gospels are accompanied by the Eusebian canon tables thereby encouraging the practice of reading and comparing all four of them with one another and thus enhancing their character as a unit.⁴⁸ The tailpiece of Acts, which follows the Gospels in Alexandrinus, includes a drawing of an amphora similar to the one found at the end of the Gospel of Matthew (Figure 2).⁴⁹ At first glance, this may appear to associate Acts with the Gospels. However, the tailpiece for Jude makes clear that Acts and the Catholic Epistles were regarded as a unit. The subscription reads: ΙΟΥΔΑ ΕΠΙΣΤΟΛΗ ΠΡΑΞΙΣ ΤΩΝ ΑΓΙΩΝ ΑΠΟΣΤΟΛΩΝ ΚΑΙ ΚΑΘΟΛΙΚΑΙ (Figure 3).⁵⁰

A coronis similar to the one following Jude is also found after Philemon, the final letter in the Pauline corpus. Regrettably, the page has been cut along the inner edge of the coronis and whatever was on that part of the page is now lost (Figure 4). Given the similarities to the tailpiece at the end of the Catholic Epistles, one might reasonably expect that the subscription within this coronis might have characterized the Pauline Epistles as a single unit much as the one after Jude did for Acts and the Catholic Epistles.⁵¹

Of course, without the text itself, only speculation is possible. Even without this subscription, the coronis and the blank page that follows on the verso of this leaf suggest a separation from the book of Revelation that follows. Thus, the treatment of the Pauline Epistles in Codex Alexandrinus adds to the evidence that this collection was treated as an edition in antiquity.

Whereas Vaticanus and Alexandrinus place the Apostolos collection in between the Gospels and the Pauline corpus, Sinaiticus places Paul in between the Gospels and the Apostolos. Sinaiticus is also distinguished among these manuscripts by its failure to utilize superscriptions or subscriptions to distinguish these collections in any meaningful way. The Pauline corpus is, however, set apart by the use of blank pages in the manuscript. A complete blank page stands between the end of the Gospel of John and the beginning of Romans. The end of the Pauline collection is similarly marked by

---

[45] Gregory Goswell, "Finding a Home for the Letter to the Hebrews," *Journal of the Evangelical Theological Society* 59, no. 4 (2016): 751.
[46] Goswell, "Early Commentary," 53.
[47] Revelation and 1–2 Clement appear to be treated independently as they are each separated by substantial tailpieces.
[48] Each of the subscriptions among the Gospels is unique, thus failing to mark any of them with distinction. The superscriptions throughout Alexandrinus are both consistent and relatively plain, similarly failing to mark particular works as distinctive in any way.
[49] Smith, *Alexandrinus*, 133. © British Library Board Royal I D.VIII f.76r. https://www.bl.uk/collection-items/codex-alexandrinus.
[50] "Jude's Epistle. Acts of the Holy Apostles and Catholic [Epistles]." © British Library Board Royal I D.VIII f. 84v. https://www.bl.uk/collection-items/codex-alexandrinus.
[51] © British Library Board Royal I D.VIII f.124r. https://www.bl.uk/collection-items/codex-alexandrinus.

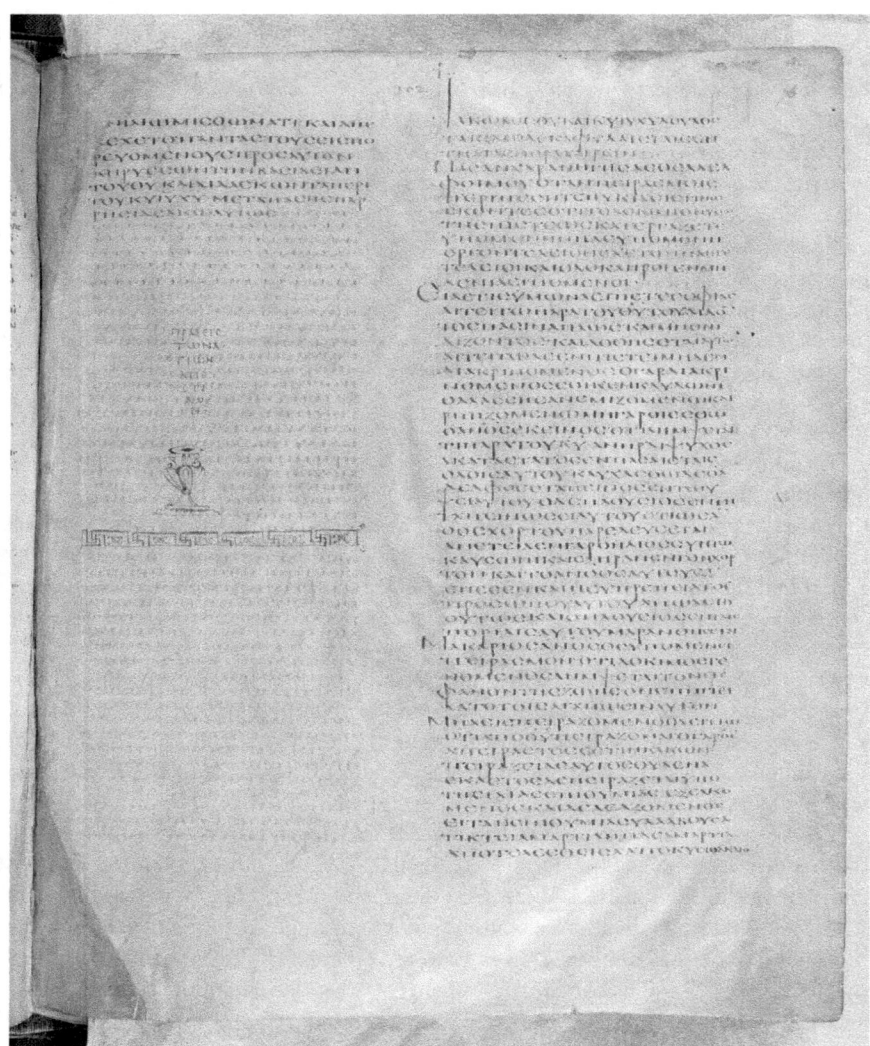

Figure 2 Tailpiece for Acts in Codex Alexandrinus. Used with permission of the British Library.

a blank page though in a slightly different manner. Philemon, the final Pauline letter in this manuscript, ends in the middle of the second column on its final page (Figure 5). This is a common occurrence in Sinaiticus, a manuscript that typically includes four columns of text on each page, and the next work typically begins in the next column of the same page.[52] In the case of Philemon, however, the page has been cut in half

---

[52] This is the case even in the transition from Revelation to the *Epistle of Barnabas*, for example.

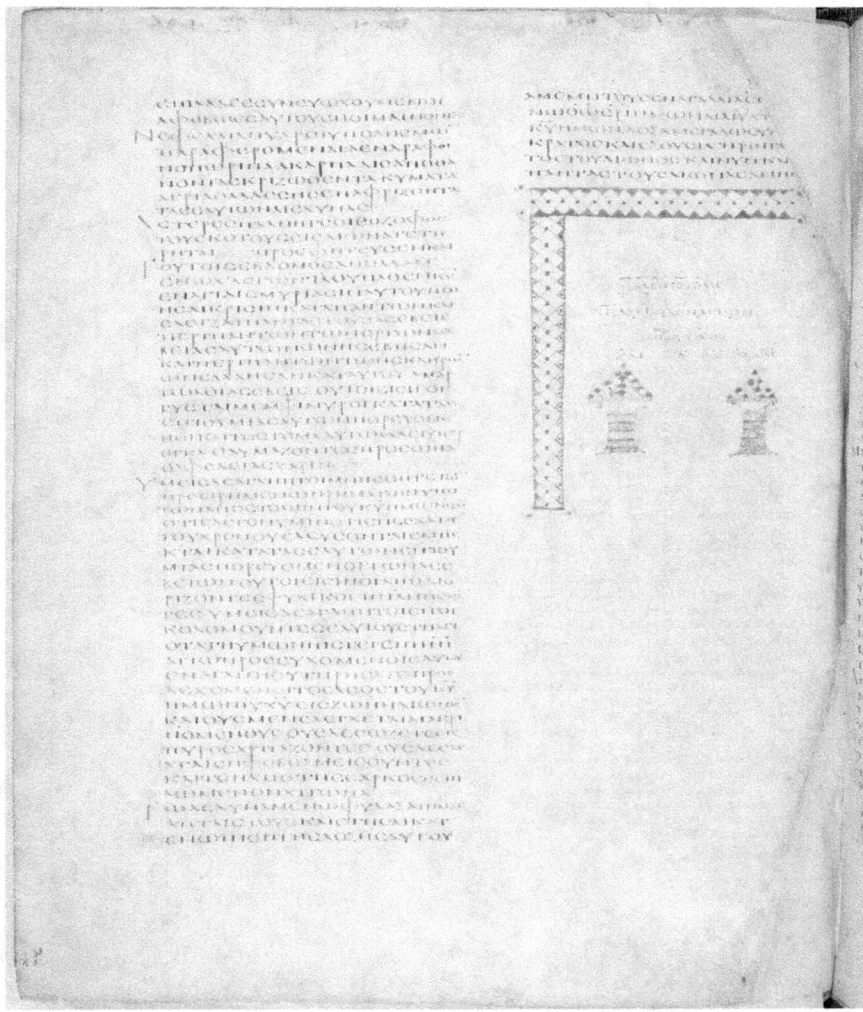

Figure 3 Tailpiece for Catholic Epistles in Codex Alexandrinus. Used with permission of the British Library.

vertically after the second column and the verso of the leaf left blank before Acts begins on the following page.[53]

Of course, it is possible that this page was cut for some other reason—some kind of error that was most easily remedied in this manner, for example—but given the corresponding blank page at the beginning of the Pauline corpus, it is not unreasonable

---

[53] © British Library Board Add. 43725 f. 298r. http://www.codexsinaiticus.org/en/.

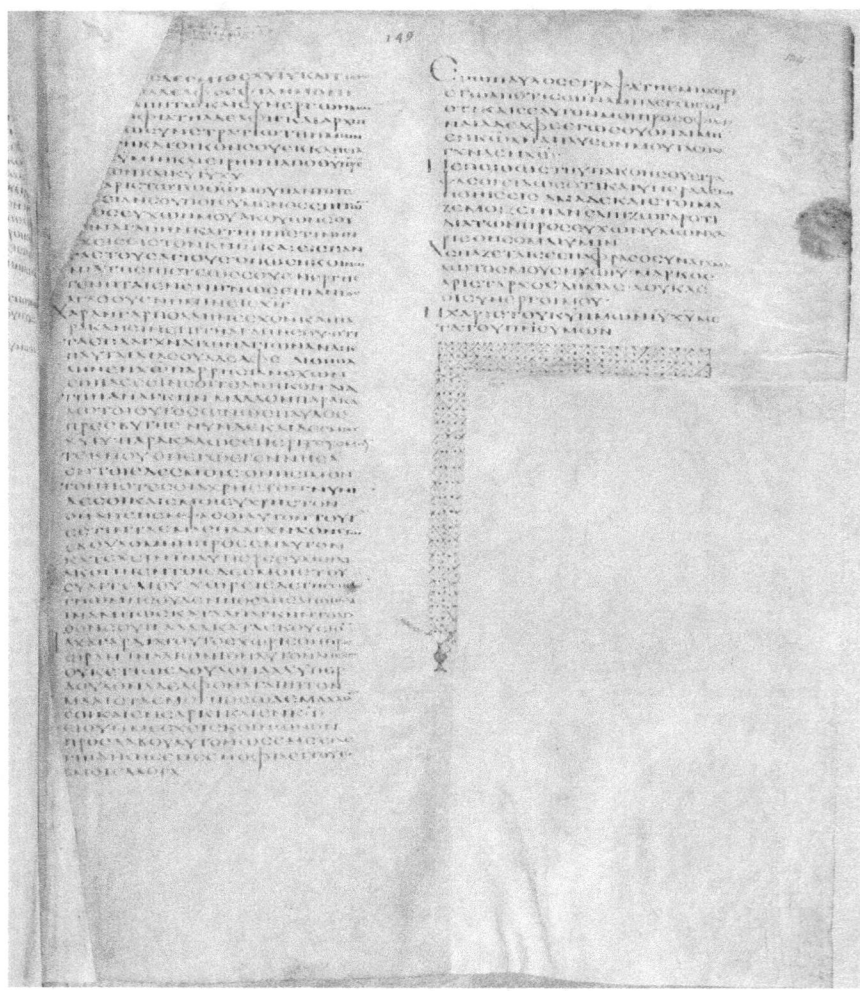

Figure 4 Tailpiece for Pauline Epistles in Codex Alexandrinus. Used with permission of the British Library.

to interpret this as further evidence for the treatment of Paul's letters as an edition within a larger edition of Christian scriptures.

The final manuscript to be considered in this section is not a pandect bible like those considered above. Codex Freerianus (I 016) is, in fact, so badly damaged that its entire contents cannot be determined with any certainty.[54] That it contained a complete

---

[54] Freerianus (Freer-Sackler Art Gallery, Smithsonian, Washington DC, F1906.275) has received little scholarly attention compared to other ancient manuscripts. For recent work on the Freer collection as a whole, see Larry W. Hurtado, *The Freer Biblical Manuscripts: Fresh Studies of an American Treasure Trove* (Leiden: Brill, 2006). Justin Soderquist, "A New Edition of Codex I (016): The Washington Manuscript of the Epistles of Paul" (PhD diss., Trinity Western University, 2014).

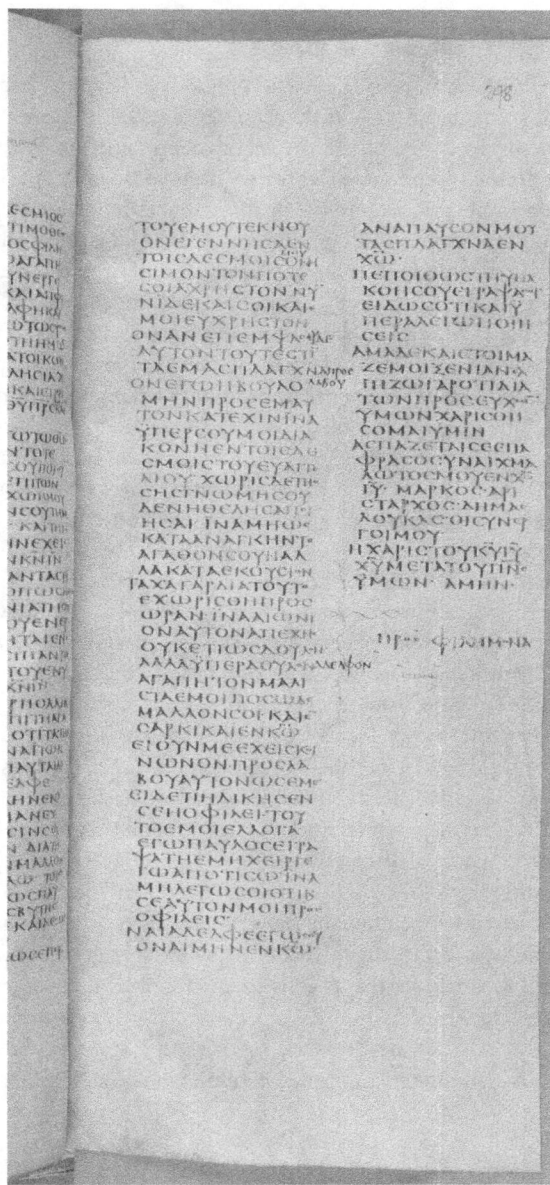

Figure 5 Subscription for Philemon in Codex Sinaiticus. Used with permission of the British Library.

edition of the *corpus Paulinum* is reasonably certain since fragments of every letter except Romans were recovered.[55] The preservation of quire numbers suggests the manuscript once consisted of between 208 and 212 leaves, leading Sanders to conclude that it likely also contained Acts and the Catholic Epistles, though no fragments of these works have survived.[56] Although the fragmentary nature of Freerianus provides limited insight into the reception of Hebrews within editions of Paul's letters, it does share at least two important features with the pandect bibles described above and thereby serves to highlight certain common features among these Greek editions of Paul's letters. The first commonality among these manuscripts is the use of the "πρός + addressee" formula for the letters of Paul, the absence of Paul's name suggesting that those using the manuscript would recognize this section of its contents as an edition of Paul's letters.[57] The second important feature Freerianus shares with the other Greek majuscule manuscripts of late antiquity is the position of Hebrews after 2 Thessalonians. This position has often been characterized as a placement between Paul's letters to churches and Paul's letters to individuals; an observation that is surely correct but left as it is fails to provide an explanation for why such an arrangement would be justified.[58] The practices of organizing ancient letter collections by multiple principles, organization by addressee often being chief among them, provides context for such an editorial decision. All of the Greek editions of Paul's letters reveal that the length of the letters was an important organizing principle. P[46] follows this criterion while also demonstrating some concern for addressee, placing Hebrews after Romans but prior to 1 Corinthians so as not to separate the two letters to the Corinthians. Other Greek editors of the Pauline collection appear to have placed even greater emphasis on organizing the collection by recipient, a more common principle of organization among ancient letter collections. All of the Greek editions of Paul's letters that include letters to individuals separate these "private" letters from the more public letters addressed to churches.[59] In addition to this division between public and private letters, the Greek editions of Paul aside from P[46] also observe another division by addressee, separating the letter to the "Hebrews" from Paul's letters to predominantly gentile churches. Hebrews' position in these manuscripts is thus elucidated by the combination of multiple organizing principles at work among these Greek editions of the Pauline corpus in a manner that is consistent with other ancient letter collections. Despite the disassociation of Hebrews from Paul's letters to churches in these later Greek editions, this position nevertheless signifies that Hebrews belonged securely within the corpus of Paul's letters in the estimation of those who created these editions.

---

[55] Henry A. Sanders, *The New Testament Manuscripts in the Freer Collection* (New York: Macmillan, 1918), 252.

[56] Henry A. Sanders, "New Manuscripts of the Bible from Egypt," *American Journal of Archaeology* 12, no. 1 (1908): 55.

[57] Sanders, *Freer Collection*, 256.

[58] William H. P. Hatch, "The Position of Hebrews in the Canon of the New Testament," *Harvard Theological Review* 29, no. 2 (1936): 136.

[59] If P[46] included these letters, it may very well have observed the same distinction, though it is impossible to know as long as the contents of its final fourteen pages remain in question.

All of the manuscripts considered in this section, despite consisting of larger collections of Christian scripture than an edition of Paul's letters, exhibit evidence that they have been influenced by some ancient version of an authorial edition. The paratextual features of these manuscripts as well as the ordering of the epistles demonstrate that Paul's letters, Hebrews included, were incorporated into these manuscripts not as independent works that were judged canonical but as a whole edition of Paul's letters. As a result, the reception of the Epistle to the Hebrews is inseparably intertwined with the reception of the *corpus Paulinum* in these manuscripts. Furthermore, its placement in that corpus is illuminated by the principles of ancient editorial practice.

Coislinianus: A Witness to the Euthalian Edition of Paul's Letters

The production of large collections of Christian scriptures in the fourth and fifth centuries did not establish a new trend in Christian book production. Even after the promulgation of canon lists in these centuries and the production of codices with contents that roughly resembled those lists, smaller collections remained the norm. One such collection is Codex Coislinianus (H^p 015), a sixth-century manuscript of the *corpus Paulinum* written on fine parchment.[60] The manuscript is incomplete and at times difficult to read, but there is little doubt that it was created as an edition of Paul's letters.[61] This is demonstrated not only by the collection of works in the manuscript but also by the colophon inscribed in it:

> I copied and published this volume of the Apostle Paul in lines on account of its value for writing and ease of comprehension for reading. I ask for forgiveness of all the brothers present among us for my boldness, returning with prayer your indulgence on my behalf. This book was collated against a copy in Caesarea from the library of the holy Pamphilus and copied by his hand.[62]

This colophon is just one of the features of Coislinianus that has caused scholars to associate the manuscript with the so-called Euthalian apparatus, a distinctive set of

---

[60] Bibliothèque nationale de France, Coislin 202, Grec. 1074.
[61] J. Armitage Robinson, *Euthaliana, Studies of Euthalius, Codex H of the Pauline Epistles, and the Armenian Version* (London: Cambridge University Press, 1895), 48:
> A later hand has covered over the letters of Codex H with a thick coating of dark ink which has completely hidden their original form. This ink is of a corrosive nature, and has eaten its way in places quite through the vellum of the codex ... But this ink had another quality, more deserving of our gratitude. It has left a yellow stain on the opposite leaf, and in some places the letters thus reproduced are easily legible.

[62] Scherbenske, *Canonizing Paul*, 117. ἔγραψακαιἐξεθέμην κα|τὰ δύναμιν στειχηρὸν·| τόδετοτεύχοςπαύλουτοῦ ἀποστόλου| πρὸςἐγγραμμονκαὶ εὐκατάλημ|πτον ἀνάγνωσιν·τῶν κα|θ ̓ ἡμᾶςἀδελφῶνπαρ ̓ ὧν| ἀπάντωντόλμης· συγ|νώμην αἰτῶ. εὐχῇ τῇ| ὑπερἐμῶν·την συνπε|ριφοραν κομιζόμενος·| ἀντεβλήθηδεὴ βίβλος·| πρὸςτοἐνκαισαρία ἀντί|γραφον· τῆς βιβλιοθήκης| τοῦἁγίουΠαμφίλου· χειρί| γεγραμμένον (Louis Charles Willard, *A Critical Study of the Euthalian Apparatus* [New York: Walter de Gruyter, 2009], 83–92).

paratextual features that serve to guide one's reading of the Pauline Epistles.[63] Although not all the features of the Euthalian apparatus as preserved in later manuscripts are present in the incomplete Coislinianus, the Euthalian *kephalaia*, the divine testimonies, and certain arrangements of text peculiar to Euthalian editions in addition to this colophon are included.[64]

These distinctive features not only attest to the production and reception of the manuscript as an edition of Paul's letter but also provide insight into the purpose of such an edition, namely, as a presentation of the apostle Paul as one whose ethical and hermeneutical wisdom was worthy of imitation. An allusion to such a presentation of the apostle is also present in the work's antiphrasis, which describes the manuscript as "a treasure with spiritual goods for you and for all people."[65] This notion is further reinforced by the arrangement of the text in sense lines for easier reading and comprehension, also mentioned in the colophon. What is most telling, however, is the kind of lines that stand out most prominently in this arrangement: specifically, virtue and vice lists. One such example occurs in Coislinianus' reproduction of Col 3:4–8, a list of vices that must be put to death by those who are in Christ. While this entire text is arranged in sense lines, the vices themselves are made to stand out as short, single words form the contents of an entire line in the manuscript in an arrangement like this:

πορνείαν
ἀκαθαρσίαν
πάθος…
ὀργήν
θυμόν
κακίαν
βλασφημίαν.

A similar arrangement occurs in the virtue list of Tit 2:1–5. This arrangement of text emphasizes the ethical teaching of the apostle and thus suggests that one of the primary purposes of this edition was to present Paul as a source of ethical wisdom to be emulated.[66]

While the textual arrangement of vice and virtue lists in Coislinianus point to Paul as an ethical teacher worthy of imitation, the divine testimonies, another feature of

---

[63] For a thorough treatment of manuscripts witnessing to the Euthalian edition, see Vemund Blomkvist, *Euthalian Traditions: Text, Translation and Commentary*, Texte Und Untersuchungen Zur Geschichte Der Altchristlichen Literatur Bd. 170 (Boston: De Gruyter, 2012).

[64] Scherbenske, *Canonizing Paul*, 158.

[65] Ibid., 117:

> Prosphonesis: I am coronis, teacher of divine ordinances. If you lend me to anyone, take a book in return. For those who sell are bad. Antiphrasis: I am a treasure with spiritual goods for you and for all people, having been desirably adorned with harmonious and beautiful words, indeed the truth. I will not give you to anyone rashly; furthermore, I will not sell you for profit. But I will lend you to friends, only taking a book in return as security.

This part of the colophon is missing from Coislinianus but has been reconstructed from MS 88 by Willard (*Critical Study*, 83).

[66] Scherbenske, *Canonizing Paul*, 160–8.

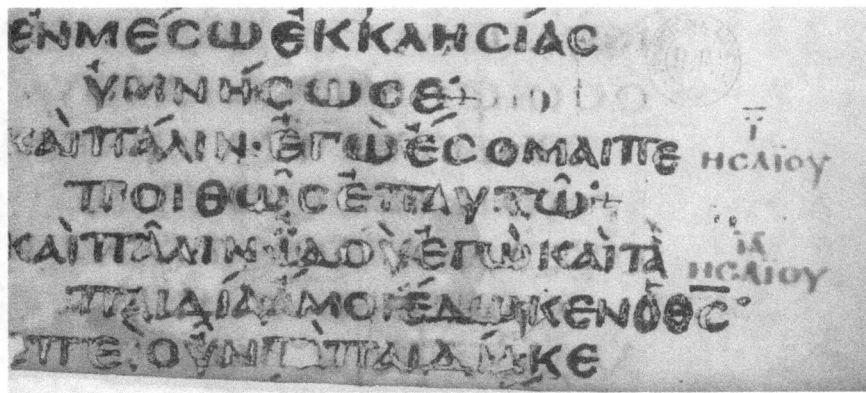

Figure 6 Divine Testimonies in Codex Coislinianus. Used with permission of the Bibliothèque nationale de France.

the Euthalian apparatus present in Coislinianus, highlight Paul as an interpreter of scripture. These testimonies consisted of a coordinating table of Septuagint citations in a given Pauline letter and the numbering of those citations throughout the epistle. Each citation was numbered in the order in which it appeared in the epistle, marked with a marginal notation of that number and the writing of the Septuagint from which it was quoted (Figure 6). These numbers were also arranged in a table at the beginning of the epistle, according to the works of the Septuagint.[67]

In more complete witnesses to the Euthalian edition, these divine testimonies not only include quotations from the Septuagint but also ones from Menander and Demades, suggesting that the source of these quotations is not what makes them "divine" testimonies but Paul's use of them. As a result, the Septuagint is not so much emphasized in these testimonies as Paul's interpretation of it.[68]

Those who produced Codex Coislinianus present Paul's ethical and interpretive goods as a treasure trove. The inclusion of the Epistle to the Hebrews in this collection marks this book also as a precious spiritual resource for those would turn to Paul for guidance. The divine testimonies in the margins of Hebrews further signal its value as an interpretative template to be imitated. Likewise, Hebrews' position after 2 Thessalonians affirms its association with the apostle Paul. Whereas this association was implied by Hebrews' position and title in other manuscripts, it is made explicit

---

[67] So, for example, "In [the epistle] to the Hebrews, 30. 3 from Genesis: #13, #15, #23. 3 from Exodus: #16, #18, #26, etc." Ibid., 138. Image of Coislinianus courtesy of Bibliothèque nationale de France. Coislin 202 f6r. https://gallica.bnf.fr/ark:/12148/btv1b8577515k/f25.item.r=.zoom.

[68] Scherbenske, *Canonizing Paul*, 141:

> The relationship between Paul and his citations has in effect been reversed: where Paul tried to legitimize his arguments by means of these sources, these sources are now legitimized as "divine testimonies" in Paul and his authority presented visually on the page. These sources, once cited by Paul to support his own argument, are now important insofar as they support Paul's interpretation of them as envisioned by Euthalius through the lens of Christ and Christianity.

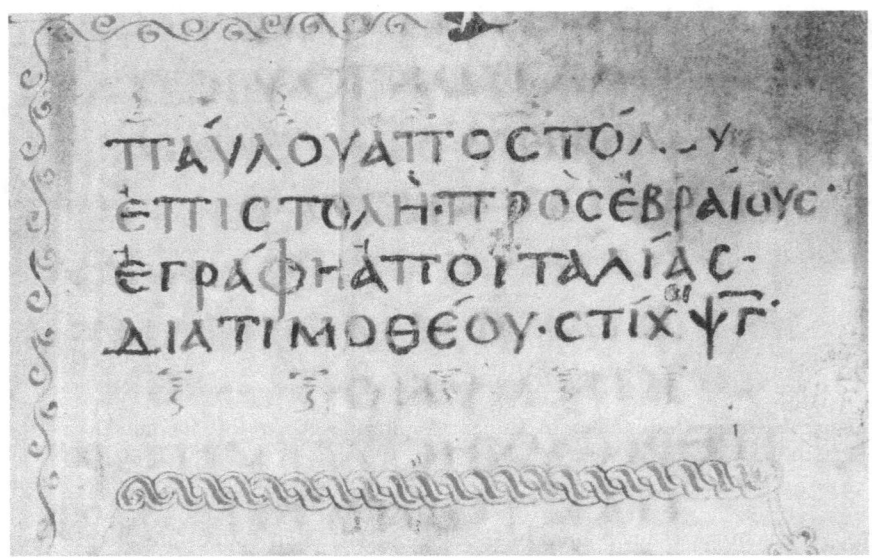

Figure 7 Subscription to Hebrews in Codex Coislinianus. Used with permission of the Bibliothèque nationale de France.

by the subscription in Coislinianus: ΠΑΥΛΟΥ ΑΠΟΣΤΟΛΟΥ ΕΠΙΣΤΟΛΗ ΠΡΟΣ ΕΒΡΑΙΟΥΣ ΕΓΡΑΦΗ ΑΠΟ ΙΤΑΛΙΑΣ ΔΙΑ ΤΙΜΟΘΕΟΥ (Figure 7).[69]

Codex Coislinianus, like the other Greek manuscripts of the third through sixth centuries that included Paul's letters, exhibits the influence of ancient editorial practice on its production. The paratextual features of these manuscripts as well as the arrangement of the epistles demonstrate that Paul's letters were incorporated into these manuscripts not as independent works that were judged canonical but as an authorial edition that was shaped by many of the same principles as other letter collections in the ancient world. Such editions were themselves vehicles of hermeneutics, having been shaped by the interpretations of Paul that preceded them and shaping subsequent interpretations by means of their editorial decisions. One such editorial decision was the inclusion of the Epistle to the Hebrews as a work that belonged in the *corpus Paulinum*. The inclusion of Hebrews in this corpus shaped the way Hebrews itself was read and understood while simultaneously shaping the readers' authorial construct of the apostle Paul as someone who would have written Hebrews in addition to the other letters included in these editions of his writings. As a result, the reception of the Epistle to the Hebrews became inseparably intertwined with the reception of the Pauline corpus among Greek speaking communities of late antiquity.

---

[69] "Paul the Apostle's letter to the Hebrews written from Italy through Timothy." Image of Coislinianus courtesy of Bibliothèque nationale de France. Grec. 1074 f6r. https://gallica.bnf.fr/ark:/12148/btv1b8594608d/f1.image.

The Reception of Hebrews in the Earliest Latin Editions of Paul's Letters

The relationship between the Epistle to the Hebrews and the *corpus Paulinum* played a decisive role in the reception of Hebrews in the Latin manuscript tradition, just as it did in the Greek manuscript tradition. However, the status of that relationship changed when the epistle was translated from Greek to Latin. Whereas Greek manuscripts of the third through sixth centuries consistently placed Hebrews firmly within the Pauline corpus, whether after Romans or after 2 Thessalonians, the two earliest extant manuscripts that include Latin translations of Hebrews, Codices Claromontanus and Fuldensis, placed it at the end of the corpus after Philemon. This shift in position to the end of the Pauline corpus is significant since works of uncertain authenticity were often relegated to precisely this position in ancient editions. Therefore, Hebrews' shift from the middle of the Pauline corpus in Greek manuscripts to its end in bilingual and Latin manuscripts may be plausibly explained by questions concerning the work's authorship in the Latin tradition.

The Distinctive Treatment of Hebrews in Codex Claromontanus

Codex Claromontanus (06, D^p) is a Greek and Latin manuscript of the *corpus Paulinum* 533 pages in length and typically dated to the late fifth or early sixth century.[70] Greek appears on the verso of one leaf with the corresponding Latin on the recto of the next leaf thereby placing the two side by side as the codex lies open to the reader.[71] Hebrews appears as the final work in Claromontanus and is distinguished by a number of features that set it apart within this Pauline collection. The position of Hebrews at the end of Claromontanus combined with the distinctive treatment of Hebrews in the codex, I argue, indicates uncertainty about the relationship between Hebrews and the Pauline corpus in a manner that is consistent with the principles of ancient editorial practice. The editor of Claromontanus likely valued Hebrews as an important work and knew of editions of Paul's works that included Hebrews but remained unconvinced regarding the writing's Pauline authorship, resulting in its inclusion in this manuscript even as a number of visual features separate it from the rest of the corpus.

The first distinctive feature of Hebrews in Claromontanus is its lack of incipit. At the conclusion of every other epistle in this edition, there is an explicit for the work just completed and an incipit for the writing to follow. The explicits typically follow a

---

[70] Bibliothéque Nationale de France, Grec. 107. Aland and Aland, *Text of the New Testament*, 110.
[71] The replacement of a few leaves in the sixth century as well as numerous corrections to the Greek text suggest its continued use throughout that century while the adjacent Latin pages appear to have been somewhat neglected. The manuscript as a whole shows very little sign of use in the seventh century and by the eighth century ends up in France where it undergoes another round of corrections in accordance with the Byzantine text. In the sixteenth century, Theodore Beza is said to have found it at the Abby of Claremont but apparently made very little use of it in preparing his edition of the New Testament. The manuscript is currently held in the Bibilothéque Nationale in Paris, France (Gr 107, 107AB). Caspar René Gregory, *Textkritik Des Neuen Testamentes* (Leipzig: J. C. Hinrichs, 1900), 160; Hermann Josef Frede, *Altlateinische Paulus-Handschriften* (Frieberg: Herder, 1964), 19.

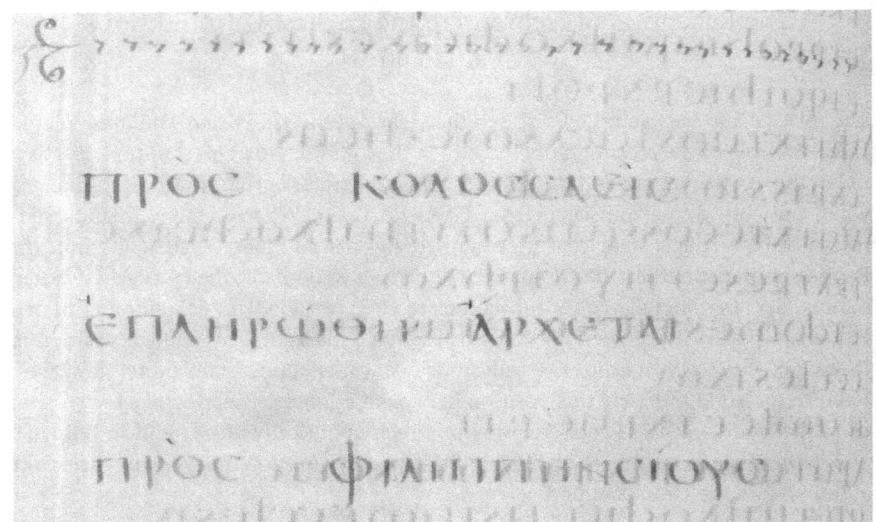

Figure 8 Subscription to Colossians, Superscription to Philippians in Codex Claromontanus. Used with permission of the Bibliothèque nationale de France.

pattern of "ΠΡΟΣ + addressee + ΕΠΛΗΡΩΘΗ" on the Greek side and "ad + addressee + explicit" on the Latin side. These are, in most cases, immediately followed by "ΑΡΧΕΤΑΙ ΠΡΟΣ + addressee" or "incipit ad + addressee," the typical pattern of the incipit for the letter to follow.[72] The transition from Colossians to Philippians provides a representative example (Figure 8).[73] Hebrews, however, lacks this incipit as Philemon ends with only the explicit and nothing more.[74]

In fact, Hebrews does not *immediately* follow Philemon. What does immediately follow Philemon in the present state of Claromontanus is a list of scriptures (Figure 9). While this list of writings has a number of interesting features, what is most relevant to the current study is the fact that this list was not originally part of the manuscript.

---

[72] "To + addressee + is completed. Begins to + addressee." Some other subscriptions have additional material from a later hand. For example, the Greek explicit for 1 Corinthians has "ΕΓΡΑ ΑΠΟ ΦΙΛΙΠΠΩΝ ΜΑΚΕΔΟΝΙΑ" written in the space between "ΠΡΟΣ ΚΟΡΙΝΘΙΟΥΣ" and "ΕΠΛΗΡΩΘΗ." For Greek superscriptions and subscriptions of the Pauline corpus in various manuscripts, see Grover Payne, "A Textual Analysis, Critical Reconstruction, and Evaluation of the Superscriptions and Subscriptions to the Corpus Paulinum" (PhD diss., Southwestern Baptist Theological Seminary, 2002).

[73] Image of Codex Claromontanus courtesy the Bibliothéque Nationale de France. Grec. 107 f349v. https://gallica.bnf.fr/ark:/12148/btv1b84683111.

[74] Brooke Foss Westcott, *The Epistle to the Hebrews: The Greek Texts with Notes and Essays*, 2nd ed. (New York: Macmillan, 1892), xxvii:

> The absence of title in D2 is contrary to the usage of the MS; and it is also to be noticed that the colophon to the Epistle to Philemon gives no notice that any other epistle is to follow, as is done in other cases. In fact, the Epistle to Philemon is followed by the Stoichometry and the Epistle to the Hebrews has been added by the Scribe as an appendix to the archetype of the other Epistles.

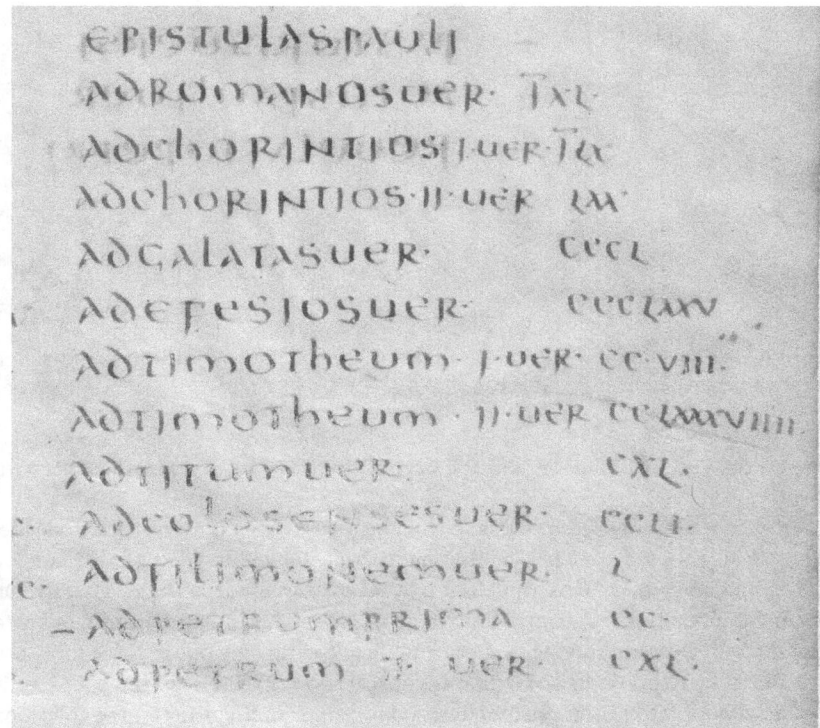

Figure 9 Catalogue of Scriptures in Codex Claromontanus. Used with permission of the Bibliothèque nationale de France.

Instead, it is thought to have circulated independently of Claromontanus and was only added later in the sixth century.[75] This means there were four blank pages

---

[75] The Gospels are listed in the typical Western order: Matthew, John, Mark, and Luke. The Pauline Epistles are listed in the atypical order of Romans, 1 and 2 Corinthians, Galatians, Ephesians, 1 and 2 Timothy, Titus, Colossians, and Philemon. Metzger notes,

> The absence of Philippians, 1 and 2 Thessalonians, and Hebrews is probably to be accounted for by an error of the scribe (or translator?) whose eye must have jumped from Εφεσιους to Εβραιους. That the scribe was not very attentive is shown by his continuing the list with the two epistles *to* Peter, followed then by James, 1, 2, and 3 John, and Jude. The list also includes the *Epistle of Barnabas*, the Shepherd of Hermas, the *Acts of Paul*, and the *Apocalypse of Peter*. Each of these has a short horizontal line next to them perhaps noting their lesser authority than the other works listed. [See appendix]. (*Textual Commentary*, 230)

"Ebenfalls im 6. Jahrhundert trug eine westliche Hand auf drei der leer gebliebenen Seiten zwischen Phlm und Hbr ein lateinishes Verzeichnis der biblischen Bucher mit Angaben uber ihre Stichenzahl ein" (Frede, *Altlateinische Paulus-Handschriften*, 25). See also Hatch, "Position of Hebrews," 137; Metzger, *Textual Commentary*, 230. Image of Codex Claromontanus courtesy the Bibliothèque Nationale de France. Grec. 107 f467v–486r. https://gallica.bnf.fr/ark:/12148/btv1b84683111.

Figure 10 Subscription to Philemon in Codex Claromontanus. Used with permission of the Bibliothèque nationale de France.

between the end of Philemon and the beginning of Hebrews when the codex was first produced.[76]

Another feature of Hebrews that distinguishes it from the rest of the collection is the various uses of red ink in the manuscript. Olive-brown is the default ink color throughout the manuscript. Red is used for three purposes: to identify Old Testament quotations, to identify the first three lines of each epistle, and in some of the embellishments around the explicits and incipits. The only one of these three uses to be found in Hebrews in a way that is consistent with the rest of the codex is the identification of the epistle's opening lines. Unlike the other epistles in the collection, red ink is not used in Hebrews to identify Old Testament quotations.[77] With regard to the embellishments, it has already been noted that Hebrews does not have an incipit following Philemon. However, red ink is used in the embellishment that separates Philemon's explicit from the text of Philemon. What is noteworthy in this instance is that the embellishment preceding Philemon's explicit is a thick band in contrast to the thin red line present with other explicits in the collection (Figure 10). This would appear to suggest a certain kind of closure or finality following Philemon that the other embellishments do not.[78]

---

[76] Trobisch suggests that the scribe originally intended to fill this space with the Epistle to the Laodiceans, which he knew from Latin manuscripts, but was unable to find a corresponding Greek text. Trobisch offers little evidence for this suggestion, but neither has any other plausible explanation for these blank pages been put forth to my knowledge. Trobisch, *First Edition*, 35. Schlossnikel raises this possibility as well but points out that there would have only been about half the space needed for both a Greek and Latin copy of Laodiceans. And if only the Latin was intended as the space suggests, why was it not included? Reinhard Franz Schlossnikel, *Der Brief an die Hebräer und das corpus Paulinum: eine linguistische "Bruchstelle" im codex Claromontanus (Paris, Bibliothèque Nationale Grec 107 + 107A + 107B) und ihre Bedeutung im Rahmen von Text- und Kanongeschichte* (Frieberg: Herder, 1991), 30.

[77] In addition to the use of red ink, quotations are also set off in the manuscript by indentation. This feature is shared by the quotations in Hebrews even while the use of red ink is not.

[78] Schlossnikel, *Der Brief an die Hebräer*, 23. Image of Codex Claromontanus courtesy the Bibliothèque Nationale de France. Grec. 107 f466v. https://gallica.bnf.fr/ark:/12148/btv1b84683111.

The final feature that sets Hebrews apart from the rest of Codex Claromontanus is its Latin translation. Reinhard Franz Schlossnikel analyzed 559 instances he deemed appropriate for comparison of the Greek and Latin texts and found that 113 of those instances demonstrated a special word choice in Hebrews as compared to the same word in the other Pauline Epistles. Based on these observations, he concluded that the translator of Hebrews was not the same individual who translated the rest of the Pauline collection into Latin.[79] The combination of all these features separates Hebrews as distinct from the rest of the writings in Codex Claromontanus even as they are bound together in a single volume. The treatment of Hebrews in Codex Claromontanus is consistent with what one might expect from an ancient editor of Paul's letters who was uncertain about the relationship between the Epistle to the Hebrews and the *corpus Paulinum*.

The Competing Traditions Regarding Hebrews in Codex Fuldensis

The hesitation concerning Hebrews' authorship exhibited in Codex Claromontanus is also manifested in the earliest complete Latin Vulgate manuscript of the New Testament, Codex Fuldensis. Hebrews appears at the end of the Pauline corpus after Philemon in Fuldensis as it does in Claromontanus. Although the paratextual features of Fuldensis do not separate Hebrews from the rest of Paul's letters as they do in Claromontanus, Fuldensis does include materials that attest to competing traditions regarding Hebrews' relationship to the *corpus Paulinum*. The presence of these competing traditions in Fuldensis further support the hypothesis that Hebrews' position at the end of the Paul's letters is an editorial decision that represents uncertainty about the epistle's relationship to the Pauline corpus.

Produced in 546 by Victor of Capua, Fuldensis includes a wealth of interesting features; the most relevant of these for the present study is the introductory prologue known as the *Primum Quaeritur (PQ)*.[80] The *PQ* is thought to have been created by Rufinus of Syria as a part of the translation that later came to be known as the Vulgate.[81] In his introduction of Paul's letters, Rufinus acknowledges the controversy concerning the Pauline authorship of Hebrews and sides decisively for including it

---

[79] He thereby also concluded that Hebrews had circulated independently from the rest of the collection at some earlier time in its development. I have already argued that there is no conclusive evidence that Hebrews circulated independently in Greek. Of course, that does not mean that it could not have done so for a time in Latin. I think it is more likely, as I will argue below, that Hebrews was excluded from the initial translation of the Pauline corpus into Latin. When it was later reincorporated at the end of the Pauline collection, as it is here in Claromontanus, I see no reason to assume that it was incorporated from an independent translation of Hebrews as a solitary document. Given the evidence surveyed throughout this chapter, it seems more likely that the scribe who wished to add Hebrews to his Latin edition of Paul had to translate Hebrews from a Greek edition of Paul rather from a Greek copy of Hebrews alone. Schlossnikel, *Der Brief an die Hebräer*, 122–4.

[80] It includes the oldest Latin harmony of the Gospels, canon tables, a collection of Paul's letters that includes Laodiceans, and numerous prologues, *argumenta*, and capitula. H. A. Houghton, *The Latin New Testament: A Guide to Its Early History, Texts, and Manuscripts* (Oxford: Oxford University Press, 2016), 256.

[81] Hermann Josef Frede, *Epistulae Ad Thessalonicenses Timotheum Titum Philemonem Hebraeos* (Frieberg: Herder, 1975), 42–3.

among Paul's writings, arguing that Paul did not attach his name to it so as not to prejudice his Jewish audience against it.[82] Rufinus does not stop at merely arguing for the inclusion of Hebrews as an authentic Pauline letter but goes on to argue that it is the very apex, the capstone, of Pauline thought. The Pauline corpus, in Rufinus' opinion, has not been arranged by the length of the letters, a distinction between churches and the "Hebrews," or any concern about Hebrews' authenticity. Instead, he states, Hebrews has been placed as the last of Paul's public letters (thereby exhibiting knowledge concerning the placement of Hebrews after 2 Thessalonians) purely out of pedagogical concerns because it is the most mature of the Pauline Epistles. One can only read Hebrews after progressing through the spiritually lower writings of the other epistles.[83] Rufinus has essentially substituted one well-known organizational principle (pedagogical) operative in ancient authorial editions for another (authenticity) in order to justify Hebrews' position in the corpus. By doing so, he has radically transformed the meaning of Hebrews' position in the corpus without changing the position itself.

Although Rufinus is adamant about the Pauline authorship of Hebrews, his own argument for this position acknowledges the well-known objections against it. Rufinus' arguments for the authenticity of Hebrews thus become further evidence of its questionable status among Latin editions of Paul's letters. Such suspicions are further confirmed by the position of Hebrews in Codex Fuldensis. The actual arrangement of the Pauline corpus in Codex Fuldensis places Hebrews after Philemon, the position more typical of the Latin tradition, despite Rufinus' placement of Hebrews after 2 Thessalonians in the *PQ* and his insistence that Hebrews really is Pauline. Therefore,

---

[82] John Wordsworth and Henry Julius White, *Nouum Testamentum Latine, Secundum Editionem Sancti Hieronymi* (London: Simon Wallenerg, 1911), 1–5:

> Epistulam sane quae ad Hebraeos scribitur quidam Pauli non esse contendunt, eo quod non sit eius nomine titulata, et propter sermonis stilique distantiam, sed aut Barnabae iuxta Tertullianum aut Lucae iuxta quosdam uel certe Clementis discipuli apostolorum et episcopi Romanae ecclesiae post apostolos ordinati. Quibus respondendum est: si propterea Pauli non erit quia eius non habet nomen, ergo nec alicuius erit quia nullius nomine titulatur; quod si absurdam est, ipsius magis esse credenda est quae tanto doctrinae suae fulget eloquio. Sed quoniam apud Hebraeorum ecclesias quasi destructor legis falsa suspicione habebatur, uoluit tacito nomine de figuris legis et ueritate Christi reddere rationem, ne odium nominis fronte praelati utilitatem excluderet lectionis. Non est sane mirum si eloquentior uideatur in proprio id est hebraeo quam in peregrino id est graeco, quo ceterae epistulae sunt scriptae sermone.

> Some men, however, contend that the letter, which is written to the Hebrews, is not Paul's, for the reason that it is not entitled with his name, and due to the discrepancy of wording and style, but that it is either Barnabas's according to Tertullian, or Luke's according to some others, or surely Clement's, a disciple of the apostles and bishop of the Roman Church, who was ordained after the apostles. To these it is necessary to respond: now then, if it is not Paul's because it does not have his name, it is nobody's because it is entitled with no name. But if this is absurd, that which shines with such eloquence of his own doctrine, ought all the more to be believed to be his. But since among the assemblies of the Hebrews by false suspicion he was thought of as a destroyer of the law, he wished to narrate the relationship of the example of the law and the truth of Christ without mentioning his name lest the hatred of his name displayed in front exclude the utility of reading. It is certainly not surprising, if he seems more eloquent in his own [language], i.e. Hebrew, than in a foreign one, i.e. Greek, the language in which the other letters are written. (Scherbenske, *Canonizing Paul*, 187)

[83] Scherbenske, *Canonizing Paul*, 191.

Codex Fuldensis has preserved evidence of competing traditions about the Pauline authorship of Hebrews within its pages. Victor, the creator of this edition of Paul's letters, is clearly aware of the tradition that Hebrews was authored by Paul as that tradition was repeated by Rufinus and preserved in the very pages of this edition. Nevertheless, Victor chose to imitate those manuscripts that placed Hebrews at the end of the Pauline corpus, thereby calling into question that very tradition.

Codex Claromontanus and Codex Fuldensis, the earliest Latin editions of Paul's letters, both place Hebrews at the end of the Pauline corpus. The treatment of Hebrews in these Latin manuscripts stands in sharp contrast to the placement of Hebrews in Greek editions of Paul's letters, which frequently placed Hebrews after 2 Thessalonians. The principles of ancient editorial practice outlined above suggest that the placement of Hebrews at the end of the Pauline corpus was an editorial decision that indicated questions about Hebrews' authorship. This conclusion is reinforced by several other features of these manuscripts, which also attest to potential questions about the authenticity of Hebrews and its relationship to the *corpus Paulinum* in the Latin tradition. Although these manuscripts exhibit hesitancy about the Pauline authorship of Hebrews, their editors were also aware of traditions that regarded Hebrews' as Pauline, an awareness that likely prevented the complete exclusion of Hebrews from these collections. Hebrews' position in these Latin manuscripts was likely an editorial compromise that resulted from two competing tradition regarding Hebrews' authorship.

Conclusions

Ancient editorial practice provides a particularly illuminating context for evaluating the reception of the Epistle to the Hebrews in the Greek and Latin manuscript tradition. The majority of surviving manuscripts that include Hebrews indicate that it was reproduced as a part of an edition of Paul's letters, and there is no surviving manuscript in which Hebrews is known to have been reproduced apart from such an edition. Even the fourth- and fifth-century pandect bibles that roughly resemble the canon of Athanasius attest to the inclusion of Paul's letters not as individual works but as a previously established collection. Although a thorough evaluation of these larger collections of scripture is well beyond the parameters of the current work, a cursory study suggests that even these large codices were not prepared with the category of canon as their guiding principle. They exhibit the same characteristics of ancient editorial practice observed in smaller collections, presenting themselves as a kind of edition of editions. Furthermore, these pandect bibles did not become the norm in the reproduction of Christian scriptures after they first appeared. On the contrary, the vast majority of Christian scriptures continued to be reproduced in smaller collections well beyond the fourth century. Therefore, the most common material reproduction and reception of the Epistle to the Hebrews throughout early Christianity was as a part of the *corpus Paulinum*. There is little, if any, evidence to suggest that those responsible for the reproduction of Hebrews had any concern about its canonical status and quite a lot of evidence to suggest that the reproduction of this epistle was guided by the editorial principles that were commonly applied to other collections in antiquity.

The principles for creating an edition in antiquity also help to explain the significance of the various positions that Hebrews occupies in Greek and Latin manuscripts. Greek editions of Paul's letters exhibit many of the same principles of organization present in the editions of other letter collections in antiquity. These organizing principles highlight that the placement of Hebrews in Greek editions of Paul's letters in the third through sixth centuries reflect a belief in the Pauline authorship of Hebrews among Greek speaking Christians. Those same editorial principles also attest to the significance of Hebrews' position in the two earliest Latin manuscripts that include Paul's letters. Whereas the early Greek editions of Paul place Hebrews securely within the corpus of Paul's writings, Codex Claromontanus and Codex Fuldensis both place Hebrews at the end of the Pauline corpus, a position typically reserved for works of questionable status in the creation of an edition. This position, along with a number of other distinctive features in these two codices, indicates questions about Hebrews' authorship and its relationship to the *corpus Paulinum* in the Latin manuscript tradition. The reason for this correlation between the relationship of Hebrews to the Pauline corpus and the language in which that corpus was reproduced is the subject of the next chapter.

5

Translating Paul: The Role of Latinity in the Reception of Hebrews

Introduction

Ancient editorial practices highlight the significant difference in receptions of Hebrews in the manuscript tradition; the earliest surviving Greek editions of the Pauline corpus represent Hebrews as one of Paul's letters by placing it securely within the *corpus Paulinum* whereas the earliest surviving Latin editions of Paul's letters raise questions about Hebrews' association with Paul by placing it at the end of the corpus. What prompted this suspicion regarding the Pauline authorship of Hebrews among Latin editors, especially when its association with Paul had been so firmly established among Greek editors? The initial translation of the *corpus Paulinum* into Latin, I argue, did not include Hebrews. As a result, it seems likely to conclude that Latin-speaking Christians who encountered these early Latin editions of Paul that did not include Hebrews had no reason to associate the treatise with Paul. This likely remained the case until a wider push toward Latinity in the imperial administration of the fourth century, which included both a broad effort to universalize Christianity and a corresponding rise in imperial patronage for Christian book production.[1] Seeking to systematize Latin editions of Paul in consultation with Greek editions, fourth-century editors and translators needed to make a decision: should Hebrews be included in the Pauline corpus or not? This comparison between Greek and Latin editions of the *corpus Paulinum* was likely the catalyst for the kinds of editorial decisions preserved by later bilingual and Latin copies of Hebrews.[2]

---

[1] Andrew James Carriker, *The Library of Eusebius of Caesarea* (Leiden: Brill, 2003), 16; Anthony Grafton and Megan Hale Williams, *Christianity and the Transformation of the Book: Origen, Eusebius, and the Library of Caesarea* (Cambridge, MA: Belknap Press of Harvard University Press, 2008), 13–21; Jennifer Knust and Tommy Wasserman, *To Cast the First Stone: The Transmission of a Gospel Story* (Princeton, NJ: Princeton University Press, 2018), 191.

[2] The manuscript evidence postdates the era in which these changes first occurred. Nevertheless, scribes were generally conservative, copying what they found in their exemplars, so what one sees in, for example, a ninth-century manuscript may well reflect a decision made much earlier. D. C. Parker, *An Introduction to the New Testament Manuscripts and Their Texts* (New York: Cambridge University Press, 2008), 151–4.

Latin and Greek were the most commonly utilized languages in the Roman Empire, though certainly many other languages were spoken in specific localities as well. Latin may be considered the principal language of Rome to the extent that certain legal documents could only be produced in Latin.[3] However, there was no coordinated, empire-wide effort on the part of Rome to impose Latin on its inhabitants. On the contrary, Greek functioned as the *lingua franca* in large portions of the empire, and, even in locations where Latin was most commonly spoken, Greek was held in high regard among educated Romans.[4] Although it would be overly simplistic to regard Latin as the language of bureaucracy and Greek as the language of arts and literature, the Greek language did retain an exceptional status, even among the Romans, while Latin was sometimes used to symbolize Roman power.[5] The relationship between these two languages among the literate elite is best understood as "dynamic rather than mechanical," as J. N. Adams points out, "in the sense that it was related to the relationships being negotiated on particular occasions between writer/speaker and addressee."[6] This dynamic relationship between Greek and Latin provides the linguistic context in which the earliest translations of Hebrews and the Pauline corpus were completed.

The Omission of Hebrews from the Initial Translation of the *Corpus Paulinum*

A direct comparison of the earliest Greek and Latin editions of Paul's letters may give the impression that Latin editors of Paul simply demoted Hebrews to the end of the corpus. Yet another conclusion is possible: the inclusion of Hebrews after Philemon in the two earliest Latin editions of Paul's letters may well have involved a *promotion* of Hebrews relative to its place, or lack thereof, in previous Latin editions of the Pauline corpus. That is, one plausible explanation for the difference in Hebrews' position in Greek and Latin manuscripts is an initial omission of Hebrews from an early translation of the *corpus Paulinum* into Latin. The Epistle to the Hebrews was simply absent from Latin editions of the Pauline corpus, I propose, until efforts aimed at uniformity led Latin

---

[3] These documents were required in Latin even if the person requiring the documents did not know Latin. After 212, wills were allowed to be written in Greek. J. N. Adams, *Bilingualism and the Latin Language* (New York: Cambridge University Press, 2002), 758.

[4] Felix Racine, "Servius' Greek Lessons," in *Learning Latin and Greek from Antiquity to the Present*, ed. Elizabeth P. Archibald, William Brockliss, and Jonathan Gnoza (Cambridge: Cambridge University Press, 2015), 52.

[5] Adams, Bilingualism and the Latin Language, 757.

[6] Ibid., 754, 761:

> First, lower-class Greeks at Rome treated Latin as the language of bureaucracy and Greek as the language of the family … Or to put it another way, there was a tendency at least among administrators in Egypt to define Greek as the language of culture but Latin as the language of political dominance … Finally, in the archive of Tiberianus, though Terentianus up to a point uses both languages for the same purposes to the same addressee, he does seem to have been treating Greek as the bureaucratic language of civil administration, and Latin as the family language. … Thus the relative status and functions of the two languages were constantly shifting according to the circumstances.

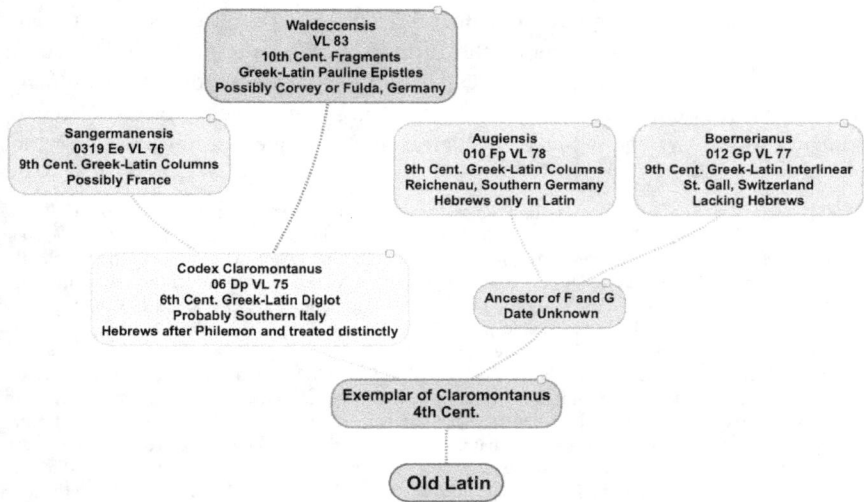

Figure 11 Bilingual Editions of Paul.

editors to consult Greek editions of Paul, which included Hebrews. The placement of Hebrews after Philemon was most likely a compromise—one consistent with the principles of ancient editorial practice—between the inclusion of Hebrews in Greek editions of the Pauline corpus and its absence from earlier Latin editions of the same.

The most compelling evidence for the absence of Hebrews from an early Latin translation of the Pauline corpus is provided by Codex Claromontanus and the other manuscripts that derived from its exemplar. The exemplar of Codex Claromontanus is no longer extant but is believed to have been a bilingual edition of Paul's letters created in the middle of the fourth century.[7] The absence of Hebrews from this exemplar is attested by its relationship to two other manuscripts, Codex Augiensis (010 F^p VL78) and Codex Boernerianus (012 G^p VL 77), both ninth-century Greek-Latin bilinguals.[8] As Hatch demonstrated in 1951, these two manuscripts share a common ancestor, which in turn derived from the exemplar of Claromontanus (Figure 11).[9]

---

[7] "The archetype (Z), a bilingual set out in sense-lines, was written in about 350" (D. C. Parker, *Codex Bezae: An Early Christian Manuscript and Its Text* [New York: Cambridge University Press, 1992], 67).

[8] Codices Sangermanensis (0319 Ee VL 76) and Waldeccensis (032 VL 83) are also copies of Codex Claromontanus even to the point of replicating some of its corrections and paratextual features. "The exemplar for the manuscript (VL 76) was VL 75, which was already missing 1 Corinthians 14:8–18: this was supplied from another Old Latin source. The Catalogus Claromontanus was also copied. Various corrections from VL 75 are incorporated (some erroneously), and there are occasional adjustments towards the Vulgate. VL 76 may have been the exemplar for VL 83." Waldeccensis consists of fragments of the Pauline Epistles copied in the second half of the tenth century, probably in Corvey or Fulda. H. A. Houghton, *The Latin New Testament: A Guide to Its Early History, Texts, and Manuscripts* (Oxford: Oxford University Press, 2016), 244–6.

[9] "This relationship is proved by the omission of certain passages in the Greek text of the two manuscripts and by many identical readings found in them" (William H. P. Hatch, "On the Relationship of Codex Augiensis and Codex Boernerianus of the Pauline Epistles," *Harvard Studies in Classical Philology*

Hebrews is missing entirely from Boernerianus (VL77) and exists only in Latin in Augiensis (VL78). Furthermore, the Latin of Augiensis is primarily Vulgate in character while Boernerianus is of the Old Latin text type.[10] Thus, one may reasonably deduce that the common ancestor of Boernerianus and Augiensis lacked Hebrews, which is why it was also omitted in Boernerianus.[11] Augiensis, on the other hand,

---

60 [1951]: 187). See also Eldon Jay Epp, *Perspectives on New Testament Textual Criticism: Collected Essays, 1962–2004* (Leiden: Brill, 2005), 622–3; Bruce M. Metzger, *The Early Versions of the New Testament: Their Origin, Transmission, and Limitations* (Oxford: Oxford University Press, 1977), 319; David Trobisch, "The Need to Discern Distinctive Editions of the New Testament in the Manuscript Tradition," in *The Textual History of the Greek New Testament: Changing Views in Contemporary Research*, ed. Klaus Wachtel and Michael W. Holmes (Boston: Brill, 2012), 45.

[10] Hatch, "Codex Augiensis and Codex Boernerianus," 191.

[11] Codex Boernerianus was produced in St. Gall, just 50 km from Reichenau, the origin site of Augiensis. The text of this common exemplar was rearranged in Boernerianus, however, so that Greek ran across the page while Latin glosses were placed above each Greek word. This interlinear format appears to have been an innovation in manuscript production for the purposes of learning Greek for which no evidence exists prior to the ninth century. Two other interlinears were also produced at St. Gall around the same time: Codex Sangallensis (037 VL 27), a Greek-Latin interlinear of the four Gospels, and the Basel Psalter. Codex Sangallensis is noteworthy in its treatment of the pericope adulterae.

> Consequently, of the thirteen Latin manuscripts with a mixed or predominantly Vulgate text in John extant in this portion of the Gospel—VL 7, 9A, 11A, 12, 15, 27, 29, 30, 33, 34, 35, 47, 48—all except VL 27, Codex Sangallensis (interlinearis) 48, include the pericope adulterae in a Vulgate form. Sangallensis, however, is a Greek Gospel manuscript (Gregory-Aland 037) copied in the West with interlinear Latin text. The scribe supplied John 8:12 right after 7:52 (fol. 348r), but then stopped after λέγων and left the rest of the page blank. The text commences again on the fourth line of the next page where he repeats the first words of 8:12. He thus left a space for the pericope, which was probably missing from his Greek exemplar but present in the Latin exemplar used for his translation. (Knust and Wasserman, *To Cast the First Stone*, 230)

The Psalter represents the only portion of biblical text that maintained an unbroken tradition of bilingual reproduction throughout the middle ages. This unique property of Psalter manuscripts demonstrates just how little demand there was for bilingual manuscripts in this time period while also highlighting how the familiarity of the Psalter made it an ideal text for those who did wish to learn Greek.

> The first important text the students read was the Psalter, from which they imbibed both spiritual and educational nourishment. This first and deep study of the Psalms remained with the students the rest of their lives. Those few who went on to become authors found that verses from the Psalms came to mind involuntarily when they wrote. The Psalter is the most frequently cited biblical book in Carolingian writings. (John J. Contreni, "The Carolingian Renaissance," in *Renaissances before the Renaissance: Cultural Revivals of Late Antiquity and the Middle Ages*, ed. Warren T. Treadgold [Stanford: Stanford University Press, 1984], 66–7; Walter Berschin, *Greek Letters and the Latin Middle Ages: From Jerome to Nicholas of Cusa* [Washington, DC: Catholic University of America Press, 1988], 39)

> The monastery of St. Gall took a leading part in the transmission of these texts. Of the thirty-two Psalters listed by Allgeier, four were copied at St. Gall, one served as a model for later St. Gall recensions, and five derive from St. Gall prototypes. In other words, nearly one-third of surviving Greek-Latin Psalters can be connected with the monastery. Of the nine bilingual New Testament manuscripts, three were copied at St. Gall and one at the neighboring monastery of Reichenau (from a prototype shared with St. Gall). The total figures are provisional, since more bilingual texts from elsewhere in Europe are sure to be identified in the future. But there is already enough evidence to point to a considerable interest on the part of St. Gall scholars in the Greek text of the Bible. (Bernice M. Kaczynski, *Greek in the Carolingian Age: The St. Gall Manuscripts* [Cambridge, MA: Medieval Academy of America, 1988], 77)

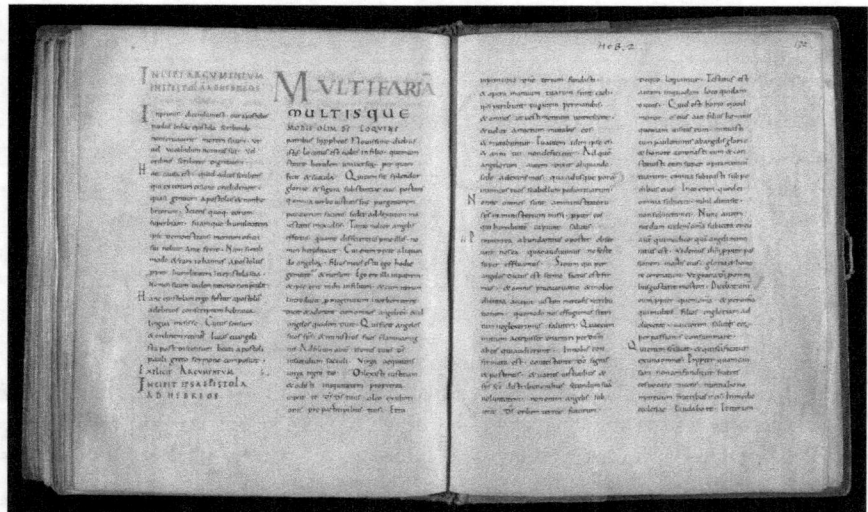

Figure 12 Prologue and Beginning of Hebrews in Codex Augiensis. Used with permission of the Wren Library, Cambridge.

included Hebrews because it relied only on the Greek text of this common ancestor for the rest of the Pauline corpus (excluding Hebrews) while utilizing a Vulgate copy of the Pauline Epistles, which included Hebrews after Philemon for its Latin text (Figure 12).[12] If Hebrews was missing from the common ancestor of Boernerianus and Augiensis, as seems likely, then one may also reasonably conclude that it was missing from the exemplar of Claromontanus since the common ancestor of these two ninth-century manuscripts also derived from this exemplar.[13]

The absence of Hebrews from the initial archetype for this tree of bilingual manuscripts also helps to explain the many distinguishing features of Hebrews in Claromontanus discussed in the previous chapter. The lack of incipit for Hebrews, the distinctive use of red ink, and the pages originally left blank between Philemon and Hebrews all visually signal the inclusion of a work previously excluded. It seems that the editor of this bilingual edition of Paul's letters had to navigate two competing traditions concerning the relationship of Hebrews to the Pauline corpus: the Greek

---

[12] Image of beginning of Hebrews in Codex Augiensis courtesy The Master and Fellows of Trinity College, Cambridge. Cambridge, Trinity College, MS B 17.1, f131v. https://mss-cat.trin.cam.ac.uk/manuscripts/uv/view.php?n=B.17.1&n=B.17.1#?c=0&m=0&s=0&cv=0&xywh=-1785%2C-168%2C6008%2C3354.

[13] Herren notes the distinct purpose in the production of these medieval bilinguals as opposed to their late antique counterparts. Unlike earlier bilingual manuscripts that may have been produced for use in liturgical settings, these later bilinguals were produced "exclusively for scholarly purposes, chief among them being biblical exegesis." Michael W. Herren, "Pelasgian Fountains: Learning Greek in the Early Middle Ages," in *Learning Latin and Greek from Antiquity to the Present*, ed. Elizabeth P. Archibald, William Brockliss, and Jonathan Gnoza (Cambridge: Cambridge University Press, 2015), 68; Kaczynski, *Greek in the Carolingian Age*, 95.

Table 2 Latin Translations of Hebrews

Manuscript	Text Type	Text of Hebrews
Codex Claromontanus	Old Latin (and Greek)	Independent Translation
Codex Boernerianus	Old Latin	Omitted
Codex Augiensis	Vulgate	Vulgate
AN Paul VL 89	Old Latin similar to Claromontanus	Pre-Vulgate similar to Complutensis Primus (VL 109)
Freising Fragments	Old Latin	Independent Translation

editions that placed Hebrews after 2 Thessalonians and the earliest Latin editions that omitted Hebrews entirely. Hebrews' position and distinctive treatment at the end of Codex Claromontanus might be reasonably expected from an editor forced to reconcile these competing traditions; Hebrews is included in the corpus while simultaneously being distinguished from the other works included in it.

Hebrews' absence from this initial translation of the Pauline corpus into Latin is further attested by the Anonymous Commentary on Paul (AN Paul VL 89). The Commentary appears to have been composed in Rome in the fourth century and is preserved in a ninth-century Carolingian minuscule manuscript. The quotations of the Pauline Epistles in this commentary have a text similar to Codex Claromontanus except in the case of Hebrews, which has a pre-vulgate form similar to Complutensis primus (VL 109), a tenth-century Latin Vulgate Bible, as Hugh Houghton has shown.[14] This suggests that the commentator had an Old Latin text of Paul's letters at his disposal but had to turn to another source in order to quote from the Epistle to the Hebrews. The omission of Hebrews from the earliest Latin editions of the *corpus Paulinum* is also detected in the various surviving Latin translations of Hebrews (Table 2). The fact that Hebrews survives in a variety of Old Latin translations stands in contrast to the current scholarly consensus regarding the translation of the rest of the Pauline corpus; the vast majority of existing Old Latin manuscripts of the Pauline letters aside from Hebrews appear to derive from a single translation.[15] In contrast to the single translation that serves as the source for the rest of Paul's letters, Reinhard Franz Schlossnikel's analysis of Hebrews in Codex Claromontanus demonstrated that Hebrews was translated by a different person than the rest of this Pauline collection.[16] Additionally, the Freising Fragments, sixth-century fragments of the Pauline and the Catholic Epistles, preserve an entirely separate branch of Hebrews' translation into Latin from that found in Claromontanus.[17] The existence of multiple Old Latin

---

[14] Houghton, *Latin New Testament*, 249.
[15] "Editors of Old and New Testament books in the Vetus Latina series have reached the conclusion that in each case a single Latin translation underlies all the surviving evidence for the Old Latin tradition. This does not remove the possibility that other translations were made at an early stage, but little if anything of these remains" (Houghton, *Latin New Testament*, 12).
[16] Reinhard Franz Schlossnikel, *Der Brief an die Hebräer und das corpus Paulinum: eine linguistische "Bruchstelle" im codex Claromontanus (Paris, Bibliothèque Nationale Grec 107 + 107A + 107B) und ihre Bedeutung im Rahmen von Text- und Kanongeschichte* (Frieberg: Herder, 1991), 122–4.
[17] Houghton, *Latin New Testament*, 239; Metzger, *Early Versions*, 360.

translations of Hebrews in contrast to the single Old Latin translation of the Pauline collection proposed by scholars further suggests Hebrews' initial independence from that collection.

Hebrews' exclusion from an early Latin version of the Pauline corpus is also consistent with the patristic evidence observed in previous chapters. Clement and Origen, who would have likely encountered Hebrews within Greek editions of Paul's letters, regularly referred to Hebrews as Pauline. On the other hand, the Latin theologian Tertullian attributed the epistle to Barnabas, a possible indication that the Latin Pauline corpus in North Africa did not include Hebrews. Jerome's much later comments corroborate this narrative as well. He emphasized that Greek writers accepted Hebrews as Pauline while the Latins did "not receive it among the canonical Scriptures." Jerome, however, accepted it because earlier writers quoted it "as canonical and churchly."[18] Although Jerome combined ideas about the authorship of Hebrews and quotations of the epistle by earlier writers into a concept of canon that would have been foreign to those earlier writers, his description of Hebrews' reception is consistent with the rest of the evidence considered above: those who encountered the epistle in Greek counted it as Pauline while those who read it in Latin did not but both regarded it as a useful work.[19]

---

[18] *Epist.* 129; Edmon Gallagher and John Meade, *The Biblical Canon Lists from Early Christianity: Texts and Analysis* (New York: Oxford University Press, 2017), 215:

> Illud nostris dicendum est, hanc epistulam, quae scribitur ad Hebraeos, non solum ab ecclesiis orientis sed ab omnibus retro ecclesiae graeci sermonis scriptoribus quasi Pauli apostoli suscipi, licet plerique eam uel Barnabae uel Clementis arbitrentur, et nihil interesse, cuius sit, cum ecclesiastici uiri sit et cotidie ecclesiarum lectione celebretur. quodsi eam latinorum consuetudo non recipit inter scripturas canonicas, nec graecorum quidem ecclesiae Apocalypsin Iohannis eadem libertate suscipiunt, et tamen nos utramque suscipimus nequaquam huius temporis consuetudinem sed ueterum scriptorum auctoritatem sequentes, qui plerumque utriusque abutuntur testimoniis, non ut interdum de apocryphis facere solent—quippe et gentilium litterarum raro utantur exemplis—, sed quasi canonicis et ecclesiasticis.

> The Epistle which is inscribed to the Hebrews is received not only by the churches of the East but also by all Church writers of the Greek language before our days, as of Paul the apostle, though many think that it is from Barnabas or Clement. And it makes no difference whose it is, since it is from a churchman, and is celebrated in the daily readings of the Churches. And if the usage of the Latins does not receive it among the canonical Scriptures, neither indeed do the same liberty do the Church of the Greeks receive the Revelation of John. And yet we receive both, in that we follow by no means the habit of today, but the authority of ancient writers, who for the most part quote each of them, not as they are sometimes to do the apocrypha, and even also as they rarely use the examples of secular books, but as canonical and churchly. (Metzger, *Early Versions*, 236; Patrick W. Skehan, "St. Jerome and the Canon of the Holy Scriptures," in *A Monument to St. Jerome: Essays On Some Aspects of His Life, Work, and Influence*, ed. Xavier Murphy [New York: Sheed and Ward, 1952], 269–70)

[19] The absence of Hebrews from the so-called Cheltenham canon, a Latin stichometric list that counts only thirteen letters of Paul, may also serve as evidence of Hebrews' omission from the earliest Latin editions of Paul, though there are many characteristics of Hebrews' omission from this document that remain unclear. Gallagher and Meade, *Biblical Canon Lists*, 188–93.

The Rise of Latinity

It therefore seems likely that the position of Hebrews at the end of the Pauline corpus was an editorial decision that attempted to reconcile two competing traditions about Hebrews' authorship: the early Greek manuscripts of Paul's letters that regarded Hebrews as Pauline and early Latin collections of Paul's letters that omitted Hebrews entirely. But why should these two competing traditions have been reconciled at all? One plausible explanation is that the rise of Latinity and the corresponding patronage of Christian book production produced a fresh encounter between Greek and Latin editions of Christian scriptures. The fourth century witnessed the ascension of the Latin language to a place of dominance that it had not previously held.[20] This rise in Latinity coincided with an increasing Christianization of the Roman Empire with the result that patronage was frequently directed toward those Christian scholars who could produce Latin editions of important Christian works originally composed in Greek.[21] The desire for Christian writings in Latin combined with the financial means to support such projects provides a plausible context for the production of Christian scriptures, which sought to reconcile differences between Greek and Latin editions.

The earliest evidence for the prominence of the Latin language among Christian writings is derived from North Africa. The account of the Scillitan Martyrs, seven North African Christians prosecuted in Carthage, provides the earliest Latin reference to the Pauline Letters.[22] Tertullian is the earliest Latin Christian author whose works survive in that language and the biblical quotations of Cyprian, the bishop of Carthage, provide the earliest evidence for a Latin translation of the New Testament.[23] Greek remained the primary language of Christian intellectuals throughout much of the rest of the empire into the third century, although there are some signs of Latin influence even outside of North Africa.[24] Knowledge of Greek declined quickly throughout

---

[20] Maura K. Lafferty, "Translating Faith from Greek to Latin: Romanitas and Christianitas in Late Fourth-Century Rome and Milan," *Journal of Early Christian Studies* 11, no. 1 (2003): 26. Berschin, *Greek Letters*, 48. Racine, "Servius' Greek Lessons," 53.

[21] Berschin, *Greek Letters*, 41–55; Megan Hale Williams, *The Monk and the Book: Jerome and the Making of Christian Scholarship* (Chicago: University of Chicago Press, 2006), 235.

[22] "Saturninus proconsul dixit: Quae sunt res in capsa uestra? Speratus dixit: Libri et epistulae Pauli uiri iusti" ["Saturninus the proconsul said: What are the objects in your carrying case? Speratus said: Books and letters of Paul, a righteous man"] (Houghton, *Latin New Testament*, 3).

[23] Only Tertullian's Latin works survive though he also knew Greek, and many of his biblical citations may be his own translation. At the very least, they do not appear to represent a fixed form of the Latin bible. The biblical quotations of Cyprian, on the other hand, exhibit a consistency that suggests a fixed version of the Latin text. Houghton, *Latin New Testament*, 6–9. Matthew V. Novenson, "The Pauline Epistles in Tertullian's Bible," *Scottish Journal of Theology* 68, no. 4 (2015): 471–83; Thomas P. O'Malley, *Tertullian and the Bible: Language, Imagery, Exegesis*, Latinitas Christianorum Primaeva (Utrecht: Dekker & Van de Vegt, 1967).

[24] Philip Burton, "The Latin Version of the New Testament," in *The Text of the New Testament in Contemporary Research: Essays on the Status Quaestionis*. 2nd ed., ed. Bart D. Ehrman and Michael William Holmes (Boston: Brill, 2014), 167–200; Jennifer Knust, "Latin Versions of the Bible," in *New Interpreter's Dictionary of the Bible* (Nashville: Abingdon Press, 2006) 5:765–69.

> Even so, there is also evidence for the use of Latin at this time. In the Greek text of the Shepherd of Hermas, the Latin word *statio* is borrowed as a way to speak of 'fasting'. Jerome identifies Victor, bishop of Rome in the 190s, and his contemporary Apollonius as 'Latins',

Latin-dominant areas in the fourth century; Greek instruction would never disappear entirely, however, as it continued to be an important language among educated elites. With the exception of Southern Italy, however, Greek was never again utilized as widely as it had been in the first few centuries of the Common Era. In his edict of 367 concerning the pay rates for rhetors and grammarians, for example, the emperor Gratian expressed some doubt that a grammarian properly trained in Greek could be found to fill posts in Trier.[25] In the churches at Milan and Rome, Latin was adopted for the Eucharistic prayers thereby "establishing Latin as *the* language of the liturgy."[26] Even in elite contexts where Greek continued to be taught, it was utilized to teach an ideal form of Latin. As Felix Racine points out, Servius' commentary on Virgil, written in Rome around the year 400, exemplifies the vision of a Latin grammarian who reads Greek and acknowledges the debt of Latin to Greek literature but is mostly interested in utilizing that knowledge to expound on the intricacies of Latin literature.[27] Augustine, who mentions how poor his own knowledge of Greek was before developing it further later in life, employed his limited Greek knowledge to similar ends.[28] With Greek knowledge waning, the demand for Greek literary texts to be translated into Latin grew steadily.[29]

This shift toward Latinity in the West was not, however, a mere accident of history that happened to shape Christian identity. Christian leaders made intentional choices in the shift toward Latinity as a way of constructing a unified Christian, Latin identity.

---

   implying that their theological treatises and writings against the Montanists may have been in Latin. (Houghton, *Latin New Testament*, 15)

[25] Robert A. Kaster, "A Reconsideration of 'Gratian's School-Law,'" *Hermes* 112, no. 1 (1984): 110–14. Racine, "Servius' Greek Lessons," 53.

[26] Lafferty, "Translating Faith from Greek," 22. However, on the Greek Odes sung by Latin-speaking Christians long after Greek had largely disappeared from daily use, see Jennifer Knust and Tommy Wasserman, "The Biblical Odes and the Text of the Christian Bible: A Reconsideration of the Impact of Liturgical Singing on the Transmission of the Gospel of Luke," *Journal of Biblical Literature* 133, no. 2 (2014): 341–65.

[27] Racine, "Servius' Greek Lessons," 55, 62:

   We should then minimize the extent of Servius' Greek culture acquired at first hand. But this is not to say that he does not care about Greek literature and the Greek language. The sheer number of Greek technical terms of grammar or rhetoric found in his commentary, as well as his general understanding of the Greek citations he reproduces confirms that he read Greek himself. More importantly, Servius and his contemporaries could not ignore Virgil's debt to Greek literature, a debt that was extended by some late Roman scholars to the whole Latin language ... All in all, Servius is interested in Greek language only to help him define good Latin practice, and this definition often takes the form of an opposition between Greek and Latin.

[28] He describes his study of Greek as "very little, in fact scarcely at all" (perparum assecutus sum et prope nihil). Contra litteras Petilliani 2.38.91; Racine, Servius' Greek Lessons," 53.

[29] Lafferty, "Translating Faith from Greek," 26:

   In the fourth century, the balance between the two languages shifted perceptibly. Greek continued to be the major language of learning, particularly in the realms of philosophical and theological debate. While the study of Greek in the West, at least among the elite classes, certainly does not disappear, the demand for and number of translations into Latin of major religious, theological, and philosophical works (Christian and non-Christian) in Greek grew rapidly. Many Latin-speakers were either unwilling or unable to tackle these works in the original. At the same time, the association between Latin and empire was strengthened under Diocletian, Constantine, and the later emperors of the fourth century.

Constantine replicated Roman institutions in Constantinople and made Latin the language of his official documents and speeches.³⁰ Eusebius reports that Constantine spoke in Latin in his official capacity during the opening ceremony at the Council of Nicea though his audience was Greek. When he greeted individuals in person, however, he spoke to them in their own language.³¹ Damasus of Rome, perhaps the first bishop of that city to aim to fashion himself as a member of the Roman aristocracy, portrayed Christianity as the natural descendant of Roman preeminence. Like the purveyors of Roman identity before him, Damasus represented Rome as the greatest city on earth but that greatness, he asserted, was founded in the ministries of Peter and Paul in the city; their ministry, he suggested, surpassed that of the heroes of Roman literature.³² Ambrose, bishop of Milan, similarly aligned himself with Rome as a vanguard of Christian identity. He further cemented the connection between Christian identity and *Romanitas* by characterizing his Christian "Arian" opponents as non-Latin barbarians.³³ Christian leaders in the Latin West repeatedly chose to identify

---

³⁰ Ibid., 27.
³¹ *Vit. Const.* 3.13.1-2; Eusebius, *Life of Constantine*, trans. Averil Cameron and Stuart G. Hall (Oxford: Clarendon Press, 1999), 127:

> When he had spoken these words in Latin, with someone interpreting, he made way for the leaders of the Council to speak. Some then began to accuse their neighbors, while the others defended themselves and made countercharges. A great many proposals were made by each side, and there was at first much controversy. The Emperor listened to all, without resentment, and received the proposals with patient flexibility; he took up what was said by each side in turn, and gently brought together those whose attitudes conflicted. He addressed each person gently, and by speaking Greek for he was not ignorant of that language either he made himself pleasant and agreeable, persuading some and shaming others with his words, praising those who were speaking well, urging all towards agreement, until he had brought them to be of one mind and one belief on all the matters in dispute.

³² Damasus set up a monumental inscription at the traditional burial site of the apostles. Lafferty translates it as follows:

> You, who seek the names of Peter and Paul, should know that the saints once lived here. The East sent the disciples; we willingly admit it. But, because of the merit of their blood and because they followed Christ through the stars, they sought the heavenly havens and the realms of the pious. Rome rather has earned the right to defend them as her own citizens. Let Damasus relate these things to your praise, o new stars.

Lafferty elaborates,

> His inscription honors them like the funerary elogia set up to celebrate the great citizens of Rome's past … it redeploys the language and imagery of traditional Latin literature. Not only does Damasus use Vergilian hexameters, but he also borrows a commonplace of classical literature, the emperor's apotheosis or ascent to heaven in the form of a star or constellation, to describe Christian resurrection. Thus Peter and Paul, like the Roman emperors before them, ascend to heaven and become new constellations. ("Translating Faith from Greek," 41–2)

Kristina Sessa also highlights the manner in which Roman household management served as a model for the early formation of the papacy. Kristina Sessa, *The Formation of Papal Authority in Late Antique Italy: Roman Bishops and the Domestic Sphere* (New York: Cambridge University Press, 2012).

³³ Lafferty, "Translating Faith from Greek," 56. McLynn highlights the extent to which Ambrose's treatises are actually aimed less at defeating these opponents in debate and more at impressing Emperor Gratian.

> But Ambrose chose not to engage in a point-by-point debate with his opponent. Perhaps he had only heard of Palladius' work at second hand … Preferring to take the offensive, he

Christianity with a concept of Latinitas or Romanitas as a way of creating a unified Christian identity in contrast to the non-Latin, barbarian world.

Yet this intentional shift toward Latinity did not result in a rejection of Greek literature. On the contrary, the decline of Greek knowledge in the West led to the translation of an enormous number of Greek works into Latin, demonstrating that a decline in Greek knowledge did not mean a decline in a desire for Greek literature. In fact, one might argue that the value of Greek literature was enhanced to a certain degree since this linguistic distance had helped to produce certain "classics" as the works that were worth translating for a broader audience.[34] The rise of Christian Latinity provided a context in which significant patronage could be directed toward the translation of "Christian classics" as well, thereby prompting a fresh encounter between Greek and Latin editions of Christian writings. Such translation projects provided Latin elites who were interested in performing their proficiency at "Greek letters" an opportunity to advance their own careers. In some instances, particular works of translation might be requested and funded by a patron while in other instances a scholar might tailor an existing project to a patron's interest or offer a scholarly project as a gift to a potential patron.[35] In any case, works of translation, like nearly all scholarly projects in late antiquity, were typically dependent upon and prompted by systems of patronage. The ability to fund, produce, consume, or collect such projects served to mark one as an elite member of Latin society.[36] The availability

---

embarked upon a series of fresh attacks on positions attributed to the Arians. The material was again drawn from various polemical sources, chiefly Athanasius, but this time the bishop's organizing hand is less in evidence: in the last two books particularly, the bulk of the text seems to have been transcribed almost directly from his sermons. Haste offers the most plausible explanation, as Ambrose strove to assemble as imposing a set of credentials as possible to present to the emperor. (Neil B. McLynn, *Ambrose of Milan: Church and Court in a Christian Capital* [Los Angeles: University of California Press, 1994], 119)

[34] "Learning to read is always a matter of learning to read something. Late ancient grammarians formed their discipline by teaching their students how to read the classics—or rather, by teaching their students how to read in a way that created classics" (Catherine M. Chin, *Grammar and Christianity in the Late Roman World* [Philadelphia: University of Pennsylvania Press, 2007], 11).

[35] Williams's description of Jerome's work provides an illustrative example.

Jerome often had to defer a cherished project in order to meet the demands of a correspondent. Occasionally, texts that he had already written, in accordance with his own pre-established research programs, could be pressed into service as gifts offered to patrons in recognition of their support. The prestige of the series of commentaries and translations for which he became known could justify their insertion into relations of exchange. But these cases were the exception. In general, Jerome's readers knew what they wanted him to write, and it was not what he had planned for. This was true of Jerome's exegetical writings, but even more so of his polemics: as in the cases we shall examine, many of Jerome's controversial works were written on another's initiative, not his own. (Williams, *Monk and the Book*, 247)

[36] Grafton and Williams, *Christianity and the Transformation*, 14:

The linkage of collection to production integrated libraries in the Roman world into an economy of gift exchange that connected literate elites across the Mediterranean. This economy involved the circulation of a variety of material objects, and also of social and political interventions. Within it, books could hold social and emotional charges that they rarely carry today, even when given as gifts. The book, in antiquity, was not a commodity, but had a status closer to that of a work of art—as Martial's positioning of the long list of books he includes in his *Apophoreta*, or *Holiday Gifts*, immediately before an even more

of patronage for the translation of Greek Christian writings into Latin thus served as an opportunity to reinforce the identity of those who produced and consumed them as both Latin and cultured.

Western Europe continued on roughly this same linguistic trajectory through late antiquity and into the Middle Ages; Greek knowledge had become the skill of an increasingly narrow segment of the populace. Eventually, the use of Latin itself became somewhat challenging since it was also no longer anyone's native language.[37] Latin was required for certain official functions in liturgy or government, but it had become decidedly a second language for those who learned it rather than their first.[38] A quip by a student of Greek is quoted by Walter Berschin to sum up the state of Greek and Latin knowledge in the early Middle Ages: "I would like to be Greek, my lady, although I am scarcely a Latin."[39] Of course, the retreat of Greek knowledge was not uniform across time or space. Certain locales remained bastions of bilingual learning at different times, including southern Italy in the sixth century and the monasteries founded by Irish missionaries in the ninth century, for example.[40] The context in which these bilingual learning centers existed, however, had shifted significantly from that of earlier centuries. Whereas Greek had once been the *lingua franca* for many inhabitants of the empire, outside of southern Italy, the study of Greek in much of the early Middle Ages was primarily undertaken to better understand the writings of scripture through some knowledge of the original language.

The Impact of Latinity on the Reproduction of Christian Scriptures

In an intellectual climate increasingly shaped by Christian institutions and patronage, the rise of Latinity and a corresponding interest in Greek translation projects naturally extended to Christian scriptures as well. Many Christian scriptures already existed in Latin translations prior to the fourth century and had already been utilized in Latin

> impressive list of objets d'art, implies. Books, like other costly gifts, traveled the Roman world from one member of the literate elite to another.

[37] Kaczynski, *Greek in the Carolingian Age*, 1:

> In the course of the preceding centuries people had become increasingly accustomed to using their own vernacular tongues for speech and the necessities of daily life. Latin - the language of religion, scholarship, and government - had to be taught in school. If a knowledge of Latin could be acquired only with effort, a knowledge of Greek was all the more elusive. There were few teachers of Greek, and there were few textbooks with which to study.

[38] There were, nevertheless, considerable resources expended in Latin instruction.

> All through the ninth century, Carolingian abbots and bishops repeated for their own congregations the prescriptions first announced by the kings and their advisers. Scholars emended ancient texts and wrote new works designed to undergird both the study of the liberal arts and sacred studies. Teams of scribes toiled in scriptoria, or writing centers, to produce manuscripts for their own libraries or for loan or donation to less fortunate libraries. The latinity of Carolingians authors improved. (Contreni, "Carolingian Renaissance," 65)

[39] Berschin, Greek Letters, 18.
[40] Ibid., 26.

Christian communities for quite some time. The fourth-century demand for new Latin translations of scripture was, therefore, probably not a matter of merely providing Latin translations where none previously existed.⁴¹ These scriptural translation projects were intertwined with the new systems of patronage available in a post-Constantinian context as well as with encounters with existing Latin editions; a fresh encounter with Greek editions provided an opportunity for both patrons and scholars to exhibit their cultured, Latin identity.⁴² Grammatical, philosophical, and rhetorical training prompted a return to Greek and thereby created a renewed interaction between Greek editions and Latin editors.⁴³ When such editors were faced with Greek and Latin editions that had developed out of their own contexts in the preceding centuries, they had to reconcile competing copies and decide, for example, which writings to include, the order in which to arrange them, and the layout of the text on the page. These editorial decisions are evident in the earliest surviving manuscript of Paul's letters with a Vulgate text type as well as in Greek-Latin bilingual manuscripts. As both late antique scholarship and surviving Greek-Latin diglot manuscripts show, interactions between Greek scholarship and Latin learning had an important impact on the Pauline corpus.

---

[41] Jerome and Augustine both complained about the existence of several Latin translations that do not agree with one another.

> For if the faith must be summoned from Latin copies, then to this they will respond: they are almost as diverse as the [number of] codices. But if truth ought to be sought from multiplicity, why do we not, by reverting back to the original Greek, correct them which either were edited poorly by bad translators or more perversely emended by reckless dolts or interpolated or changed by sleeping copyists? (Jerome, Epistula ad Damasum (Preface to the Four Gospels) NPNF 6.488)

"Qui enim scripturas ex hebrea in graecam uerterunt, numerari possunt, latini autem interpretes nullo modo. Vt enim cuique primis fidei temporibus in manus uenit codex graecus et aliquantum facultatis sibi utriusque linguae habere uidebatur, ausus est interpretari" (CCSL 32 42:21-26).

> They are able to be enumerated who have translated the scriptures from Hebrew into Greek; but not at all the Latin translators. For in the beginning of the faith whenever a Greek codex found its way into the hands of anyone and he seemed to have some faculty of his own tongue and the other, he ventured to translate it. (Augustine, Doctr. chr. 2.11.16; Eric W. Scherbenske, *Canonizing Paul: Ancient Editorial Practice and the Corpus Paulinum* [New York: Oxford University Press, 2013], 182; Knust and Wasserman, *To Cast the First Stone*, 216)

[42] Scherbenske, *Canonizing Paul*, 182:

> Such diversity, as Jerome intimated, threatened to undermine the unity of the faith predicated on these writings with the result that, in the face of theological disputes, their multiplicity could seriously compromise insistence upon unanimous church doctrine. Thus the revision of the OL texts at the end of the fourth century, which eventually became known as the Vulgate, was more than a scholastic enterprise undertaken to improve the Latin text, though it did do that: it also was an attempt to impose unity on the diversity of Latin manuscripts and to harmonize them with the Greek tradition. One of the aims of this effort was to foster theological unity.

[43] Eleanor Dickey, *Ancient Greek Scholarship: A Guide to Finding, Reading, and Understanding Scholia, Commentaries, Lexica, and Grammatical Treatises, from Their Beginnings to the Byzantine Period* (New York: Oxford University Press, 2007), 31–2; Chin, *Grammar and Christianity*, 40.

The Latin Revisions of Jerome and Rufinus

The translation of the Christian scriptures into Latin that would later come to be known as the Vulgate is commonly credited to Jerome, though he was not responsible for the whole of this translation. Bishop Damasus requested that Jerome make a new translation directly from Greek copies of the scriptures while also being mindful of the tradition of currently existing Latin translations.[44] Jerome describes his own translation philosophy as an attempt to represent the Greek text quite literally, following a word-to-word correspondence as closely as possible when translating scripture as opposed to the more dynamic method he would employ in the case of non-scriptural works.[45] After completing his translation of the Gospels, Jerome turned his attention to the Old Testament, a project that began with the Septuagint but eventually led him to utilize the Hebrew text as the basis for his translation.[46] This massive undertaking, as well as the task of defending it as a legitimate one, occupied Jerome's attention for much of the rest of his life, with the result that he never completed a new translation of the rest of the New Testament.[47] That Jerome was not responsible for the revision of the Pauline Epistles later received as the Vulgate is made evident by the dissimilarity between his own quotations of Paul and the Vulgate text of the epistles; he even criticizes manuscripts that contain what are now labeled "Vulgate readings" of Paul's letters. Jerome's opinion about Hebrews also differs from that preserved in the *Primum quaeritur* (*PQ*), the prologue to the Pauline Epistles preserved in later Vulgate manuscripts.[48] Clearly Jerome was not responsible for these translations; the translator is actually unknown, but Rufinus the Syrian has been proposed as a likely candidate. Rufinus was a close associate of Jerome and was also well known to Pelagius (according

---

[44] Andrew Cain, *The Letters of Jerome: Asceticism, Biblical Exegesis, and the Construction of Christian Authority in Late Antiquity* (Oxford: Oxford University Press, 2009), 52; Knust and Wasserman, *To Cast the First Stone*, 228; Stefan Rebenich, "Jerome: The 'Vir Trilinguis' and the 'Hebraica Veritas,'" *Vigiliae Christianae* 47, no. 1 (1993): 50–77; Williams, *Monk and the Book*, 65–6:

> Jerome must have had a sense of the controversial nature of his revision and even took measures in the preface to the work to insulate himself pre-emptively from criticism. He opens this preface by emphasizing Damasus' ultimate accountability for the project: "You force me to make a new work out of an old one" (novum opus facere me cogis ex veteri). He strategically places "novum" as the first word in order to cast the edition as a masterful innovation while at the same time affirming, with the forceful "cogis," that it was not undertaken presumptuously at his own initiative but rather at Damasus' prodding. Later in the preface he uses another strong verb of compulsion (iubes) to underscore yet again the point that Damasus was the impetus behind the work: "You who are the supreme bishop order that it be done" (tu qui summus sacerdos es fieri iubes).

[45] Scherbenske, Canonizing Paul, 186.
[46] "With the Hexapla at hand, he began an even more ambitious project – a fresh translation of the Septuagint into Latin but from the Hebrew rather than the Greek, together with intricate Biblical commentaries and a set of reference works designed to accompany his translations (Hebrews Names, the Book of Places, and Hebrews Questions)" (Knust and Wasserman, *To Cast the First Stone*, 229; Williams, *Monk and the Book*, 149).
[47] Jerome had to fend off many attacks of his translation and his decision to base it on the Hebrew text rather than the Greek. One of the more well-known incidents involved Jerome's translation of the word referring to the plant that provides shade for Jonah. His translation of this word as "ivy" rather than "gourd" led at least one prominent Roman opponent to accuse him of sacrilege. Stefan Rebenich, *Jerome* (London: Routledge, 2002), 57.
[48] Scherbenske, *Canonizing Paul*, 184.

to Augustine and Marius Mercator). Such a connection is significant since Pelagius' commentary on the Pauline Epistles is generally held to be the earliest witness to the revision of these epistles later known as the Vulgate.[49] Rufinus' responsibility for this revision of Paul's letters is further supported by the resemblance it bears to his citations of Paul in *Liber de Fide*.[50]

The specific nature of Rufinus' revision of the Pauline Epistles suggests that he consulted Greek as well as Latin copies. Although no writings survive that describe Rufinus' methodological aims, a close study of the text itself reveals a relatively strict adherence to Greek readings, particularly Alexandrian ones, even to the point of replicating Greek word order in a manner similar to that described by Jerome.[51] Such a strict adherence to Greek word order suggests that Rufinus was knowledgeable concerning Greek editions of Paul's letters even as he created his own Latin edition. As a result, it is probable that he encountered Greek editions of the Pauline corpus that included Hebrews after 2 Thessalonians, the common location in the Greek manuscript tradition. This probability is further supported by Rufinus' summary of Paul's letters in the *PQ* in which he places Hebrews after 2 Thessalonians. Rufinus' defense of Hebrews' Pauline authorship in the *PQ* additionally suggests that he may have not only known Greek manuscripts that included Hebrews among Paul's works but also some of the Greek discourses justifying this inclusion; his reasoning in the *PQ* for the omission of Paul's name from Hebrews is remarkably similar to Eusebius' reports concerning Clement's thoughts on the epistle.[52]

Rufinus' *PQ* is included in Codex Fuldensis, along with its defense of Hebrews' Pauline authorship and the placement of Hebrews after 2 Thessalonians. In the actual arrangement of Paul's letters in the codex, however, Hebrews appears after Philemon,

---

[49] Houghton, *Latin New Testament*, 39.
[50] Though I cannot be certain that Rufinus was responsible both for the *PQ* and this translation, for the sake of convenience I will call the writer "Rufinus." Scherbenske, *Canonizing Paul*, 185.
[51] Ibid., 186.
[52] Rufinus in the *PQ*:

> Some men, however, contend that the letter, which is written to the Hebrews, is not Paul's, for the reason that it is not entitled with his name, and due to the discrepancy of wording and style, but that it is either Barnabas's according to Tertullian, or Luke's according to some others, or surely Clement's, a disciple of the apostles and bishop of the Roman Church, who was ordained after the apostles. To these it is necessary to respond: now then, if it is not Paul's because it does not have his name, it is nobody's because it is entitled with no name. But if this is absurd, that which shines with such eloquence of his own doctrine, ought all the more to be believed to be his. But since among the assemblies of the Hebrews by false suspicion he was thought of as a destroyer of the law, he wished to narrate the relationship of the example of the law and the truth of Christ without mentioning his name lest the hatred of his name displayed in front exclude the utility of reading. It is certainly not surprising, if he seems more eloquent in his own [language], i.e. Hebrew, than in a foreign one, i.e. Greek, the language in which the other letters are written." Scherbenske, 187. Clement according to Eusebius: "And as for the Epistle to the Hebrews, he says indeed that it is Paul's, but that it was written for Hebrews in the Hebrew tongue, and that Luke, having carefully translated it, published it for the Greeks; hence, as a result of this translation, the same complexion of style is found in this Epistle and in the Acts: but that the [words] 'Paul an apostle' were naturally not prefixed. For, says he, "in writing to Hebrews who had conceived a prejudice against him and were suspicious of him, he very wisely did not repel them at the beginning by putting his name." (Eusebius, *Hist. eccl.* 6.14 [Oulton, LCL 265:47])

as it does in the vast majority of Vulgate manuscripts.[53] The inclusion of material that preserves Greek traditions regarding Hebrews' relationship to the Pauline corpus even as this manuscript preserves an arrangement of Paul's letters traditional in Latin manuscripts speaks to the continuing interactions between these traditions even into the middle of the sixth century when Codex Fuldensis was produced. Fuldensis is, in fact, a veritable storehouse of potentially contradictory traditions incorporated into the pages of a single codex; it includes the so-called Marcionite prologues, *capitula* drawn from various sources, a concordance often characterized as "Pelagian," and the epistle to the Laodiceans.[54] Perhaps its most notable feature is the gospel harmony that Victor of Capua, the patron of the manuscript, discusses at length in his preface.[55] "When

---

[53] So far as I know, there is only one Vulgate manuscript that places Hebrews after 2 Thessalonians: S (Paul) [VgSp S] St. Gall MS 70. Interestingly, it derives from a source similar to Fuldensis. Houghton, *Latin New Testament*, 261.

[54] Scherbenske, *Canonizing Paul*, 175.

[55] Ernst Ranke, *Codex Fuldensis: Novum Testamentum latine interprete Hieronymo* (Marburgi: Sumtibus N.G. Elwerti, 1868), 1–2:

> Cum fortuito in manus meas incideret unum ex quattuor euangelium conpositum et absente titulo non invenirem nomen auctoris· diligenter inquirens quis gesta uel dicta domini et saluatoris nostri euangelica lectione discreta in ordinem quo se consequi uidebantur· non minimo studii labore redegerit· repperi ammonium quemdam alexandrinum· qui canonum quoque euangelii fertur inuentor· matthei euangelio reliquorum trium excerpta iunxisse· ac sic in unam seriem euangelium nexsuisse· sicut eusebius episcopus carpiano cuidam scribens in praefatione editionis suae· qua canones memorati euangelii edidit supra dicti uiri imitatus studium refert· in hunc modum· ammonius quidam alexandrinus multum ut arbitror laboris et studii impendens unum ex quattuor nobis abreliquit euangelium ex historia quoque eius comperi· quod tatianus uir eruditissimus et orator illius temporis clarus· unum ex quattuor conpaginauerit euangelium cui titulum diapente conposuit· hic beati iustini philosophi et martyris· dum aduiueret discipulus fuit· quo migrante ad dominum cum palma martyrii· magistri sanctam deserens disciplinam et doctrinae supercilio elatus in lapsum encratitarum heresim marcionis potius amplexus errorem quam iustini· christi philosophi ueritatem· suae uitae perniciosus excoluit· asserens inter alia nuptias et stupra pari crimini subiacere· sed et dictis apostolicis· manus profanae emendationis· uel ut dicam uerius corruptionis dicitur intulisse· sed quia et hominum perfidorum christi dei nostri operante potentia confessione uel opere saepe triumphat gloria ueritatis· nam et daemones christum fatebantur· et filii sceuae in actibus apostolorum· in nomine ihesu quem praedicaret paulus demonia fugabant· tatianus quoque licet profanis inplicatus erroribus non inutile tamen exhibens studiosis exemplum hoc euangelium ut mihi uidetur sollerti conpaginatione disposuit· et forsitan adhuc beati iustini adherens lateri illius eruditionis merito hoc opus explicuit· arbitror enim propterea non ammonii sed huius esse editionem memorati uoluminis quod ammonius matthei fertur relationi euangelistarum reliquorum relatione discretos adnexuisse sermones hic uero sancti lucae principia sunt adsumpta. Licet ex maxima parte euangelio sancti matthei reliquorum trium dicta coniunxerit· ut iure ambigi possit· ammonii an tatiani inuentio eiusdem operis debeat extimari· Uerumtamen uel si iam heresiarces huius editionis auctor exstitit tatianus uerba domini mei cognoscens libenter amplector interpretationem si fuisset eius propria procul abicerem.

Scherbenkse, *Canonizing Paul*, 177–8:

> When by chance a gospel harmony prepared from the four fell into my hands and, since it was without title, I did not find the name of the author, after diligently inquiring who, with no small labor of study, [both] rearranged the words and deeds of our Lord and savior [and also] separated for gospel reading in the order in which they appear to have followed, I discovered a certain Alexandrian, Ammonius, who is also said [to be] the author of the canons of the gospel joined with the gospel of Matthew excerpts from the remaining three and in this way wove together a gospel in one ... I also learned from his [i.e. Eusebius's] history that Tatian, a most learned and renowned orator of that time put together a gospel

by chance a gospel harmony prepared from the four" came into Victor's possession, he sat about investigating who had produced such a distinctive version of the text of the Gospels by utilizing the scholarship of Eusebius. Upon discovering the text's potentially "heretical" connections, he offers further research he believes may serve to ameliorate those connections. Chief among this research is his own examination of the text of the Gospels that he judges as uncorrupted, an observation that leads Victor to regard the gospel harmony as a useful tool of study even if it was produced by an individual whose orthodoxy had been subject to question.[56] Victor's preface and the eclectic inclusion of textual aids in Codex Fuldensis serve as examples of the interest in the production of superior Latin editions of scriptural texts in consultation with previously existing editions and scholarship that characterized late antiquity.

Greek-Latin Bilinguals

The direct interaction between Greek and Latin editions of New Testament writings is perhaps most evident in the surviving Greek-Latin bilingual manuscripts of these writings. The very existence of such manuscripts serves as evidence for the intersection of different Greek and Latin traditions regarding Christian scripture and the impact of these traditions upon one another. Discrepancies between these different traditions required editorial decisions regarding the number and order of books to include in these bilingual editions. Furthermore, the completion of these labor-intensive and costly projects could only be completed with the support of patronage.[57] Therefore,

> harmony from the four, for which he composed the title Diapente. This one [i.e. Tatian] was a disciple of the blessed philosopher and martyr Justin while he was living, but when departing to the Lord with the crown of martyrdom, after deserting the sacred instruction of his teacher and becoming puffed up with arrogance and cleaving to the error of the lapsed heresy of Marcion, the Encratites, rather than to the truth of the philosopher of Christ, Justin, this baleful man perfected his ruinous life, asserting among other things that marriage and defilement are to be made equal [and] liable to judgment; but he [i.e. Tatian] is even said to have introduced to the apostolic writings the hand of profane emendation or, as I say, more accurately corruption. But because the glory of the truth working by the power of Christ, our God, often triumphs even through confession or deeds of faithless men (for even demons used to confess Christ and in the Acts of the Apostles the sons of Sceva put demons to flight in the name of Jesus, whom Paul preached) Tatian also, even if implicated in profane error, nevertheless is not useless, by producing an example for the learned, as it seems to me, he set in order this gospel with expert arrangement. And perhaps he developed this work while cleaving to side of the blessed Justin on account of the latter's erudition. For I think for this reason that it is this one's [Tatian's] not Ammonius's edition of the celebrated volume, since Ammonius appears to have joined the words separated from the narrative of the remaining evangelists to Matthew's narrative; but this one adopts the beginning of Saint Luke. Although for the most part he joins the words of the remaining [gospels] to the gospel of Saint Matthew, with the result that it is rightfully possible to be uncertain whether this invention of the same work ought to be reckoned Ammonius's or Tatian's. Nevertheless, now even if the author of this edition appears to be Tatian the heresiarch, I willingly embrace the version, since I examine and recognize the words of my Lord, [but] if they had been his [i.e. Tatian's] own, I would have thrown it away.

[56] Scherbenske, *Canonizing Paul*, 178.
[57] The Price Edict posted by Diocletian at the beginning of the fourth century provides a reference point for such a project. Using the figures listed there, Marichal estimated a cost of 3,400 denarii for a high-quality copy of the Aeneid. Robert Marichal, "L'écriture Latine et La Civilisation Occidentale Du Ier Au XVIe Siècle," in *L'écriture et La Psychologie Des Peuples: XXIIe Semaine de Synthèse*, ed.

Greek-Latin bilingual New Testament manuscripts provide meaningful evidence for Latinity as a focus of patronage and its impact on the production of Christian writings.

Perhaps due in part to the significant costs involved in the production of these manuscripts, Greek-Latin bilinguals are relatively rare; there are only twenty-four among the thousands of manuscripts that exist in these two languages.[58] The earliest surviving Greek-Latin manuscript of the Pauline Letters comes from fourth-century Egypt. 0230 (VL 85) is a small papyrus fragment with only a few verses of Ephesians inscribed on it. The fragment may have been part of a bilingual edition of the Pauline corpus with Greek on the verso and Latin on the recto, though given the limited remains of the manuscript, this is mostly a matter of speculation.[59] The only other extant Greek-Latin New Testament manuscript from the fourth century is not a biblical manuscript in the traditional sense but a glossary and grammar organized according to Paul's letters. P. Chester Beatty 1499 (P99) contains Greek words listed in the order in which they occur in Paul's writings with a Latin translation immediately following each word. The manuscript was likely created by a Greek speaker who utilized Greek and Latin editions of Paul's letters as a source for learning Latin and perhaps also improving his own native language.[60] In this respect, P99 represents the use of Christian scriptural texts in a manner similar to the use of Greek and Latin classics by those who wished to learn these languages.[61] Many of the extant non-biblical bilingual manuscripts divided up the text into small units that allowed the student to find the translation of a word or phrase in the corresponding column or page.[62] This division of text into sense lines is

---

Marcel Cohen (Paris: Librairie Armand Colin, 1963), 214–16. Grafton and Williams estimate the cost of Origen's Hexapla at 150,000 denarii (*Christianity and the Transformation*, 106). Parker estimates the cost of Codex Sinaiticus at 19.7 solidi. A solidus was a gold coin weighing about 4.5 grams. The annual income of priests and deacons has been estimated at 20–25 solidi a year. D. C Parker, *Codex Sinaiticus: The Story of the World's Oldest Bible* (Peabody, MA: Hendrickson, 2010), 62–3. Although the manuscripts discussed here contain far fewer works than Sinaiticus and the Hexapla, they were still large codices owing to their bilingual nature.

[58] Parker, *Codex Bezae*, 60.
[59] Houghton, *Latin New Testament*, 28, 247.
[60] Although this manuscript indicates a use of Paul's letters for language acquisition, which would have been familiar to language learners in the ancient world, the method used to create the glossary is actually quite distinct from other surviving Greek-Latin glossaries from antiquity.

It is perhaps somewhat similar to the Greek word-lists on Latin authors, but compilers of such word-lists provided for the Latin lemmata a Greek translation which they knew by heart or adopted from a bilingual glossary. The author of Ac. 1499, on the contrary, added to each of the Greek (/or Latin) Pauline lemmata the corresponding lemmata from a current Latin (/or Greek) Pauline text. He clearly worked either from a bilingual copy or from separate Greek and Latin Pauline texts. (Alfons Wouters, *The Chester Beatty Codex AC 1499: A Graeco-Latin Lexicon on the Pauline Epistles and a Greek Grammar* [Paris: Peeters, 1988], 105)

[61] "Ancient Latin students thus seem to have engaged in most of the elements of language learning practiced in today's Latin classrooms: they used dictionaries, learned paradigms, studied syntax, started reading on easy texts specially created for them, read Virgil and other canonical authors, and translated paragraphs into Latin" (Eleanor Dickey, "Teaching Latin to Greek Speakers in Antiquity," in *Learning Latin and Greek from Antiquity to the Present*, ed. Elizabeth P. Archibald, William Brockliss, and Jonathan Gnoza [Cambridge: Cambridge University Press, 2015], 50).
[62] Parker, *Codex Bezae*, 69:

Only in the use of sense lines are the oldest New Testament Graeco-Latin bilinguals consistent. The lack of consistency in all other respects, even among so few examples, suggests that there was not a strong tradition of specialism in copying Graeco-Latin biblical texts. The need will

the only formatting feature that is consistent across all the oldest extant biblical Greek-Latin manuscripts, suggesting that ease of transition from one language to the other was a high priority in the production of these manuscripts.[63]

The order of the Gospels in Codex Bezae (D/*d* 05 VL 5), a bilingual manuscript that includes the four Gospels, 3 John, and Acts with Greek on the verso and Latin on the recto, may also serve as an example of an editorial decision impacted by the interaction between distinct Greek and Latin editions of Christian scriptures. David Parker has argued persuasively that Bezae was copied in Berytus near the beginning of the fifth century by a scribe whose primary language was Latin but who also had a working knowledge of Greek.[64] The presence of the law school at Berytus created an environment in which a bilingual manuscript was required, a community where Latin was the dominant language but where Greek continued to be employed because of its "sacred character."[65] Parker has shown that there were two exemplars from which

> have arisen only rarely, and then the scribe employed will have been whoever could be found to have the necessary competences. This explains the lack of agreement, the way in which the general features of book production simply reflect those current at the time, and the fact that such untypical hands were used for writing these texts.

[63] Interestingly, this is not a feature shared by Greco-Coptic manuscripts. Parker argues that this commonality among the Greco-Latin manuscripts suggested some shared tradition of copying though he sees it as a weak one.

> However, there must have been a tradition of some kind. There will have been a reason for the ways in which the earliest copies were produced, and their descendants will have imitated them. It seems very probable indeed that the biblical texts, or some of them, were modelled on the typical bilingual Virgil that we have described. The contrast with the Graeco-Coptic manuscripts written in blocks, which we discussed earlier, supports this: there was no similar precedent for Coptic copyists to follow, so they created a format based on the use of church lections in two languages, the one followed by the other. In the codices where pairs of columns are written in the same language, the Copts created another format. (Ibid., 58)

[64] Ibid., 267:

> First, there is the paleographical requirement: the manuscript was written in the East, by a Latin-trained scribe who was used to copying legal texts and who had a working knowledge of Greek. Second, the chronology and character of the early correctors must fit in with the historical information that can be gathered from other sources. Third, there is the requirement to find a place where Latin was spoken, so that Latin scriptures were needed, but where the reading of Greek was still possible. ... Our conclusions about the sense lines of D require a community old enough already to have worn out at least one copy (the exemplar). On the other hand, a place must be sought where the existence of such a *Greek* text as that of D is also within the bounds of possibility. ... It must be recognized that the number of Eastern locations where Codex Bezae could have been copied is severely limited by the fact that Latin was not commonly spoken.

[65] Although the rise of Latinity was primarily a Western phenomenon, there was a short-lived spike in the prominence of Latin even in some Eastern centers as Constantine and other fourth-century emperors promulgated Latin influence through their policies. By the early fifth century, however, this spike in Latinity had already started to fade in the East; a transition reflected in the change of the official teaching language of the law school at Berytus from Latin to Greek. The corrections in Codex Bezae bear witness to this shift as the first corrections were made to the Latin side of the text shortly after the manuscript was produced, but not much later the Latin side of the text is ignored as the prominence of Latin quickly declined in Berytus. The Greek side, on the other hand, continued to receive corrections throughout the fifth century and the beginning of the sixth. After the sixth century the manuscript shows no signs of use until the ninth century when missing leaves were replaced in Lyons, one of the significant locales for the preservation of ancient texts in early medieval Europe. By 1562 the codex was in the possession of its namesake, Theodore Beza, until

the single scribe of Codex Bezae copied, one for Acts and the other for the Gospels. The Gospels in Bezae, however, preserve certain scribal features which diverge in the fifth chapter of John. Parker has suggested that this divergence may be explained if the exemplar of Bezae was copied by two scribes who split their work at John 5, which would have been roughly the midway point of the four Gospels if they were arranged in the order Matthew-Mark-John-Luke.[66] If this is true, it means that the scribe of Codex Bezae rearranged the order of the Gospels in his edition of the Gospels relative to his exemplar. Although the reason for this change cannot be known with certainty, Parker suggests as a possibility that the scribe chose to conform his edition to what he understood to be the new standard for gospel editions.[67] The order of the Gospels in Codex Bezae (Matthew-John-Luke-Mark) is most widely attested among Old Latin manuscripts of the Gospels, many of which are thought to come from Italy.

If the scribe of Codex Bezae adapted the order of the Gospels in his bilingual exemplar to match the order more common in Latin editions of the Gospels, Bezae would serve as another example of editorial decisions influenced by interactions between Greek and Latin editions akin to those proposed here regarding the place of Hebrews in editions of Paul's letters. These editorial decisions would not be exactly the same in each manuscript since the editors of Bezae appear to have conformed this bilingual manuscript to the Latin tradition. The scenario I have proposed for Hebrews, on the other hand, assumes a kind of compromise in the later bilingual and Latin copies between earlier Greek and Latin traditions. Despite these differences, both manuscripts attest to plausible interactions between Greek and Latin editions of Christian scriptures throughout late antiquity.[68]

---

he donated it to the Cambridge library where it has resided ever since. Ibid., 265, 282. The missing folia may have been replaced by Florus. It was also utilized by the Ado of Vienne as he wrote his *Martyrologium*. Knust and Wasserman, *To Cast the First Stone*, 239.

[66] Parker, *Codex Bezae*, 112–13.
[67] Ibid., 118.
[68] The later history of Claromontanus also bears some resemblance to that of Bezae at many points though the origin of the two manuscripts are thought to be quite distinct. Claromontanus is typically dated roughly a century later than Bezae and its origins attributed to southern Italy. The presence of a bilingual community, the b-d uncial script of the codex, and a few other distinctive calligraphic features associated with Italy are often the reasons cited for this location. It should be noted that Bezae shares this same script. Despite the similarities in layout and script, Frede argues that Claromontanus and Bezae should not be regarded as related in anyway. "Trotz großer Ähnlichkeit in der Anlage und trotz Verwendung der bd-Unziale in beiden Handschriften darf man jedoch den Claromontanus nicht als mit dem Codex Bezae irgendwie zusammengehörig betrachten" (Hermann Josef Frede, *Altlateinische Paulus-Handschriften* [Frieberg: Herder, 1964], 19). The scribe of Claromontanus appears not to have been exceptionally skilled in either Latin or Greek but, like the scribe of Bezae, Latin was his more familiar language. H. J. Vogels, "Der Codex Claromontanus Der Paulinischen Brief," in *Amicitiae Corolla*, ed. H. G. Wood (London: University of London Press, 1933), 280. Claromontanus is also like Bezae in that corrections were made to its Latin text shortly following its production after which the manuscript shows no signs of use for over a century until it appeared in France in the second half of the eighth century where its Greek text was corrected according to a Byzantine text type. Frede, *Altlateinische Paulus-Handschriften*, 29–31. Theodore Beza came into possession of this manuscript as well, reportedly having found it at the Abby of Claremont. Caspar René Gregory, *Textkritik Des Neuen Testamentes* (Leipzig: J.C. Hinrichs, 1900), 107.

The other great Greek-Latin New Testament manuscript of late antiquity, Codex Laudianus, bears some significant differences relative to Bezae and Claromontanus. Nevertheless, it serves as yet another example of a manuscript in which editorial decisions have been influenced by the intersection of Greek and Latin editions. Laudianus is a bilingual text of Acts that was written near the end of the sixth century by a scribe who was more proficient in Greek than Latin.[69] Sardinia has been the most commonly suggested location for the origin of Laudianus due to the mention of the city in an inscription on the end flyleaf of the codex.[70] Sardinia was also one of the more prominent multilingual locations in the West of late antiquity where Greek continued to be spoken as well as Latin. Whereas the Greek and Latin text appear on opposing pages in Bezae and Claromontanus, they appear in parallel columns of the same page in Laudianus, with Latin taking the "place of honor" in the left column typically reserved for Greek as the original language.[71] The layout of the manuscript is further distinguished by its extremely short sense lines—frequently only a word or two—suggesting that its purpose was to aid readers who knew Greek and were still developing their acquisition of Latin.[72] Although this bilingual situation is the reverse of those in which Bezae and Claromontanus were created, the distinctively short sense lines of Laudianus suggest that its format was an editorial decision influenced by the intersection of Greek and Latin. The production of a bilingual manuscript of Acts in a community that already spoke the language in which Acts was written, especially a manuscript of this kind that appears to have been designed specifically as a Latin learning aid and gave the place of prominence on the page to the Latin column, speaks to the prevalent interest in producing Latin editions of Christian scriptures.[73]

This brief survey of scriptural translation projects in late antiquity illustrates the continued interaction between Greek and Latin on the production and use of biblical manuscripts in late antiquity. The prominence of Latin Christianity in the fourth century led to considerable patronage of Christian scholarship, including a number

---

[69] This is evidenced by the higher number of mistakes in the Latin text and the adjustment of some Latin letter forms to the Greek script of the text. Margaret T. Gibson, *The Bible in the Latin West* (Notre Dame: University of Notre Dame, 1993), 22. Otto Walther, "Codex Laudianus G35 A Re-Examination of the Manuscript: A Reproduction of the Text and Accompanying Commentary" (PhD diss., University of St. Andrews, 1980), 13.

[70] Gibson, *Bible in the Latin West*, 22.

[71] Parker, *New Testament Manuscripts*, 289–90. Walther, "Codex Laudianus," 7.

[72] Parker likens the text to a bilingual copy of Virgil created for the same purpose. Parker, *Codex Bezae*, 69.

[73] It may also be worth noting that the text of *both* columns were corrected soon after the manuscript's production; the Latin column having been brought into closer accord with the text of the Vulgate. Walther, "Codex Laudianus," 42. The subsequent history of Laudianus also bears certain resemblance to that of Bezae and Claromontanus insofar as it too began to be utilized by those with a knowledge of Latin to improve their knowledge of Greek. Laudanius left Sardinia shortly after its production, traveling first to Jarrow in Northumbria, where Bede used it as he wrote his commentary on Acts early in the eighth century, and then to Wurzburg by the end of that century. Kaczynski, *Greek in the Carolingian Age*, 76; Parker, *New Testament Manuscripts*, 290. Around this time the manuscript also acquired three significant additions that indicate its use in a predominantly Latin context; section divisions indicated by Roman numerals, an Old Roman version of the Apostle's creed written in Latin on folio 226, and Latin translations written above words in the Greek column of the text. The first two of these additions were probably made in the eighth century while the third was more likely in the ninth or tenth. Walther, "Codex Laudianus," 19–20.

of sizeable translation projects of earlier Greek works. Although these projects served to translate works written in an increasingly unknown language into Latin, they also provided an opportunity for scholars to display their scholarly abilities and patrons an opportunity to display their own elite, Latin identity. In the case of the Christian scriptures, the patronage of these translation projects, I have argued, brought together previously distinct Greek and Latin editions of the scriptures in a manner that required editorial decisions in the production of new manuscripts.

Conclusions

The earliest editions of Paul's letters manifested competing traditions about the Epistle to the Hebrews and its relationship to the *corpus Paulinum*. All evidence suggests that Hebrews was included among Greek editions of Paul's letters at a very early stage. There is also considerable evidence to indicate that the earliest Latin editions of Paul's letters, on the other hand, did not include Hebrews. None of these earliest Latin editions survive today, but the absence of Hebrews from their pages is attested by the varied transmission of Hebrews in the manuscripts that do survive as well as the witness of early Latin theologians. The increase of patronage for scriptural translation projects substantially impacted the production and utilization of biblical manuscripts throughout late antiquity. The new editions of the *corpus Paulinum* that were created as a part of these larger trends, I have argued, forced the competing traditions regarding Hebrews' authorship together in a way that they had not previously intersected, compelling the editors of these collections to reconcile the inclusion of Hebrews in Greek editions and its exclusion from Latin ones. The editorial reconciliation of these different traditions provides a plausible explanation for the placement of Hebrews at the end of the Pauline corpus, an editorial decision consistent with Hebrews' questionable Pauline status and one that would determine its place in the vast majority of the subsequent manuscript tradition as well as modern print editions of the Bible.

6

Concluding Reflections

The category of canon, I have argued, was the exclusive concern of a limited number of fourth-century Christian intellectuals. Scholars like Eusebius and Athanasius utilized their training in bibliographic methods to reconstruct the past history of Christian writings, noting which works had been quoted by earlier Christian writers and reporting the prevailing opinions about the authorship of those works. They also employed these tools to new ends, however, directing their reconstructions of the past toward the construction of lists of scriptures intended as authoritative for their present. In doing so, they forged a new concept of Christian scripture that had not previously existed but has significantly shaped subsequent history. Their reconstructions of the past not only were shaped by their present circumstance but also participated in the construction of that present as well as the future. In this respect the work of these ancient scholars was not so different from the work of current biblical scholarship, which continues to offer its reconstructions of the past that are shaped by and shape the present, simultaneously forging new concepts of scripture that shape the future and scripture's place in it.

Hebrews' reception in early Christianity was influenced by a number of factors that had little to do with the fourth-century category of canon: its utility in theological arguments, its relationship to the Pauline corpus, and its omission from that corpus when it was first translated into Latin. The reception of the Epistle to the Hebrews suggests a model for the reception of early Christian writings that cannot be captured by the supposedly rational decisions of church leaders concerning the inclusion or exclusion of certain works. The reception of these works was informed by a complex interplay between the citation habits of educated writers, the assumptions that guided book production and ancient editorial practice, and the impact of bibliographic methodology on catalogues of Christian scriptures. If any of these factors had been different in the case of Hebrews—for example, if Clement and Origen had not so frequently cited Hebrews as Pauline, if Justin and Tertullian had not found Hebrews useful to their theological arguments, if later Latin editors of Paul's letters had not chosen to include Hebrews where it had previously been excluded, if fourth-century scholars had not set about the task of cataloguing acceptable Christian scriptures—the reception of the epistle may have turned out very differently.

Allusions to and quotations of Hebrews by early Christian writers attest to the early and broad appeal of Hebrews in the first centuries of its existence. Clement of Rome alluded to the epistle sometime near the end of the first century. Justin Martyr and Tertullian both mined Hebrews as a source for Christian readings of the Septuagint in their arguments about the proper interpretation of scripture. Both Clement and Origen of Alexandria quoted the epistle frequently. These writers employed the text of Hebrews in various social contexts in order to promote specific rhetorical goals. There is, however, no hint of "rejection" of the epistle among any of them, whether Greek or Latin.

Even so, traces of conflicting opinions about the place of Hebrews within the *corpus Paulinum* also arose early. Tertullian was the first writer to mention the authorship of the treatise but he attributed it to Barnabas, not Paul. The position of Hebrews in P[46], on the other hand, suggests that the creators of this codex attributed Pauline authorship to the epistle. Clement and Origen of Alexandria both regularly referred to the epistle as one of Paul's in their own writings. Eusebius later reported the same opinion in his presentation of Clement and Origin's statements about the epistle though he also claimed that these scholars were not ignorant of the questions that could be posed to Pauline authorship. The fourth-century scholar presented Origen as a highly educated individual who could not ignore the difference between the style of Hebrews and the rest of Paul's letters; similarly, he stated, Pantaenus and Clement also acknowledged the peculiarity of an epistle attributed to Paul without his name attached to it. Eusebius thereby portrayed the attribution of Pauline authorship to Hebrews as a tradition that prevailed in Alexandria at least as far back as Pantaenus even as he noted possible objections to such a claim. Although Eusebius' own agenda informed his presentation of Hebrews' authorship as a well-established tradition, he nevertheless appears to have accurately represented the reception of Hebrews as Pauline among Greek speaking Christians in that region.

A disparity in the treatment of Hebrews in early Greek and Latin editions of the *corpus Paulinum* appears to have contributed to a disparity in the reception of the book by later readers, editors, and scribes. Though many copies have been lost, the earliest extant Greek editions of the Pauline corpus all include Hebrews, most commonly after 2 Thessalonians. Evidence from surviving Latin and bilingual manuscripts, however, suggests that Hebrews was omitted from the earliest translation of Paul's letters into Latin. Eusebius reported that some in Rome, particularly Gaius, rejected the Pauline authorship of Hebrews; that rejection may well have been tied to available editions. Still, if available Latin copies of the *corpus Paulinum* rarely (if ever?) included the book, its place as an authentic letter would have been called into question, irrespective of any concerns either about the book's style or its lack of direct attribution to the Apostle. Hebrews' omission from the Muratorian Fragment may reflect a similar problem. Jerome confirms this situation: near the beginning of the fifth century, after he had moved from Rome to Palestine and likely encountered a number of Greek editions of Paul, he stated that Hebrews was received among the Greeks but not the Latins, a statement that just as likely reflects the different manuscript editions in the two languages as attitudes about the apostolic status of the letter. By the time he was writing, Greek-speaking communities had encountered editions of Paul that included Hebrews for quite some time while Latin-speaking communities regularly encountered ones that did not, perhaps for more than a century.

Jerome's perspective on Hebrews' reception, however, was also heavily shaped by the Christian intellectual projects that characterized the fourth century. Debates about Hebrews' status in the fourth century fit within larger efforts at transforming Christian knowledge into a sophisticated, intellectual endeavor that employed methods familiar to other educated elites at the time. Jerome's language in his statement about Hebrews reflects this transformation: he began by discussing Hebrews' standing with regard to Pauline authorship but concluded with remarks about its "canonical" status. The question of the epistle's authorship had thus become one of the criteria that functioned to authorize the epistle's status. The effort to delimit which works are "classics," why, and on what basis was a central project of fourth-century Christian scholars like Jerome. Eusebius, Athanasius, and Rufinus participated in this scholarly project as well by producing catalogues of Christian scriptures, each one counting Hebrews' among the fourteen letters of Paul. The practice of producing such lists was itself an intellectual habit, a scholarly custom, and, by engaging in it, these writers signal their participation in the *paideia* of the age.

Such efforts toward systematization coincided with an increase in imperial patronage for Christian scholarship, an additional factor that may have impacted the relationship of Hebrews to the *corpus Paulinum*. Manuscripts that include Paul's letters exhibit characteristics consistent with the creation of an authorial edition, one of the central tasks of which was the separation of an author's authentic works from those deemed spurious. In the case of Paul's letters, the support of imperial patronage for Christian book production may have led to a renewed encounter between Greek editions, which included Hebrews after 2 Thessalonians and Latin editions that omitted it entirely. This may have subsequently resulted in a compromise consistent with the principles of editorial practice; Hebrews was placed at the end of the Pauline corpus, not only in Claromontanus but also in Latin Vulgate manuscripts, signaling its status as a work with an uncertain relationship to the *corpus Paulinum*. The placement of Hebrews at the end of Paul's letters was its most common position among these manuscripts, a practice that can be detected in copies from the sixth century up to modern printed editions of the Bible available today.

Appendix

Name G.-A. no. VL no.	Inventory Number	Contents	Position of Hebrews/ Other Features	Language	Date
P¹³	P. Oxy. IV. 657.- Ägyptisches Museum. PSALMI 1292	Extensive portions from five chapters of Hebrews on the verso of a roll with portions of a Latin epitome of a history of Rome by Livy on the recto	Uncertain. Possibly between Romans and 1 Corinthians	Greek	3rd or 4th century
P⁴⁶	University of Michigan. P. Mich. Inv. 6238.	Nearly complete Pauline collection. Missing first five chapters of Romans. Content of final pages uncertain	Between Romans and 1 Corinthians	Greek	3rd century
P⁹⁹	Chester Beatty Library. P. 1499	Glossary and Grammar arranged according to Paul's letters	NA	Greek and Latin	4th century
01 ℵ Codex Sinaiticus	British Library. Add. 43725	Pandect Bible	After 2 Thessalonians	Greek	4th century

Name G.-A. no. VL no.	Inventory Number	Contents	Position of Hebrews/ Other Features	Language	Date
02 A Codex Alexandrinus	British Library. Royal I D.VIII	Pandect Bible	After 2 Thessalonians	Greek	5th century
03 B Codex Vaticanus	Vatican Library. Vat. gr. 1209	Pandect Bible	After 2 Thessalonians, though after Heb 9:14 is replaced with later minuscule writing	Greek	4th century
04 C Ephraemi Rescriptus	Bibliothèque Nationale de France. Grec 9	Pandect Bible, reused in the 12th century for Greek translation of 38 tractates by Ephraem	After 2 Thessalonians	Greek	5th century
05 D VL 5 Codex Bezae Cantabrigiensis	Cambridge Library. Nn II. 41	Gospels, 3 John, Acts	NA	Greek and Latin (VL) on facing pages	*ca.* 400
06 Dp VL 75 Codex Claromontanus	Bibliothèque Nationale de France. Grec 107	Pauline Epistles	After Philemon, originally with blank pages in between, list of writings inserted in blank pages later. Also lacks incipit, explicit, and use of red ink characteristic of rest of collection. Hebrews translation different from rest of corpus	Greek and Latin (VL) on facing pages	6th century

Name G.-A. no. VL no.	Inventory Number	Contents	Position of Hebrews/ Other Features	Language	Date
08 Ea VL 50 Codex Laudianus	Oxford, Bodleian Library, MS Laud Gr. 35	Acts	NA	Greek and Latin (VL) columns on each page	6th or 7th century
010 Fp VL 78 Codex Augiensis	Cambridge, Trinity College. Cambridge B. XVII.1	Pauline Epistles	After Philemon with lengthy introduction, no explicit for Philemon Ancestor shares exemplar with 06	Greek and Latin (VL) columns on each page. Hebrews only in Latin	9th century
012 Gp VL77 Codex Boernerianus	Dresden, Landesbibliothek Dresden A 145b	Pauline Epistles	Lacks Hebrews. Ancestor shares exemplar with 06	Interlinear Latin (VL) above Greek text	9th century
015 Hp Codex Coislinianus	Bibliothèque Nationale de France. Grec 1074. Coislin 202, Lavra Athos s.n., Turin A.1, Moscow F.270. 1a.70.1 (Gr. 166,1), Moscow 563, St. Petersburg Gr. 14, Kiev F.301	Pauline Epistles	After 2 Thessalonians, include Euthalian Apparatus	Greek	6th century

Name G.-A. no. VL no.	Inventory Number	Contents	Position of Hebrews/ Other Features	Language	Date
016 I Codex Freerianus	Freer Art Gallery, Smithsonian Institute. F1906.275	1 Cor. - Hebrews, Badly damaged. May have originally contained Pauline Epistles, Acts, and Catholic Epistles	After 2 Thessalonians	Greek	5th century
032 VL 83 Codex Waldeccensis	i) formerly Mengeringhausen (Waldeck), Stiftsarchiv, s.n. ii) Marburg, Hessisches Staatsarchiv, Best. 147	Fragments of the Pauline Epistles	NA	Greek and Latin (VL) on facing pages	10th century
037 VL27 Codex Sangallensis	St Gall, Stiftsbibliothek, 48	Gospels	NA	Greek and Latin (Vg) Interlinear	860/70
0319 Ee VL 76 Codex Sangermanensis	St. Petersburg Gr. 20, Dabs 1	Pauline Epistles	After Philemon, copy of 06	Greek and Latin (VL) columns on each page	9th century
VL 64 Freising Fragments	Various Holding Institutions	Fragments of the Pauline and Catholic Epistles	Uncertain. Represents a translation of Hebrews distinct from 06	Latin (VL)	6th and 7th century

Name G.-A. no. VL no.	Inventory Number	Contents	Position of Hebrews/ Other Features	Language	Date
VL 85 0230	Biblioteca Medicea Laurenziana, P.S.I. 13.1306	Fragment of Ephesians	NA	Greek and Latin (VL) columns on each page	4th or 5th century
VL 89 AN Paul Anonymous Commentary on Paul	Budapest, National Széchényi Library, Cod. Lat. 1	Text of Pauline Epistles Alternates with Commentary	After Philemon, Text of Hebrews is similar to VL 109 while rest of collection resembles VL 75	Latin (VL)	9th century
VL 109 Complutensis Primus	Madrid, Biblioteca de la Universidad Complutense, 31	Pandect Bible, including Laodiceans	Between Philemon and Laodiceans	Latin (mixed)	927
VgF Codex Fuldensis	Fulda, Hochschul- und Landesbibliothek Bonifatianus 1	Harmony of the Gospels followed by the rest of the New Testament, including Laodiceans. Includes prologues, capitula, and arguments for many writings	After Philemon but listed after 2 Thessalonians in *PQ*	Latin (Vg)	546
P Vg Op P	Bibliothèque Nationale de France. Latin 1063	Gospels and Pauline Epistles	Laodiceans included between Philemon and Hebrews	Latin (Vg)	7th century
S Vg SP S. St	Gall, Stiftsbibliothek. 70	Pauline Epistles	After 2 Thessalonians. Derives from source similar to VgF	Latin (Vg)	8th century

Bibliography

Ackroyd, Peter R. C. Evans, G. W. H. Lampe, and S. L. Greenslade, eds. *The Cambridge History of the Bible*. New York: Cambridge University Press, 1963.
Adams, J. N. *Bilingualism and the Latin Language*. New York: Cambridge University Press, 2002.
Adams, J. N. *Bilingualism in Ancient Society: Language Contact and the Written Text*. New York: Oxford University Press, 2002.
Aichele, George. *The Control of Biblical Meaning: Canon as Semiotic Mechanism*. Harrisburg: Trinity Press International, 2001.
Aland, Kurt. *The Problem of the New Testament Canon*. London: A.R. Mowbray, 1962.
Aland, Kurt, and Barbara Aland. *The Text of the New Testament: An Introduction to the Critical Editions and to the Theory and Practice of Modern Textual Criticism*. 2nd ed. Grand Rapids, MI: Eerdmans, 1989.
Albl, Martin C. *And Scripture Cannot Be Broken: The Form and Function of the Early Christian Testimonia Collections*. Supplements to Novum Testamentum 96. Boston: Brill, 1999.
Allert, Craig D. *Revelation, Truth, Canon, and Interpretation: Studies in Justin Martyr's Dialogue with Trypho*. Supplements to Vigiliae Christianae 64. Boston: Brill, 2002.
Andrist, Patrick, ed. *Le Manuscrit B de La Bible (Vaticanus Graecus 1209)*. Lausanne: Editions du Zebre, 2009.
Aragione, Gabriella, Eric Junod, and Enrico Norelli, eds. *Le canon du Nouveau Testament: regards nouveaux sur l'histoire de sa formation*. Genève: Labor et Fides, 2005.
Archibald, Elizabeth P., William Brockliss, and Jonathan Gnoza, eds. *Learning Latin and Greek from Antiquity to the Present*. Cambridge: Cambridge University Press, 2015.
Aristotle. *Art of Rhetoric*. Translated by J. H. Freese. Cambridge, MA: Harvard University Press, 1926.
Armstrong, Jonathan J. "Victorinus of Pettau as the Author of the Canon Muratori." *Vigiliae Christianae* 62, no. 1 (2008): 1–34.
Arnal, William E., Richard S. Ascough, Robert A. Derrenbacker, and Philip A. Harland, eds. *Scribal Practices and Social Structures among Jesus Adherents: Essays in Honour of John S. Kloppenborg*. Leuven: Peeters, 2016.
Attridge, Harold W. *Hebrews: A Commentary on the Epistle to the Hebrews*. Philadelphia: Fortress Press, 1989.
Attridge, Harold W., and Gōhei Hata. *Eusebius, Christianity, and Judaism*. Studia Post-Biblica 42. New York: Brill, 1992.
Babcock, William S. *Paul and the Legacies of Paul*. Dallas: Southern Methodist University Press, 1990.
Bagnall, Roger S. *Reading Papyri, Writing Ancient History*. New York: Routledge, 1995.
Bagnall, Roger S. *Early Christian Books in Egypt*. Princeton, NJ: Princeton University Press, 2009.
Bagnall, Roger S. *Egypt in Late Antiquity*. Princeton, NJ: Princeton University Press, 2014.

Band, Erster. *Die Handschriften Der Hessichen Landesbibliothek Fulda*. Weisbaden: Harrossowitz, 1992.
Barker, Don. "The Dating of New Testament Papyri." *New Testament Studies* 57, no. 4 (2011): 571–82.
Barnes, Timothy David. *Tertullian: A Historical and Literary Study*. New York: Oxford University Press, 1985.
Barnes, Timothy David. *From Eusebius to Augustine: Selected Papers, 1982–1993*. Aldershot: Ashgate, 1994.
Barton, John, and Michael Wolter, eds. *Die Einheit Der Schrift Und Die Vielfalt Des Kanons*. New York: Walter de Gruyter, 2003.
Batovici, Dan. "The Apostolic Fathers in Codex Sinaiticus and Codex Alexandrinus." *Biblica* 97, no. 4 (2016): 581–605.
Baum, A.D. "Der Neutestamentliche Kanon Bei Eusebius (Historia Ecclesiastica 3.25.1–7) Im Kontext Seiner Literaturgeschichtlichen Arbeit." *ETL* 73 (1997): 307–48.
Berschin, Walter. *Greek Letters and the Latin Middle Ages: From Jerome to Nicholas of Cusa*. Washington, DC: Catholic University of America Press, 1988.
Bindley, T. H., trans. *Tertullian: On the Testimony of the Soul and on the Prescription of Heretics*. London: SPCK, 1914.
Bischoff, Bernhard. *Latin Paleography: Antiquity and the Middle Ages*. Cambridge: Cambridge University Press, 1990.
Black, Matthew, Ernest Best, and R. Wilson. *Text and Interpretation: Studies in the New Testament Presented to Matthew Black*. New York: Cambridge University Press, 1979.
Blomkvist, Vemund. *Euthalian Traditions: Text, Translation and Commentary*. Texte Und Untersuchungen Zur Geschichte Der Altchristlichen Literatur Bd. 170. Boston: De Gruyter, 2012.
Blum, Rudolf. *Kallimachos: The Alexandrian Library and the Origins of Bibliography*. Madison: University of Wisconsin Press, 1991.
Blumell, Lincoln H., and Thomas A. Wayment. *Christian Oxyrhynchus: Texts, Documents, and Sources*. Waco, TX: Baylor University Press, 2015.
Boer, E. A. de. "Tertullian on 'Barnabas' Letter to the Hebrews' in De Pudicitia 20.1–5." *Vigiliae Christianae* 68, no. 3 (2014): 243–66.
Bordier, Henri-Léonard. *Description Des Peintures et Autres Ornements Contenus Dans Les Manuscrits Grecs de La Bibliothèque Nationale. Quatrième Livraison*. Paris: Champion, 1884.
Bowersock, G. W. *Hellenism in Late Antiquity: Thomas Spencer Jerome Lectures*. Ann Arbor: University of Michigan Press, 1996.
Bowman, Alan K, and Greg Woolf. *Literacy and Power in the Ancient World*. New York: Cambridge University Press, 1994.
Brakke, David. "Canon Formation and Social Conflict in Fourth-Century Egypt: Athanasius of Alexandria's Thirty-Ninth '*Festal Letter*.'" *Harvard Theological Review* 87, no. 4 (1994): 395–419.
Brakke, David. *The Gnostics: Myth, Ritual, and Diversity in Early Christianity*. Cambridge, MA: Harvard University Press, 2010.
Brakke, David. "A New Fragment of Athanasius's Thirty-Ninth *Festal Letter*: Heresy, Apocrypha, and the Canon." *Harvard Theological Review* 103, no. 1 (2010): 47–66.
Breed, Brennan W. *Nomadic Text: A Theory of Biblical Reception History*. Bloomington: Indiana University Press, 2014.
Bright, Pamela, ed. *Augustine and the Bible*. Notre Dame: University of Notre Dame Press, 1986.

Brown, Michelle. *In the Beginning: Bibles before the Year 1000.* Washington, DC: Freer Gallery of Art and Arthur M. Slacker Gallery, Smithsonian Institution, 2006.

Brown, Peter Robert Lamont. *Power and Persuasion in Late Antiquity: Towards a Christian Empire.* The Curti Lectures; 1988. Madison, WI: University of Wisconsin Press, 1992.

Brown, Peter Robert Lamont. *The Rise of Western Christendom: Triumph and Diversity, A.D. 200–1000.* The Making of Europe. Malden, MA: Blackwell Publishers, 2003.

Bruyn, Theodore de, ed. *Pelagius's Commentary on St Paul's Epistle to the Romans: Translated with Introduction and Notes.* Oxford: Clarendon Press, 1993.

Bruyn, Theodore de. *Making Amulets Christian: Artefacts, Scribes, and Contexts.* Oxford: Oxford University Press, 2017.

Burns, J. Patout, and Robin Margaret Jensen. *Christianity in Roman Africa: The Development of Its Practices and Beliefs.* Grand Rapids, MI: Eerdmans, 2014.

Burton, Philip. *The Old Latin Gospels: A Study of Their Texts and Language.* New York: Oxford University Press, 2000.

Cain, Andrew. *The Letters of Jerome: Asceticism, Biblical Exegesis, and the Construction of Christian Authority in Late Antiquity.* Oxford: Oxford University Press, 2009.

Campenhausen, Hans von. *The Formation of the Christian Bible.* Translated by J. A. Baker. Philadelphia: Fortress Press, 1972.

Carr, David McLain. *Writing on the Tablet of the Heart: Origins of Scripture and Literature.* New York: Oxford University Press, 2005.

Carriker, Andrew James. *The Library of Eusebius of Caesarea.* Leiden: Brill, 2003.

Casiday, Augustine, and Frederick W. Norris. *Constantine to C. 600.* New York: Cambridge University Press, 2007.

Cernuskova, Veronika, Judith L. Kovacs, and Jana Platova, eds. *Clement's Biblical Exegesis.* Boston: Brill, 2016.

Charlesworth, James H., and Lee Martin McDonald, eds. *Sacra Scriptura: How "Non-Canonical" Texts Functioned in Early Judaism and Early Christianity.* New York: T&fT Clark, 2014.

Chin, Catherine M. *Grammar and Christianity in the Late Roman World.* Philadelphia: University of Pennsylvania Press, 2007.

Clabeaux, John James. *A Lost Edition of the Letters of Paul: A Reassessment of the Text of the Pauline Corpus Attested by Marcion.* Washington, DC: Catholic Biblical Association of America, 1989.

Clark, Kenneth. *A Descriptive Catalogue of Greek New Testament Manuscripts in America.* Chicago: University of Chicago Press, 1937.

Clarke, M. L. *Rhetoric at Rome: A Historical Survey.* D. H. Berry, ed. London: Routledge, 1996.

Clement of Alexandria. *Stromateis.* Translated by John Ferguson. Washington, DC: Catholic University of America Press, 1991.

Clivaz, Claire. *Reading New Testament Papyri in Context = Lire Des Papyrus Du Nouveau Testament Dans Leur Contexte.* Leuven: Peeters, 2011.

Comfort, Philip Wesley. *Encountering the Manuscripts: An Introduction to New Testament Paleography & Textual Criticism.* Nashville: Broadman and Holman, 2005.

Cosgrove, Charles H. "Justin Martyr and the Emerging Canon." *Vigiliae Christianae* 36 (1982): 209–32.

Cribiore, Raffaella. *Gymnastics of the Mind: Greek Education in Hellenistic and Roman Egypt.* Princeton, NJ: Princeton University Press, 2001.

Davies, Philip R. *Writing the Bible: Scribes, Scribalism and Script.* New York: Routledge, 2016.

Dawson, David. *Allegorical Readers and Cultural Revision in Ancient Alexandria*. Berkeley: University of California Press, 1992.

Den Hollander, August, Ulrich Schmid, and Willem Smelik, eds. *Paratext and Megatext as Channels of Jewish and Christian Traditions: The Textual Markers of Contextualization*. Boston: Brill, 2003.

Derrenbacker, Robert A. *Ancient Compositional Practices and the Synoptic Problem*. Dudley, MA: Peeters, 2005.

Dickey, Eleanor. *Ancient Greek Scholarship: A Guide to Finding, Reading, and Understanding Scholia, Commentaries, Lexica, and Grammatical Treatises, from Their Beginnings to the Byzantine Period*. New York: Oxford University Press, 2007.

Dionysius of Halicarnassus. *Roman Antiquities*. Translated by Earnest Cary. vol. 319. Cambridge, MA: Harvard University Press, 1937.

Duff, J. "Papyrus-Codex-46 (P46) and the 'Pastorals': A Misleading Consensus? (Scribal Compression and Miscalculation as Evidence for an Omitted Pastoral Epistle Section in the Pauline Corpus)." *New Testament Studies* 44, no. 4 (1998): 578–90.

Dungan, David L. *Constantine's Bible: Politics and the Making of the New Testament*. Minneapolis, MN: Fortress Press, 2007.

Dunn, Geoffrey D. "Tertullian's Scriptural Exegesis in de Praescriptione Haereticorum." *Journal of Early Christian Studies* 14, no. 2 (June 12, 2006): 141–55.

Dunn, Geoffrey D. *Tertullian's Aduersus Iudaeos: A Rhetorical Analysis*. Washington, DC: Catholic University of America Press, 2008.

Duplacy, J., and Joël Delobel. *Etudes de Critique Textuelle Du Nouveau Testament*. Leuven: Peeters, 1987.

Ebojo, Edgar Battad. "A Scribe and His Manuscript: An Investigation Into the Scribal Habits of Papyrus 46 (P. Chester Beatty II – P. Mich. Inv. 6238)." PhD diss., University of Birmingham, 2014.

Eden, Kathy. *Hermeneutics and the Rhetorical Tradition: Chapters in the Ancient Legacy & Its Humanist Reception*. Yale Studies in Hermeneutics. New Haven, CT: Yale University Press, 1997.

Edwards, James. "The Hermeneutical Significance of Chapter Divisions in Ancient Gospel Manuscripts." *New Testament Studies* 56, no. 3 (2010): 413–26.

Ehrman, Bart D, ed. *The Apostolic Fathers, Volume I: I Clement. II Clement. Ignatius. Polycarp. Didache*. Cambridge, MA: Harvard University Press, 2003.

Ehrman, Bart D. *Lost Christianities: The Battles for Scripture and the Faiths We Never Knew*. Oxford: Oxford University Press, 2005.

Ehrman, Bart D. *Forgery and Counterforgery: The Use of Literary Deceit in Early Christian Polemics*. New York: Oxford University Press, 2013.

Ehrman, Bart D., and Michael William Holmes, eds. *The Text of the New Testament in Contemporary Research: Essays on the Status Quaestionis*. 2nd ed. Boston: Brill, 2014.

Ellingworth, Paul. *Hebrews*. Grand Rapids, MI: Eerdmans, 2015.

Elliott, J K. "Manuscripts, the Codex and the Canon." *Journal for the Study of the New Testament* 19, no. 63 (January 1997): 105–23.

England, Emma and William John Lyons, ed. *Reception History and Biblical Studies: Theory and Practice*. London: Bloomsbury, 2015.

Epp, Eldon Jay. *The Theological Tendency of Codex Bezae Cantabrigiensis in Acts*. New York: Cambridge University Press, 1966.

Epp, Eldon Jay. *Studies in the Theory and Method of New Testament Textual Criticism*. Grand Rapids, MI: Eerdmans, 1993.

Epp, Eldon Jay. *Perspectives on New Testament Textual Criticism: Collected Essays, 1962–2004*. Leiden: Brill, 2005.

Epp, Eldon Jay. "Text-Critical Witnesses and Methodology for Isolating a Distinctive D-Text in Acts." *Novum Testamentum* 59, no. 3 (2017): 225–96.

Eusebius. *Life of Constantine*. Translated by Averil Cameron and Stuart G. Hall. Oxford: Clarendon Press, 1999.

Eusebius. *Ecclesiastical History*. Translated by Jeffrey Henderson. Cambridge, MA: Harvard University Press, 2001.

Evans, Robert. *Reception History, Tradition and Biblical Interpretation: Gadamer and Jauss in Current Practice*. London: Bloomsbury, 2014.

Ferguson, Everett. "Canon Muratori: Date Provenance." *Studia Patristica* 17 (1982): 677–83.

Finegan, Jack. "The Original Form of the Pauline Collection." *Harvard Theological Review* 49, no. 2 (1956): 85–103.

Fischer, Bonifatius. *Vetus Latina: Die Reste Der Altlateinischen Bibel*. Frieberg: Herder, 1986.

Fotopoulos, John, ed. *The New Testament and Early Christian Literature in Greco-Roman Context: Studies in Honor of David E. Aune*. Supplements to Novum Testamentum 122. Boston: Brill, 2006.

Foucault, Michel. *Language, Counter-Memory, Practice: Selected Essays and Interviews*. Ithaca, NY: Cornell University Press, 1977.

Frede, Hermann Josef. *Altlateinische Paulus-Handschriften*. Frieberg: Herder, 1964.

Frede, Hermann Josef. *Epistulae Ad Thessalonicenses Timotheum Titum Philemonem Hebraeos*. Frieberg: Herder, 1975.

Gallagher, Edmon. "Origen via Rufinus on the New Testament Canon." *New Testament Studies* 62 (2016): 461–76.

Gallagher, Edmon, and John Meade. *The Biblical Canon Lists from Early Christianity: Texts and Analysis*. New York: Oxford University Press, 2017.

Gamble, Harry Y. *The New Testament Canon: Its Making and Meaning*. Philadelphia: Fortress Press, 1985.

Gamble, Harry Y. *Books and Readers in the Early Church: A History of Early Christian Texts*. New Haven, CT: Yale University Press, 1995.

Gameson, Richard. *The Early Medieval Bible: Its Production, Decoration, and Use*. Cambridge: Cambridge University Press, 1994.

Gibson, Margaret T. *The Bible in the Latin West*. Notre Dame: University of Notre Dame, 1993.

Gibson, Roy. "On the Nature of Ancient Letter Collections." *Journal of Roman Studies* 102 (2012): 56–78.

Goswell, Gregory. "An Early Commentary on the Pauline Corpus: The Capitulation of Codex Vaticanus." *Journal of Greco-Roman Christianity and Judaism* 8 (2011): 51–82.

Goswell, Gregory. "Finding a Home for the Letter to the Hebrews." *Journal of the Evangelical Theological Society* 59, no. 4 (2016): 747–60.

Grafton, Anthony, and Megan Hale Williams. *Christianity and the Transformation of the Book: Origen, Eusebius, and the Library of Caesarea*. Cambridge, MA: Belknap Press of Harvard University Press, 2008.

Grant, Robert. *Eusebius as Church Historian*. Oxford: Clarendon Press, 1980.

Grant, Robert. *Irenaeus of Lyons*. New York: Routledge, 1996.

Graves, Michael. *Biblical Interpretation in the Early Church*. Minneapolis, MN: Fortress Press, 2017.

Greer, Rowan A. *The Captain of Our Salvation: A Study in the Patristic Exegesis of Hebrews.* Tübingen: Mohr, 1973.
Greer, Rowan A., and Margaret Mary Mitchell. *Belly-Myther of Endor: Interpretations of 1 Kingdoms 28 in the Early Church.* Atlanta: Society of Biblical Literature, 2007.
Gregory, Caspar René. *Textkritik Des Neuen Testamentes.* Leipzig: J.C. Hinrichs, 1900.
Gregory, Caspar René. *Das Freer-logion.* Leipzig: J. C. Hinrichs, 1908.
Grenfell, Bernard P., and Arthur S. Hunt. *The Amherst Papyri: Part I.* London: H. Frowde, 1900.
Grenfell, Bernard P., and Arthur S. Hunt. *The Oxyrhynchus Papyri. Vol. IV.* London: Egypt Exploration Fund, 1904.
Grenz, Jesse R. "Textual Divisions in Codex Vaticanus: A Layered Approach to the Delimiters in B (03)." *TC: A Journal of Biblical Textual Criticism* 23 (2018): 1–22.
Guillory, John. *Cultural Capital: The Problem of Literary Canon Formation.* Chicago: University of Chicago Press, 1993.
Gurd, Sean Alexander. *Work in Progress: Literary Revision as Social Performance in Ancient Rome.* New York: Oxford University Press, 2011.
Hahneman, Geoffrey Mark. *The Muratorian Fragment and the Development of the Canon.* Oxford: Clarendon Press, 1992.
Haines-Eitzen, Kim. *Guardians of Letters Literacy, Power, and the Transmitters of Early Christian Literature.* New York: Oxford University Press, 2000.
Hall, Jonathan M., and William Dominik, eds. *A Companion to Roman Rhetoric.* Williston, UK: John Wiley, 2008.
Hall, Linda Jones. *Roman Berytus: Beirut in Late Antiquity.* Oxford: Routledge, 2004.
Hammond Bammel, C. "Products of Fifth-Century Scriptoria Preserving Conventions Used by Rufinus of Aquileia." *Journal of Theological Studies* 35 (1984): 347.
Harrison, Rebecca. "Jerome's Revision of the Gospels (Vulgate)." PhD diss., University of Pennsylvania, 1986.
Hatch, William H. P. "The Position of Hebrews in the Canon of the New Testament." *Harvard Theological Review* 29, no. 2 (1936): 133–51.
Hatch, William H. P. "On the Relationship of Codex Augiensis and Codex Boernerianus of the Pauline Epistles." *Harvard Studies in Classical Philology* 60 (1951): 187–99.
Hausmann, Regina. *Die Handschriften Der Hessischen Landesbibliothek Fulda Bd. 2. Die Historischen, Philologischen Und Juristischen Handschriften Der Hessischen Landesbibliothek Fulda Bis Zum Jahr 1600.* Weisbaden: Otto Harrassowitz, 1992.
Head, P., and M. Warren. "Re-Inking the Pen: Evidence from P. Oxy. 657 (P13) Concerning Unintentional Scribal Errors." *New Testament Studies* 43, no. 3 (1997): 466–73.
Heine, Ronald E. *Origen: Scholarship in the Service of the Church.* Oxford: Oxford University Press, 2010.
Hill, Charles E., and Michael J. Kruger, eds. *The Early Text of the New Testament.* Oxford: Oxford University Press, 2014.
Holmes, Michael W., and Daniel M. Gurtner. *Studies on the Text of the New Testament and Early Christianity: Essays in Honour of Michael W. Holmes on the Occasion of His 65th Birthday.* Boston: Brill, 2015.
Horbury, William. "The Wisdom of Solomon in the Muratorian Fragment." *Journal of Theological Studies* 45, no. 1 (1994): 149–59.
Houghton, H. A. "Augustine's Adoption of the Vulgate Gospels." *New Testament Studies* 54, no. 3 (2008): 450–64.

Houghton, H. A. *Augustine's Text of John: Patristic Citations and Latin Gospel Manuscripts.* New York: Oxford University Press, 2008.

Houghton, H. A. *The Latin New Testament: A Guide to Its Early History, Texts, and Manuscripts.* Oxford: Oxford University Press, 2016.

Humphries, Mark. "Rufinus's Eusebius: Translation, Continuation, and Edition in the Latin Ecclesiastical History." *Journal of Early Christian Studies* 16, no. 2 (2008): 143–64.

Hurtado, Larry W. *The Earliest Christian Artifacts: Manuscripts and Christian Origins.* Grand Rapids, MI: Eerdmans, 2006.

Hurtado, Larry W. *The Freer Biblical Manuscripts: Fresh Studies of an American Treasure Trove.* Leiden: Brill, 2006.

Jacobsen, Anders-Christian, ed. *The Discursive Fight Over Religious Texts in Antiquity.* Aarhus, DK: Aarhus University Press, 2009.

Jaeger, Werner. *Early Christianity and Greek Paideia.* Cambridge, MA: Belknap Press of Harvard University Press, 1961.

Jansen, Laura. *The Roman Paratext: Frame, Texts, Readers.* Cambridge: Cambridge University Press, 2014.

Johnson, Luke Timothy. *Hebrews: A Commentary.* Louisville: Westminster John Knox Press, 2006.

Johnson, William A. "Toward a Sociology of Reading in Classical Antiquity." *American Journal of Philology* 121, no. 4 (2000): 593–627.

Johnson, William A., and Holt N. Parker. *Ancient Literacies: The Culture of Reading in Greece and Rome.* New York: Oxford University Press, 2009.

Jongkind, Dirk. *Scribal Habits of Codex Sinaiticus.* Piscataway, NJ: Gorgias Press, 2007.

Joosten, Jan. "The Dura Parchment and The Diatessaron." *Vigiliae Christianae* 57, no. 2 (2003): 159–75.

Justin. *Dialogue with Trypho.* Translated by Thomas B. Falls. Washington, DC: Catholic University of America Press, 2003.

Kaczynski, Bernice M. *Greek in the Carolingian Age: The St. Gall Manuscripts.* Cambridge: Medieval Academy of America, 1988.

Kalin, Everett R. "Re-Examining New Testament Canon History: 1. The Canon of Origen." *Currents in Theology and Mission* 17 (1990): 274–82.

Kannengiesser, Charles. *Handbook of Patristic Exegesis: The Bible in Ancient Christianity, Volumes 1–2.* Leiden: Brill Academic, 2004.

Kaster, Robert A. "A Reconsideration of 'Gratian's School-Law.'" *Hermes* 112, no. 1 (1984): 100–14.

Kaster, Robert A. *Guardians of Language: The Grammarian and Society in Late Antiquity.* Berkeley: University of California Press, 1988.

Kennedy, George A. "The Earliest Rhetorical Handbooks." *American Journal of Philology* 80, no. 2 (1959): 169–78.

Kennedy, George A. *Greek Rhetoric under Christian Emperors.* Princeton, NJ: Princeton University Press, 1983.

Kennedy, George A. *A New History of Classical Rhetoric.* Princeton, NJ: Princeton University Press, 2011.

Kilpatrick, G. D. "Western Text and Original Text in the Gospels and Acts." *Journal of Theological Studies* 44, no. 173/174 (1943): 24–36.

King, Karen L. "Factions, Variety, Diversity, Multiplicity: Representing Early Christian Differences for the 21st Century." *Method & Theory in the Study of Religion* 23, no. 3 (2011): 216–37.

Knust, Jennifer. "Early Christian Re-Writing and the History of the Pericope Adulterae." *Journal of Early Christian Studies* 14, no. 4 (2006): 485–536.
Knust, Jennifer. "Latin Versions of the Bible." In *New Interpreter's Dictionary of the Bible*, vol. 5. Nashville: Abingdon Press, 2006.
Knust, Jennifer, and Claudia Moser, eds. *Ritual Matters: Material Remains and Ancient Religion*. Ann Arbor: University of Michigan Press, 2017.
Knust, Jennifer, and Tommy Wasserman. "The Biblical Odes and the Text of the Christian Bible: A Reconsideration of the Impact of Liturgical Singing on the Transmission of the Gospel of Luke." *Journal of Biblical Literature* 133, no. 2 (2014): 341–65.
Knust, Jennifer, and Tommy Wasserman.. *To Cast the First Stone: The Transmission of a Gospel Story*. Princeton, NJ: Princeton University Press, 2018.
Koester, Craig R. *Hebrews*. New Haven, CT: Yale University Press, 2001.
Kolbas, E. Dean. *Critical Theory and the Literary Canon*. Ann Arbor: University of Michigan Press, 2001.
Korpel, Marjo C. A. *Layout Markers in Biblical Manuscripts and Ugaritic Tablets*. Assen: Koninklijke Van Gorcum, 2005.
Kraus, Thomas J. *New Testament Manuscripts: Their Texts and Their World*. Leiden: Brill, 2006.
Kries, Douglas, and Catherine Brown Tkacz, eds. *Nova Doctrina Vetusque: Essays on Early Christianity in Honor of Fredric W. Schlatter, S.J.* New York: Peter Lang, 1999.
Kruger, Michael J. *Canon Revisited: Establishing the Origins and Authority of the New Testament Books*. Wheaton, IL: Crossway, 2012.
Kruger, Michael J. *The Question of Canon: Challenging the Status Quo in the New Testament Debate*. Downers Grove, IL: IVP Academic, 2013.
Lafferty, Maura K. "Translating Faith from Greek to Latin: Romanitas and Christianitas in Late Fourth-Century Rome and Milan." *Journal of Early Christian Studies* 11, no. 1 (2003): 21–62.
Lang, T., and Matthew Crawford. "The Origins of Pauline Theology: Paratexts and Priscillian of Avila's Canons on the Letters of the Apostle Paul." *New Testament Studies* 63, no. 1 (2017): 125–45.
Latour, Bruno. *Reassembling the Social: An Introduction to Actor-Network-Theory*. New York: Oxford University Press, 2005.
Lowe, E. A. "Some Facts about Our Oldest Latin Manuscripts." *Classical Quarterly* 19, no. 3/4 (1925): 197–208.
Lowe, E. A. "More Facts about Our Oldest Latin Manuscripts." *Classical Quarterly* 22, no. 1 (1928): 43–62.
Luijendijk, AnneMarie. "Sacred Scriptures as Trash: Biblical Papyri from Oxyrhynchus." *Vigiliae Christianae* 64, no. 3 (2010): 217–54.
Lunn-Rockliffe, Sophie. *Ambrosiaster's Political Theology*. Oxford: Oxford University Press, 2007.
Mansfeld, Jaap. *Prolegomena: Questions to Be Settled before the Study of an Author, or a Text*. New York: Brill, 1994.
Marichal, Robert. "L'écriture Latine et La Civilisation Occidentale Du Ier Au XVIe Siècle." In *L'écriture et La Psalmychologie Des Peuples: XXIIe Semaine de Synthèse*, ed. Marcel Cohen, 199–247. Paris: Librairie Armand Colin, 1963.
McDonald, Lee Martin. *The Formation of the Christian Biblical Canon*. Nashville: Abingdon Press, 1988.
McDonald, Lee Martin. *The Formation of the Biblical Canon: 2 Volumes*. New York: T&T Clark, 2017.

McDonald, Lee Martin, and James A. Sanders, eds. *The Canon Debate*. Peabody, MA: Hendrickson, 2002.

McGurk, P. "The Canon Tables in the Book of Lindisfarne and in the Codex Fuldensis of St. Victor of Capua." *Journal of Theological Studies* 6, no. 2 (1955): 192–98.

McGurk, P. *Latin Gospel Books from A.D.400 to A.D.800*. Paris: Éditions "Érasme," 1961.

McKendrick, Scot. *In a Monastery Library: Preserving Codex Sinaiticus and the Greek Written Heritage*. London: British Library, 2006.

McKendrick, Scot, and Orlaith O'Sullivan. *The Bible as Book: The Transmission of the Greek Text*. London: Oak Knoll Press, 2003.

McKenzie, D. F. *Bibliography and the Sociology of Texts*. New York: Cambridge University Press, 1999.

McLynn, Neil B. *Ambrose of Milan: Church and Court in a Christian Capital*. Los Angeles: University of California Press, 1994.

Meade, David G. *Pseudonymity and Canon: An Investigation into the Relationship of Authorship and Authority in Jewish and Earliest Christian Tradition*. Grand Rapids, MI: Eerdmans, 1987.

Metzger, Bruce M. *The Early Versions of the New Testament: Their Origin, Transmission, and Limitations*. Oxford: Oxford University Press, 1977.

Metzger, Bruce M. *Manuscripts of the Greek Bible: An Introduction to Greek Paleography*. New York: Oxford University Press, 1981.

Metzger, Bruce M. *The Canon of the New Testament: Its Origin, Development, and Significance*. New York: Oxford University Press, 1987.

Metzger, Bruce M. *A Textual Commentary on the Greek New Testament*. 2nd ed. New York: United Bible Societies, 1994.

Migne, J. P. *Patrologia Graeca*. Chicago: Brepols, 2003.

Millar, F. "Linguistic Co-Existence in Constantinople: Greek and Latin (and Syriac) in the Acts of the Synod of 536 C.E." *Journal of Roman Studies* 99 (2009): 92–103.

Mitchell, Margaret Mary. *Paul, the Corinthians, and the Birth of Christian Hermeneutics*. New York: Cambridge University Press, 2012.

Mohrmann, Christine. *Liturgical Latin, Its Origins and Character; Three Lectures*. Washington: Catholic University of America Press, 1957.

Mroczek, Eva. *The Literary Imagination in Jewish Antiquity*. New York: Oxford University Press, 2016.

Murphy, Xavier, ed. *A Monument to St. Jerome: Essays On Some Aspects of His Life, Work, and Influence*. New York: Sheed and Ward, 1952.

Myshrall, Amy, David C. Parker, Scot McKendrick, and Cillian O' Hogan, eds. *Codex Sinaiticus: New Perspectives on the Ancient Biblical Manuscript*. London: British Library, 2015.

Najman, Hindy. "The Vitality of Scripture Within and Beyond the 'Canon.'" *Journal for the Study of Judaism* 43, nos. 4–5 (2012): 497–518.

Neil, Bronwen, and Pauline Allen, eds. *Collecting Early Christian Letters. From the Apostle Paul to Late Antiquity*. Cambridge: Cambridge University Press, 2015.

Nongbri, Brent. "The Use and Abuse of P52: Papyrological Pitfalls in the Dating of the Fourth Gospel." *Harvard Theological Review* 98, no. 1 (2005): 23–48.

Nongbri, Brent. *God's Library: The Archaeology of the Earliest Christian Manuscripts*. New Haven, CT: Yale University Press, 2018.

Novenson, Matthew V. "The Pauline Epistles in Tertullian's Bible." *Scottish Journal of Theology* 68, no. 4 (2015): 471–83.

O'Malley, Thomas P. *Tertullian and the Bible. Language, Imagery, Exegesis*. Latinitas Christianorum Primaeva. Utrecht: Dekker & Van de Vegt, 1967.
Origen. *Commentary on the Gospel according to John*. Translated by Ronald E. Heine. Fathers of the Church 80. Washington, DC: Catholic University of America Press, 1989.
Origen. *Homilies on Leviticus 1–16*. Translated by Gary Wayne Barkley. Washington DC: Catholic University of America Press, 2005.
Origen. *Homilies on Luke: Fragments on Luke*. Translated by Joseph T. Lienhard. Washington, DC: Catholic University of America Press, 2009.
Osiek, Carolyn. *Shepherd of Hermas: A Commentary*. Minneapolis, MN: Fortress Press, 1999.
Otten, Willemien, Hent De Vries, and A. J. Vanderjagt, eds. *How the West Was Won: Essays on Literary Imagination, the Canon and the Christian Middle Ages for Burcht Pranger*. Leiden: Brill, 2010.
Oulton, J. E. L. "Rufinus' Translation of the Church History of Eusebius." *JTS* 30 (1929): 150–74.
Paget, James Carleton, ed. *The New Cambridge History of the Bible*. Cambridge: Cambridge University Press, 2013.
Parker, D. C. *Codex Bezae: An Early Christian Manuscript and Its Text*. New York: Cambridge University Press, 1992.
Parker, D. C. *The Living Text of the Gospels*. New York: Cambridge University Press, 1997.
Parker, D. C. *An Introduction to the New Testament Manuscripts and Their Texts*. New York: Cambridge University Press, 2008.
Parker, D. C. *Codex Sinaiticus: The Story of the World's Oldest Bible*. Peabody, MA: Hendrickson, 2010.
Parvis, Sara, and Paul Foster, eds. *Irenaeus: Life, Scripture, Legacy*. Minneapolis, MN: Augsburg Fortress, 2012.
Payne, Grover. "A Textual Analysis, Critical Reconstruction, and Evaluation of the Superscriptions and Subscriptions to the Corpus Paulinum." PhD diss., Southwestern Baptist Theological Seminary, 2002.
Payne, Philip, and Paul Canart. "The Originality of Text Critical Symbols in Codex Vaticanus." *Novum Testamentum* 42, no. 2 (2000): 105–13.
Pervo, Richard I. *The Making of Paul: Constructions of the Apostle in Early Christianity*. Minneapolis, MN: Fortress Press, 2010.
Petersen, William Lawrence. *Tatian's Diatessaron: Its Creation, Dissemination, Significance, and History in Scholarship*. New York: Brill, 1994.
Pfeiffer, Rudolf. *History of Classical Scholarship from the Beginnings to the End of the Hellenistic Age*. Oxford: Clarendon Press, 1968.
Popović, Mladen. *Authoritative Scriptures in Ancient Judaism*. Boston: Brill, 2010.
Price, Robert M. "The Evolution of the Pauline Canon." *HTS Teologiese Studies / Theological Studies* 53, no. 1/2 (December 13, 1997): 36–67.
Puech, Amie. *Historie de La Litterature Grecque Chretienne*. Paris: Societe D'Edition, 1930.
Quinn, Jerome D. "P46, the Pauline Canon." *Catholic Biblical Quarterly* 36, no. 3 (July 1974): 379–85.
Rajak, Tessa. *Translation and Survival: The Greek Bible of the Ancient Jewish Diaspora*. Oxford: Oxford University Press, 2009.
Ranke, Ernst. *Codex Fuldensis: Novum Testamentum latine interprete Hieronymo*. Marburgi: Sumtibus N.G. Elwerti, 1868.

Rebenich, Stefan. "Jerome: The 'Vir Trilinguis' and the 'Hebraica Veritas.'" *Vigiliae Christianae* 47, no. 1 (1993): 50–77.
Rebenich, Stefan. *Jerome*. London: Routledge, 2002.
Reed, Annette Yoshiko. "ΕΥΑΠΓΕΛΙΟΝ: Orality, Textuality, and the Christian Truth in Irenaeus' 'Adversus Haereses.'" *Vigiliae Christianae* 56, no. 1 (2002): 11–46.
Reicke, Bo, and William C Weinrich. *The New Testament Age: Essays in Honor of Bo Reicke*. Macon, GA: Mercer, 1984.
Reynolds, L. D. *Scribes and Scholars: A Guide to the Transmission of Greek and Latin Literature*. New York: Oxford University Press, 2013.
Robbins, Gregory Allen. "'Peri Ton Endiathekon Graphon': Eusebius and the Formation of the Christian Bible." PhD diss., Duke University Press, 1986.
Roberts, Colin H. *The Birth of the Codex*. London: Oxford University Press, 1987.
Robinson, J. Armitage. *Euthaliana, Studies of Euthalius, Codex H of the Pauline Epistles, and the Armenian Version*. London: Cambridge University Press, 1895.
Rönsch, H. "Die Doppelübersetzungen Im Lateinischen Texte Des Cod. Boernerianus Der Paulinischen Briefe." *Zeitschrift Für Wissenschaftliche Theologie* 26 (1883): 73.
Rothschild, Clare K. *Hebrews as Pseudepigraphon: The History and Significance of the Pauline Attribution of Hebrews*. Tubingen: Mohr Siebeck, 2012.
Rothschild, Clare K. "The Muratorian Fragment as Roman Fake." *Novum Testamentum* 60 (2018): 55–82.
Rousseau, Philip, and Jutta Raithel. *A Companion to Late Antiquity*. Malden, MA: Wiley-Blackwell, 2009.
Royse, James Ronald. *Scribal Habits in Early Greek New Testament Papyri*. Boston: Brill, 2008.
Rufinus. *A Commentary on the Apostles' Creed*. Translated by J. N. D. Kelly. Ancient Christian Writers. Westminster, MD: Newman Press, 1955.
Rufinus. *History of the Church*. Translated by Philip R. Amidon. Fathers of the Church. Washington, DC: Catholic University of America Press, 2016.
Runia, David T. *Philo in Early Christian Literature: A Survey*. Minneapolis, MN: Fortress Press, 1993.
Sanders, Henry A. "New Manuscripts of the Bible from Egypt." *American Journal of Archaeology* 12, no. 1 (1908): 49–55.
Sanders, Henry A. "Age and Ancient Home of the Biblical Manuscripts in the Freer Collection." *American Journal of Archaeology* 13, no. 2 (1909): 130–41.
Sanders, Henry A. *The New Testament Manuscripts in the Freer Collection*. New York: Macmillan, 1918.
Sanzo, Joseph Emanuel. *Scriptural Incipits on Amulets from Late Antique Egypt: Text, Typology, and Theory*. Tübingen: Mohr Siebeck, 2014.
Scherbenske, Eric W. *Canonizing Paul: Ancient Editorial Practice and the Corpus Paulinum*. New York: Oxford University Press, 2013.
Schlossnikel, Reinhard Franz. *Der Brief an die Hebräer und das corpus Paulinum: eine linguistische "Bruchstelle" im codex Claromontanus (Paris, Bibliothèque Nationale Grec 107 + 107A + 107B) und ihre Bedeutung im Rahmen von Text- und Kanongeschichte*. Freiberg: Herder, 1991.
Schmid, Ulrich. *Marcion und sein Apostolos: Rekonstruktion und Historische Einordnung der Marcionitischen Paulusbriefausgabe*. New York: De Gruyter, 1995.
Schmid, Ulrich. "In Search of Tatian's Diatessaron in the West." *Vigiliae Christianae* 57, no. 2 (2003): 176–99.

Schmid, Ulrich. "Marcion and the Textual History of Romans: Editorial Activity and Early Editions of the New Testament." *Studia Patristica* 54 (2013): 105–8.

Schnabel, Eckhard J. "The Muratorian Fragment: The State of Research." *Journal of the Evangelical Theological Society* 57, no. 2 (2014): 231–64.

Schröter, Jens. *From Jesus to the New Testament: Early Christian Theology and the Origin of the New Testament Canon.* Waco, TX: Baylor University Press, 2013.

Sessa, Kristina. *The Formation of Papal Authority in Late Antique Italy: Roman Bishops and the Domestic Sphere.* New York: Cambridge University Press, 2012.

Sharpe, John L., III. *The Bible as Book: The Manuscript Tradition.* London: British Library, 1998.

Shillingsburg, Peter L. "Text as Matter, Concept, and Action." *Studies in Bibliography* 44 (1991): 31–82.

Skarsaune, Oskar. *The Proof from Prophecy: A Study in Justin Martyr's Proof-Text Tradition: Text-Type, Provenance, Theological Profile.* Leiden: Brill, 1987.

Skeat, T. C. *The Collected Biblical Writings of T.C. Skeat.* Boston: Brill, 2004.

Smith, Jonathan Z. *Imagining Religion: From Babylon to Jonestown.* Chicago: University of Chicago Press, 1982.

Smith, W. Andrew. *A Study of the Gospels in Codex Alexandrinus: Codicology, Palaeography, and Scribal Hands.* Leiden: Brill, 2014.

Smith, William Benjamin. "The Pauline Manuscripts F and G. A Text-Critical Study." *American Journal of Theology* 7, no. 3 (1903): 452–85.

Soderquist, Justin. "A New Edition of Codex I (016): The Washington Manuscript of the Epistles of Paul." PhD diss., Trinity Western University, 2014.

Souter, Alexander. *The Commentary of Pelagius on the Epistles of Paul: The Problem of Its Restoration.* London: Oxford University Press, 1906.

Souter, Alexander. *The Earliest Latin Commentaries on the Epistles of St. Paul: A Study.* Oxford: Oxford University Press, 1999.

Starr, James M, and Troels Engberg-Pedersen. *Early Christian Paraenesis in Context.* New York: Walter de Gruyter, 2004.

Starr, Raymond J. "The Circulation of Literary Texts in the Roman World." *Classical Quarterly* 37, no. 1 (1987): 213–23.

Stroumsa, Guy G. *The Scriptural Universe of Ancient Christianity.* Cambridge, MA: Harvard University Press, 2016.

Sundberg, Albert C. "Canon Muratori: A Fourth-Century List." *Harvard Theological Review* 66 (1973): 1–41.

Tarrant, Harold. *Thrasyllan Platonism.* Ithaca, NY: Cornell University Press, 1993.

Taylor, David G. K. *Studies in the Early Text of the Gospels and Acts: The Papers of the First Birmingham Colloquium on the Textual Criticism of the New Testament.* Piscataway, NJ: Gorgias Press, 2013.

Tertullian. *Treatises on Penance: On Penitence and on Purity.* Ancient Christian Writers 28. Westminster, MD: Newman Press, 1959.

Tertullian. *Homily on Baptism.* London: SPCK, 1964.

Theissen, Gerd. *The New Testament: A Literary History.* Minneapolis, MN: Fortress Press, 2011.

Thomassen, Einar, ed. *Canon and Canonicity: The Formation and Use of Scripture.* Copenhagen: Museum Tusculanum Press, 2009.

Tilley, Maureen A. *The Bible in Christian North Africa: The Donatist World.* Minneapolis, MN: Fortress Press, 1997.

Tischendorf, Contantine. *Novum Testamentum Vaticanum: Post Angeli Maii Aliorumque Imperfectos Labores Ex Ipso Codici*. Leipzig: Giesecke et Devrient, 1867.
Toorn, K. van der. *Scribal Culture and the Making of the Hebrew Bible*. Cambridge, MA: Harvard University Press, 2007.
Treadgold, Warren T., ed. *Renaissances before the Renaissance: Cultural Revivals of Late Antiquity and the Middle Ages*. Stanford: Stanford University Press, 1984.
Trobisch, David. *Paul's Letter Collection: Tracing the Origins*. Minneapolis, MN: Fortress Press, 1994.
Trobisch, David. *The First Edition of the New Testament*. Oxford: Oxford University Press, 2000.
Turner, E. G. *The Typology of the Early Codex*. Haney Foundation Series 18. Philadelphia: University of Pennsylvania Press, 1977.
Ulrich, Jörg, Anders-Christian Jacobsen, and David Brakke, eds. *Invention, Rewriting, Usurpation: Discursive Fights over Religious Traditions in Antiquity*. Frankfurt am Main: Peter Lang, Internationaler Verlag der Wissenschaften, 2011.
Van Den Hoek, Annewies. "Techniques of Quotation in Clement of Alexandria: A View of Ancient Literary Working Methods." *Vigiliae Christianae* 50, no. 3 (1996): 223–43.
Wachtel, Klaus, and Michael W. Holmes, eds. *The Textual History of the Greek New Testament: Changing Views in Contemporary Research*. Boston: Brill, 2012.
Walker, Jeffrey. *Rhetoric and Poetics in Antiquity*. New York: Oxford University Press, 2000.
Walther, Otto. "Codex Laudianus G35 A Re-Examination of the Manuscript: A Reproduction of the Text and Accompanying Commentary." PhD diss., University of St. Andrews, 1980.
White, Peter. *Cicero in Letters: Epistolary Relations of the Late Republic*. New York: Oxford University Press, 2010.
Wikramanayake, G. H. "A Note on the Pisteis in Aristotle's Rhetoric." *American Journal of Philology* 82, no. 2 (1961): 193–96.
Wilhite, David E. *Ancient African Christianity: An Introduction to a Unique Context and Tradition*. New York: Routledge, 2017.
Willard, Louis Charles. *A Critical Study of the Euthalian Apparatus*. New York: Walter de Gruyter, 2009.
Williams, Megan Hale. *The Monk and the Book: Jerome and the Making of Christian Scholarship*. Chicago: University of Chicago Press, 2006.
Williams, Michael A. *Rethinking "Gnosticism": An Argument for Dismantling a Dubious Category*. Princeton, NJ: Princeton University Press, 1996.
Willison, Ian. "On the History of the Archival Library and Scholarship in the West since the Alexandrian Library: An Overview." *Alexandria* 25, no. 3 (2014): 87–110.
Wilson, N. G. *Scholars of Byzantium*. Cambridge: Medieval Academy of America, 1996.
Wiseman, T. P., ed. *Classics in Progress: Essays on Ancient Greece and Rome*. New York: Oxford University Press, 2006.
Witty, Francis J. "The Pínakes of Callimachus." *The Library Quarterly: Information, Community, Policy* 28, no. 2 (1958): 132–6.
Witty, Francis J. "The Other Pinakes and Reference Works of Callimachus." *The Library Quarterly* 43, no. 3 (1973): 237–44.
Wood, H. G., ed. *Amicitiae Corolla*. London: University of London Press, 1933.
Wordsworth, John, and Henry Julius White. *Nouum Testamentum Latine, Secundum Editionem Sancti Hieronymi*. London: Simon Wallenerg, 1911.

Wouters, Alfons. *The Chester Beatty Codex AC 1499: A Graeco- Latin Lexicon on the Pauline Epistles and a Greek Grammar*. Paris: Peeters, 1988.
Wyrick, Jed. *The Ascension of Authorship: Attribution and Canon Formation in Jewish, Hellenistic, and Christian Traditions*. Cambridge, MA: Harvard University Press, 2004.
Zimmer, F. "Der Codex Augiensis (Fpaul), Eine Abschrift Des Boernerianus (Gpaul)." *Zeitschrift Für Wissenschaftliche Theologie* 30 (1887): 76.
Zola, Nicholas. "Tatian's 'Diatessaron' in Latin: A New Edition and Translation of Codex Fuldensis." PhD diss., Baylor University, 2014.
Zuntz, G. *The Text of the Epistles: A Disquisition Upon the Corpus Paulinum*. The Schweich Lectures of the British Academy, 1946. Eugene, OR: Wipf and Stock, 2007.

Ancient Sources Index

Acts of John 20
Acts of Paul 20–2, 31, 35, 61, 70, 101
Acts of Thomas 22
Africanus 69
Ambrose of Milan 10, 40, 116–17
Apocalypse of Peter 20, 22, 31, 37, 41–4, 101
Aristotle 52, 79
Athanasius of Alexandria 1, 3–5, 29–35, 39, 41, 44–5, 85–6, 105, 117, 129, 131
Augustine 2, 7, 9, 12–13, 44, 46–7, 115, 119, 121

Barnabas 9–10, 20, 22–3, 31, 35–7, 45, 55, 58–63, 70–1, 86, 90, 101, 104, 113, 121, 130

Callimachus 16–17, 20, 78–9
Cicero 51–3, 80–1
Clement of Alexandria 10, 36, 41, 45, 55, 63–7, 72, 113, 121, 129–30
Clement of Rome 8, 10, 13, 25–30, 38, 50, 56, 70–1, 86, 89, 104, 129
Constantine 18, 23, 26, 115–16, 125
Cyprian 9, 55, 114

Damasus of Rome 116, 120
Didache 22, 31
Diocletian 115, 123
Diogenes Laertius 17–18, 20, 78
Dionysios of Halicanarssus 17

Epistle to the Alexandrians 12, 44
Epistle to the Laodiceans 12, 42, 44–5, 102–3, 122, 137
Eusebius of Caesarea 7–8, 12–13, 18–33, 35–9, 41–5, 50, 56, 69–70, 107, 116, 121–3, 129–31

Gaius 12–13, 25, 43, 56, 130
Gospel according to the Hebrews 20, 22, 31, 35, 70–2
Gospel of Peter 20, 22, 70
Gospel of Matthias 20, 22
Gospel of Thomas 20, 22

Hilary 8–10
Hippolytus 8, 13, 55

Irenaeus 3–4, 13, 27–8, 30–1, 40–1, 58, 62

Jerome 2, 7, 9, 12–13, 41–2, 44–7, 83, 110, 113–14, 117, 119–21, 130–1
Justin Martyr 13, 43, 50, 55–63, 69, 72, 123, 129–30

Livy 84, 133
Lucian 52–3
Lucifer 8

Marcion 3–4, 123
Marcionite 7, 41, 122–3

Origen 8, 10–11, 19–20, 22, 25–7, 33, 35–9, 41, 50, 52, 55, 62, 66–72, 107, 113, 124, 129–30

Pantaenus 7, 25, 45, 130
Pelagius 120–1
Plato 18, 51, 65, 78–9
Pliny the Elder 51, 80
Preaching of Peter 70
Primum quaeritur 103, 120

Rufinus of Aquileia 10, 33–9, 41, 44
Rufinus of Syria 103–5, 120–1, 131

Seneca 51–2
Servius 108, 114–15

Shepherd of Hermas 13, 25, 34, 40–2, 56, 101, 114
Susanna 69, 82

Tertullian 2–3, 8–10, 13, 50, 53, 55–6, 58–63, 69, 72, 104, 113–14, 121, 129–30

Thrasyllus 78–9

Victor of Capua 103, 105, 114, 122–3
Virgil 51, 115, 124–5, 127

Biblical Passages Index

Old Testament

Genesis	75–6, 82, 97
1:1–5	75
14:18–20	58
18–19	59
19:24	59
Exodus	97
Leviticus	
13–14	68
16:27	62
Numbers	82
Deuteronomy	82
4:2	31
Esther	31, 39, 82
Psalms	4, 58, 62, 76, 110
2	62
2:7	62
8	62
8:5	62
8:5–6	62
45:7–8	58–9
110	58, 62
110:1	28, 58–9, 62
110:4	58, 62
110:7	58
118:22	62
Isaiah	62, 69, 82
53:2–3	7–8 62
8:14	62
28:16	62
Jeremiah	70, 82

Ezekiel	82
Daniel	9, 70, 82
2:34	62
7:13	62
Jonah	120
Zechariah	
3:1–5	62

New Testament

Matthew	26, 34, 37–8, 68, 70, 87–9, 101, 122–3, 126
11	65
12:50	72
22:44	62
Mark	27, 34, 38, 65, 70, 101, 126
3:35	72
12:36	62
Luke	3, 8, 25–7, 29–30, 34, 36, 38, 42, 45, 65, 70, 101, 104, 115, 121, 123, 126
John	18, 20, 22–4, 27, 34, 38, 65, 70–1, 88–9, 101, 110, 126, 134
1:14–15	71
1:19–23	65
5	126
8:12	110
Acts	8, 20–2, 25–6, 28, 31, 34–5, 38, 42, 65, 70, 82, 85, 88–91, 94, 121, 123, 125–7, 134–6

Romans	3, 25, 46, 82–5, 87–9, 94, 99, 101, 133	Philemon	7, 14, 45–6, 77, 89–90, 93, 99–104, 108–9, 111, 121, 134–7
4	57		
8:34	62		
14:1	69	Hebrews	1–15, 20–2, 24–8, 31, 33, 35–40, 42–7, 49–50, 54–64, 66–73, 75–7, 81, 84–6, 88, 94–5, 97–114, 120–2, 126, 128–31, 133–7
1 Corinthians	69, 82, 84, 94, 100–1, 133, 136		
2	69		
2:6	69		
9:9	69	1	58
10:11	69	1–2	62
14:8–18	109	1:1	64, 75
15:25–27	62	1:3	28
		1:4	10
2 Corinthians	46, 82, 94, 101	1:3–4	13, 28, 56–7, 67
3:14	68–9	1:3–13	62
10:13	30	1:3–2:8	62
		1:14	67
Galatians	46, 82, 84, 88, 101	2:5–9	62
3:10–13	57	2:14–5:5	85
4:30	66	4:12	62
6:16	30	4:13–14	66
		5:12–14	68
Ephesians	46, 82, 84, 88, 101, 124, 137	6	63
		6:4	61
1:20–23	62	6:4–6	13, 56
5:2	69	7	58
		9	88
Philippians	46, 82, 88, 100–1	10:1	67
		10:4	68
Colossians	46, 82, 88, 100–1	10:8–22	85
3:4–8	96	10:29–11:13	85
		11:28–12:17	85
1 Thessalonians	31, 82, 83, 88, 101	12:22–23	68
		13:12	68
2 Thessalonians	14, 31, 46, 83, 88, 94, 97, 99, 101, 104–5, 112, 121, 122, 130–1, 133–7	13:24	43
		James	9, 20–3, 31–2, 34–6, 38, 43, 71, 101
1 Timothy	45	1 Peter	20–2, 24, 34–5, 43–4, 71, 101
2 Timothy	46, 83, 101	3:22	62
Titus	45–6, 101	2 Peter	20–3, 29, 31, 34–6, 38, 43–4, 71, 101
2:1–5	96		

1 John	21–3, 35, 43, 60, 71, 101	Jude	9, 20–3, 31, 34–8, 43, 89, 101
2 John	21–3, 31, 35–6, 38, 43–4, 60, 71, 101	Revelation	10, 20, 23–4, 35–6, 40, 45–6, 60, 82, 85–7, 89–90, 113
3 John	21–3, 31, 35–6, 38, 43–4, 60, 71, 101, 125		

Modern Authors Index

Adams, J. N. 108
Aland, Barbara 75, 83, 85, 86, 99
Aland, Kurt 75, 83, 85, 86, 99
Albl, Martin C. 58, 62
Allen, Pauline 80
Allert, Craig D. 57, 58
Andrist, Patrick, ed. 86
Aragione, Gabriella 22
Arbor, Ann 30
Archibald, Elizabeth P. 108, 111, 124
Armstrong, Jonathan J. 41
Arnal, William E. 18, 52, 78
Ascough, Richard S. 18, 52, 78
Attridge, Harold W. 11, 13, 28, 57

Baker, J. A. 1
Barton, John 4
Batovici, Dan 86
Baum, A. D. 22
Beard, Mary 77–8, 80–1
Berschin, Walter 110, 114, 118
Bindley, T. H. 61
Blomkvist, Vemund 96
Blum, Rudolf 16, 17, 79
Boer, E. A. 60
Brakke, David 1–4, 18, 30–3
Brockliss, William 108, 111, 124
Bruyn, Theodore de 76
Burton, Philip 114

Cain, Andrew 120
Campenhausen, Hans von 1, 11
Canart, Paul 86
Carriker, Andrew James 107
Cernuskova, Veronika 64
Charlesworth, James H. 34
Chin, Catherine M. 18, 117, 119
Clark, Kenneth 75
Contreni, John J. 110, 118
Cosgrove, Charles H. 57

Dawson, David 65
Derrenbacker, Robert A. 18, 52, 78
Dickey, Eleanor 119, 124
Duff, J. 83–4
Dungan, David L. 18, 23, 26
Dunn, Geoffrey D. 53

Ebojo, Edgar Battad 83
Eden, Kathy 53
Ehrman, Bart D. 21, 23, 29, 82, 114
Ellingworth, Paul 11
Epp, Eldon Jay 75, 82–4, 110

Ferguson, Everett 40, 42, 65
Fotopoulos, John 52
Foucault, Michel 18, 78
Frankfurter, David 76
Frede, Hermann Josef 99, 101, 103, 126

Gallagher, Edmon 9, 21, 24, 29–31, 34–5, 37–40, 44–6, 113
Gamble, Harry Y. 1, 4, 9–11, 75
Gibson, Margaret T. 127
Gibson, Roy 80–1
Gnoza, Jonathan 108, 111, 124
Goswell, Gregory 88–9
Grafton, Anthony 107, 117, 124
Grant, Robert 13, 28
Greer, Rowan A. 52
Gregory, Caspar René 99, 126
Grenfell, Bernard P. 75–85
Grenz, Jesse R. 87
Guillory, John 2, 4
Gurd, Sean Alexander 52

Hahneman, Geoffrey Mark 40–2
Harland, Philip A. 18, 52, 78
Hatch, William H. P. 7, 9–11, 94, 101, 109–10
Head, P. 85

Heine, Ronald E. 70-1
Herren, Michael W. 111
Hill, Charles E. 85
Holmes, Michael W. 82, 110, 114
Horbury, William 41
Houghton, H. A. 103, 109, 112-15, 121-2, 124
Humphries, Mark 36
Hunt, Arthur 75, 85
Hurtado, Larry W. 92

Jacobsen, Anders-Christian 1-2, 30, 32
Johnson, Luke Timothy 11
Junod, Eric 22

Kaczynski, Bernice M. 110-11, 118, 127
Kalin, Everett R. 23, 27, 39
Kaster, Robert A. 115
King, Karen L. 18-19, 52, 54, 78
Knust, Jennifer 2, 31, 72, 75-6, 107, 110, 114-15, 119-20, 126
Koester, Craig R. 11
Kolbas, E. Dean. 30
Kovacs, Judith L. 64
Kruger, Michael J. 31, 85
Kyrtatas, Dimitris J. 3

Lafferty, Maura K. 114-16
Latour, Bruno 76
Luijendijk, AnneMarie 84

Mansfeld, Jaap 79
Marichal, Robert 123
McDonald, Lee Martin 4, 10, 23, 34, 41, 75
McKenzie, D. F. 2, 76
McLynn, Neil B. 116-17
Meade, John 9, 21, 24, 29-31, 34, 38, 40, 45-6, 113
Metzger, Bruce M. 1, 7-11, 42, 45, 88, 101, 110, 113
Mitchell, Margaret Mary 5, 52-3, 69
Moser, Claudia 2, 75
Mroczek, Eva 2, 4
Murphy, Xavier 45, 113

Najman, Hindy 2
Neil, Bronwen 80
Nongbri, Brent 82, 84

Norelli, Enrico 22
Novenson, Matthew V. 60-1, 114

O'Malley, Thomas P. 114
Osiek, Carolyn 41, 56
Oulton, J. E. L. 35-6

Parker, D. C. 83, 107, 109, 124-7
Payne, Grover 86, 100
Pedersen, Nils Arne 32
Pervo, Richard I. 11
Peterson, Anders Klostergaard 30
Pfeiffer, Rudolf 16
Platova, Jana 64

Quinn, Jerome D. 83

Racine, Felix 108
Ranke, Ernst 122
Rebenich, Stefan 120
Reed, Annette Yoshiko 4, 31
Robbins, Gregory Allen 19, 22-4, 27, 38
Robinson, J. Armitage 95
Rothschild, Clare K. 7, 11-13, 41-2
Royse, James Ronald 85

Sanders, Henry A. 85, 94
Sanders, James. A. 4, 10, 23, 41, 75
Sanzo, Joseph Emanuel 76
Scherbenske, Eric W. 6, 77, 79, 95-7, 104, 119-23
Schlossnikel, Reinhard Franz 102-3, 112
Schmid, Ulrich 3
Schnabel, Eckhard J. 40, 42-4
Sessa, Kristina 116
Shillingsburg, Peter L. 76
Siebeck, Mohr 11
Skarsaune, Oskar 58-9
Skehan, Patrick W. 45, 113
Smith, W. Andrew 88-9
Soderquist, Justin 92
Starr, James M. 32
Sundberg, Albert C. 27, 40

Tarrant, Harold 78-9
Theissen, Gerd 11
Thomassen, Einar 3, 11
Tischendorf, Contantine 86

Treadgold, Warren T. 110
Trobisch, David. 1, 84, 102, 110
Turner, E. G. 75

Ulrich, Jörg 1–2

Van den Hoek, Annewies 65

Wachtel, Klaus 110
Walther, Otto 127
Warren, M. 85
Wasserman, Tommy 31, 72, 107, 110, 115, 119–20, 126

Westcott, Brooke Foss 100
White, Henry Julius 104
Wikramanayake, G. H. 52
Willard, Louis Charles 95–6
Williams, Megan Hale 35, 107, 114, 117, 120
Willison, Ian 16
Wiseman, T. P. 77
Witty, Francis J. 16–17
Wood, H. G. 126
Wordsworth, John 104
Wouters, Alfons 124

www.ingramcontent.com/pod-product-compliance
Lightning Source LLC
Chambersburg PA
CBHW061839300426
44115CB00013B/2441